# TENEMENT NATION

FRAMING THE GLOBAL
Hilary Kahn and Deborah Piston-Hatlen, series editors

Christa Ballard Tooley

# TENEMENT NATION

**WORKING-CLASS
COSMOPOLITANISM
IN EDINBURGH**

INDIANA UNIVERSITY PRESS

This book is a publication of

Indiana University Press
Office of Scholarly Publishing
Herman B Wells Library 350
1320 East 10th Street
Bloomington, Indiana 47405 USA

iupress.org

© 2023 by Christa Ballard Tooley

All rights reserved
No part of this book may be reproduced or utilized in any form or by any means, electronic or mechanical, including photocopying and recording, or by any information storage and retrieval system, without permission in writing from the publisher. The paper used in this publication meets the minimum requirements of the American National Standard for Information Sciences—Permanence of Paper for Printed Library Materials, ANSI Z39.48–1992.

Manufactured in the United States of America

First printing 2023

Cataloging information is available from the Library of Congress.

ISBN 978-0-253-06599-5 (hdbk.)
ISBN 978-0-253-06600-8 (pbk.)
ISBN 978-0-253-06601-5 (web PDF)

*To Ron and Wanda Ballard,
who saw this book coming
before I did.*

# CONTENTS

*Acknowledgments  ix*

Introduction: Working Out Class and Nation in Edinburgh  1

1. History, Heritage, and Politics in the Old Town  32
   *Interlude 1: On Conservation, Community, and Class  59*

2. Depoliticizing Development: Neoliberal Urbanism
   and Caltongate  68
   *Interlude 2: A Shop in the Canongate  98*

3. Saving the Old Town, One More Time: Ancient Concerns for
   Neoliberal Times  106
   *Interlude 3: Dumbiedykes  143*

4. The Politics of Home  153
   *Interlude 4: Doocots and Community Land Use in Glasgow  184*

5. Scottish Cosmopolitanism: From Neighborhood to Nation  194

Conclusion: Urban Scotland, Working-Class Politics,
and National Futures  231

*References  239*

*Index  257*

# ACKNOWLEDGMENTS

FIRSTLY, THIS PROJECT WOULD NOT have gotten off the ground without the support, guidance, and encouragement of Dr. Richard Baxstrom and Dr. Francesca Bray, from the initial period of fieldwork and writing through to the present. Readers Dr. Gisa Weszkalnys and Dr. Michael Rosie provided invaluable feedback and suggestions, expanding the scope of inquiry and affirming that early stage of progress.

I am grateful for grants that I received from the University of Edinburgh and from Wheaton College, which have funded the initial period of research as well as the many return visits to Scotland that have allowed this project to be sustained and continue to develop over years and across two continents. I have also depended on family and friends who stepped in to fill the gaps produced by a long-term research program: in childcare and course coverage, but also occasionally in confidence and always in good humor.

To those many individuals who have engaged this project through shared panels or conference discussions, or otherwise indulged me in thinking through my work and theirs, I want to offer my thanks and acknowledgment that in doing so, you have helped to shape this book along the way: Caroline Brettell has helped me to keep firmly in view the human aspects of both anthropological research and friendship, and Richard Rodger's expansive understanding of Edinburgh, past and present, has helped me to tie together these narratives of a complex, compact city. Elizabeth Darling's innovative historical research on women in the Canongate similarly highlighted for me the importance of the activism detailed in the chapters that follow. Julia Yezbick, Leo Coleman, Jarrett Zigon, and Andre Gingrich, your comments on papers delivered from this research along the way have provided inspiration and creative direction that I have thoroughly enjoyed pursuing. Thank you as well to the anonymous reviewers of this book, whose recommendations, insights, and direction substantially improved the contents of the chapters that follow.

My work on this project has been enriched by colleagues at Wheaton College who have read, listened to, and discussed my research; meaningfully contributed their time and disciplinary perspectives; and served as thought partners in substantive ways: Cherith Lundin, Jamie Huff, Karen Johnson, Brian Miller, Matthew Lundin, Greg Lee, Tim Larsen, and Matthew Milliner, with a special thanks to Noah Toly and Brian Howell, whose intellectual contributions have been almost as significant as their support and friendship. And to a much-appreciated writing group, you graced me with a place in a collaborative and productive community for the sharing of ideas and lives for a short but fantastic season: Amy Reynolds, Laura Yoder, Christine Folch, Larycia Hawkins, Leah Anderson, Winnie Fung, Sandra Joireman. Students in my Urban Studies and Anthropology classes have offered rich and stimulating discussions, helping me to conceive of new approaches, angles, and insights, even as they often inspired me with the earnestness of their concerns. Student research assistants have also contributed to this project in a wide and important range of ways. My thanks to Jake Adams, Jared Hackworth, Elijah Kaiss, Kie Takazawa, Joselyn Broadway, Allie Trujillo, and Eric Hoskins. Thank you to Sheldon Till Campbell, whose patient instruction guided me through the studio printing process for the cover image used on this book, a print titled "Fresh Air," that was inspired by a photograph that my eight-year-old son took on one of our research trips to Edinburgh.

To everyone who granted me an interview or conversation and who otherwise shared their experiences and perspectives with me in Edinburgh and Glasgow, you have planted seeds that bear fruit in the following pages. While some of you are named in this book, far more of my sources have not been counted here, and this book project and more than ten years of research have utterly depended on your graciousness, patience, and time. In this book, I have done my best to capture realities far more complex and interesting than any description that I have provided. I feel honored to have had this opportunity to be an ethnographer in your world.

Most of all, thanks to Andy Tooley, who has convinced me that everyone should have a historian on their core team. Without your support, encouragement, creative scheduling, and belief in me, this work would have been immeasurably more difficult. To our children: I have so enjoyed bringing you along for this ride.

# TENEMENT NATION

# INTRODUCTION
## Working Out Class and Nation in Edinburgh

IN THE NEWS COVERAGE OF Scottish independence demonstrations in Edinburgh, the crowds spilling down the High Street, bristling with blue-and-white flags and hand-lettered signs, have provided arresting front-page illustrations. Outnumbering the published images, however, participants' mobile phones have uploaded their own perspectives on these marches to social media. In my media feed, people whom I have come to know through more than ten years of fieldwork pose jubilantly for posterity: arms thrown around a neighbor's shoulders, a blue-and-white saltire painted on both cheeks, a T-shirt with a bold blue "AYE" stretched over a bulky sweater. Scrolling past such images, one might be excused for assuming these marchers to fit a model that by 2022 seems worryingly status quo for European politics: yet more exemplars of a populist nationalism borne out of working-class disaffection.

The working-class Scots discussed in this book do indeed share many of the complaints of the disaffected: properly political processes transformed into economic ones; unresponsive elected representatives; dispossession of goods, spaces, and services formerly provided by the welfare state. But the national political ideals that the Scottish independence demonstrators proclaim when they march with their neighbors bear the markings of European social democracy: multiculturalism, universalism, fairness, and equality. If this is working-class politics, as the Scots in this book claim that it is, then this political mobilization flies in the face of patterns well established in anthropological analysis, observing "the multiculturalism backlash" (Vertovec and Wessendorf 2010; Grillo 2007) and the "return of the repressed" in European political and social life elsewhere (Kalb and Halmai 2011). In light of the extraordinarily high stakes of understanding these movements, a case in which liberal democratic ideals retain their popular strategic significance for the politics of the nation warrants close consideration.

The rhetoric of Scottish independence in official channels, as well as in the everyday lives of the working-class political activists in Edinburgh whom I have observed, explicitly rejects the racialized visions of the nation that sponsor the kind of "regressive, anti-humanist policy" examined by Paul Silverstein in France (2018, 10; Grillo 2008). In their place, an aesthetic of a multicultural Scotland, supported by immigration policies more generous than in the rest of the UK and grounded in a pro-Europe philosophy of political liberalism, supports the nationalists' narrative of Scotland's political and social distinction. While optimism about European political and economic institutions can racially operationalize antisemitism and Islamophobia in the buttressing of white European identities (Bunzl 2005; Schiller 2005), the contemporary significance of Europe in Scottish national politics indexes resistance to isolationist electoral movements that have imposed Britain's exit from the EU on largely unwilling Scots. The narrative of Scotland's liberal distinction thus lends a moralized character to the public image of independent Scotland, which the Edinburgh-based activists described in this book have appropriated in the pursuit of their political ideals. Perhaps most surprisingly, to foil binaries of "leftist populism" versus "nationalist populism" (Gusterson 2017), the nation remains a viable leftist political imaginary in the pursuit of liberal democracy in Scotland.

As the following chapters show, the working-class Scots discussed in this book did not spring to political life along the independence marches. Their support for Scottish independence reflects imaginaries and ethics continuous with the rest of their political and social lives. The independence marchers who insisted on fairness, equality, and multicultural Scotland formed their sense for these values, or their political aesthetic, in the crucible of Edinburgh's processes of urban development, as they rallied against the largest project planned for Edinburgh's city center since the eighteenth century. While national politics may understandably attract the bulk of media coverage, particularly given the crises of identity now afflicting much of Europe, anthropological analyses bear the capacity to situate such activities within longer trajectories of mobilization to political activism, seeking evidence of political imaginaries, values, and objectives in the neighborhood, community, and city politics with which they intersect. This book elaborates the connections between local-level political concerns and movements addressing the nation, offering an analysis of the interpenetrating scales of political life. The capacity for such an approach to depict the influences and relationships of political entanglements in the terms that our interlocutors frame them has already become apparent in ethnographic research that has illuminated the meaningful mobilizations of working-class political actors in and of post–Brexit Britain (see Balthazar 2021; Koch 2017). Elaborating what constitutes both "the political" and "the aesthetic" in this analysis and the relationship between them foregrounds both the motivations and stakes of political action.

The study of everyday life in cities has afforded a field ripe for such analysis since at least the early twentieth century. The relationship between aesthetic practice and social and political life captured the interest of Henri Lefebvre, who from his observations of postwar urban France recognized the capacity of aesthetic practice to foment resistance—in particular, resistance to the multiple alienations imposed by capitalist commodification mechanisms. Lefebvre, however, locates the agency of aesthetic practice in the senses, which through their use in everyday life enable individuals to obtain a freedom of consciousness figured in the production of a work of art (Lefebvre 1953, 27; see also Lefebvre 1991). Art, as the quintessential product of aesthetic work, for Lefebvre is social but not, strictly speaking, political; a refusal of things as they are that effects change within the practice of a life. While aesthetic practice can inspire political practice, for Lefebvre the two remain distinct domains of action. For the residents of the Edinburgh neighborhood of the Canongate whose engagements with local and national politics are discussed in the following chapters, however, everyday practices became the primary terrain of political action, and these everyday politics obtained their moralized coherence through the cultivation and articulation of a shared aesthetic.

Rather than locating aesthetics in the social domain of everyday life and relating everyday life dialectically to politics, I argue that key to understanding the experiences of these Canongate resident campaigners is a theoretical framework attuned to the aesthetic dimensions of the political or, in Jacques Rancière's work, the political aesthetic. Indeed, the affirmations that launched Rancière's wide-ranging philosophical project parallel the political claims of the Edinburgh residents described in this book. Informed by his research on the workers' movement in France, Rancière begins with the profound assertion of equality as the foundational political act, that which constitutes political subjectivation. Politics, Rancière posits, stems from disagreement and dispute with an established order that is being asserted or upheld and is by nature polemical (Rancière 2004 47). While Michel Foucault concerns himself with the apparatuses of control and discipline, and Pierre Bourdieu with the (re)production of consciousness and practice within class structures, Rancière focuses on the means of resistance to such structures and instruments, qua politics (Abélès 2017, 73).

Essential to the aesthetic resistance of the Canongate campaigners is the particular material form of that neighborhood—the built environment that through their indwelling had obtained for them a quality of idealized communal life. Hannah Arendt's (1958) characterization of the relationship between human life and the durability of materiality as consisting in an ongoing project of "world-building" suggests the significance of the specific buildings and spaces to the Canongate residents' political activism, a material and spatial orientation that is missing from Rancière's discussion of political aesthetics. Arendt's work, echoed in Paul Connerton's (2009) observations connecting collective memory to the built environment, suggests the destabilizing impacts of accelerating the metabolism of the urban built environment, which was contested by the Canongate campaigners through their campaign and a repoliticizing discourse of home. I suggest that a theory of the aesthetic, which situates everyday practices within the sense of a place and considers both the social elements of these practices and the material forms they inhabit, is needed to represent the aesthetics of politics that emerged in the Canongate neighborhood of Edinburgh and has found resonance in the politics of the Scottish nation. Rancière's attentiveness to the inherently aesthetic dimensions of politics (elaborated in chaps. 2, 3, and 5), Arendt's (1958) explication of the "world-building quality" of material forms (engaged in chap. 4), and Connerton's conceptualization of a link between built environment and memory (chap. 3) thus afford the theoretical framework for the analysis in this book.

Discussions of aesthetics often invoke the language of moral judgment in both popular and scholarly analysis, so a note on their distinctive semantic domains for the purpose of the book follows. Morality is treated here as the interpretive system that attributes value to behavior; it offers a vernacular language of "the good" and "the bad" and a distribution of behaviors, orders, and realities between the two. Aesthetics concerns the material and social order of appearance, idealized or actualized. As in this book, the aesthetics of a material form or plan—as in the plans for a city block—are often considered through a moral lens that confers judgment as to propriety and benefit. Gisa Weszkalnys has demonstrated persuasively that planning disputes often center on divergent interpretations of the good (2010). In this book, I show that the language and practices of aesthetics permit the content of the respective visions to be elaborated and contested—not necessarily in that order.

In the following chapters, I show how working-class Edinburgh residents organized and mobilized a program of political action founded on an affirmation of their equality with other actors and groups invested in the city's built environment, from which they disputed the terms of the redevelopment of their neighborhood. Their mobilization in that campaign constituted an "effectuation of equality," which, precisely because its objectives could not be "settled once and for all" (Abélès 2017, 77), subsequently shaped their political mobilization at the national scale. The working-class Edinburgh residents discussed in this book approach national independence as a rhetorical exposition of their social ideals as well as a pragmatic expression of a political voice, which in their experiences with Edinburgh's urban development machinery had been silenced. In contrast with the depoliticizing that they observed in the municipal processes, independent Scotland for them has been appealingly repoliticized, seized from the teeth of both the technocrats and the tourism board, whose collusion had seemingly denied residents' rightful political agency—in Rancière's terms their emancipation—throughout the development process (cf. Koch 2016).

The image of an independent Scotland for these campaigners is thus rooted in the Canongate neighborhood of Edinburgh at the turning of the twentieth century, and the liberal democratic terms of that nation's appeal have been amplified by their experience of dispossession via urban development, as well as affirmed through the alliances they cultivated in an extensive and wide-ranging neighborhood campaign. The idealized images and rhetoric of a multicultural, people's Scotland that circulated through public and social media in the years following their campaign did not capture a sense of disillusionment with a decreasingly relevant state (Abélès 2017), or the instability of a postcolonial imperial capital (Silverstein 2018), but rather resonated with activists' hopes for a more politically inclusive and responsive liberal democracy. As the following chapters trace the mobilizations of these Edinburgh residents from a development campaign to the independence movement, I argue that their identification with the Scottish nation should be approached as an unfolding, agentive process, invested in the aesthetic construction of both neighborhood and nation. This book thus shows that to understand the varied political imaginaries of the nation, a promising antecedent for analysis may be the politics of a space more proximate: the city itself.

### Working-Class Edinburgh and the Problem of Visibility

Throughout the centuries-old industry of Scottish tourism, the gorse-blown hills and blackened sandstone spires of Edinburgh have staged an accommodatingly photogenic dreamscape. An air of romantic decay has been attributed to the city's Old Town since at least the eighteenth century, when pedestrian passage and a doorstep economy of production required the high tenement cliffs to be punctured by a sundry assortment of alleys, locally called *wynds* and *closes*. In its accommodations to an undulating topography, owed to the area's historic volcanic activity and long subjected to some serious Arthurian speculation (Bort 2010; Koch 1997), the city's built environment offers some genuine surprises to a first-time visitor. From the first step out of Waverley train station, a traveler faces the Old Town's stony edifice rising heavily toward the castle, and on a stroll along one of its main roads, one is apt to find that a gently sloping passage between a double row of shops opens abruptly to a bridge spanning a multistory townscape and crosscutting street below. Such architecture famously delves deep underground, and I recall vividly the shudders of a Nigerian friend whenever she descended many underground stories to take inventory in the Old Town shop where she worked.

Edinburgh's moodily charismatic built and natural environment has shaped its international image in the fields of cultural production as well, boasting the kind of literary attention often reserved for human characters. Muse to the eighteenth-century poetry of Robert Burns, the nineteenth-century novels of Sir Walter Scott and Robert Louis Stevenson, and the twentieth-century verses of Hugh MacDiarmid, Edinburgh has maintained its starring role in twentieth-first-century bestselling series by authors Ian Rankin, Alexander McCall Smith, and Irvine Welsh, and it affords a haunting cityscape that continues to captivate more recent generations of novelists, such as Kate Atkinson, Alicia Thompson, and Alex Brown. Edinburgh was designated the first UNESCO City of Literature in 2004, and its list of fictionalized accounts is too long and varied to attempt a characterization here. The city has been invoked across an impressive affective range, from mad and romantic, to somber and bleak, manic or farcical. Indeed, Edinburgh rarely fails to register as an agent of affect, rendered through its distinctive aesthetic cues.

For all its visual accessibility, however, the city's most persistent representations have authorized the occlusion of large swathes of its population or their relegation to notoriety at the urban fringes. Despite the sweeping panoramas available from Edinburgh's hills and windows, its most apparent identities and time-worn scripts obscure the considerable contributions of its working-class residents to its social, material, and political life. And where visible presence is obscured, access to the processes of urban influence tends to follow suit (Ghertner 2015; Tooley and Yezbick 2020).

Edinburgh, erstwhile "Athens of the North" and "Auld Reekie," has in Scotland long been popularly characterized by its white-collar professions and an aloofness captured in the politely inhospitable phrase "You'll have had your tea then," which is supposed to greet (and disappoint) visitors and would-be supper guests. The home of the eighteenth-century Scottish Enlightenment and Britain's second city of finance, Edinburgh seems at first glance a strange place to study working-class politics, as apparently the most culturally middle-class city in a nation known for its popular identification with the working classes (McCrone 2017). But Edinburgh's middle-class caricature has long belied a sizeable population of working-class residents (Madgin and Rodger 2013), and as this book shows, this obscurity, in both historical and present-day representations, has facilitated their exclusion from the processes of urban development and an underappreciation of their roles in the politics of city and nation. Alongside the monumental architecture more often associated with Scottish "civic symbolism" (Hearn 2003), this book foregrounds the sturdy tenement building and its council housing flats—sites not only of social solidarity but, as in campaigns described in the following chapters, of life-affirming aesthetic cum political resistance as well.

In its attention to the political life of a working-class neighborhood in Edinburgh, this book complements a rich and growing body of social science research on class and national identity in Britain, where examples from

England tend to predominate (see Biressi and Nunn 2013; Degnen and Tyler 2017), with studies on the working classes following a similar trend (Evans 2006; Koch 2015; McKenzie 2015; Mollona 2009; Tyler 2004, 2012). Representation of Scotland's working classes has often confirmed geographic and historical patterns found in many other British cities, being associated with peripheral council housing estates and narratives of postindustrial decline (Gilfillan 2011; Grill 2012; see also McGarvey 2017). Likewise, popular fiction has associated working-class life with Edinburgh's council housing estates, depicting its scenes in novels like Welsh's *Trainspotting* (popularized through the film of the same name) and Rankin's Rebus detective series. But Edinburgh's estates, much like their counterparts in England, house more varied populations than such fictionalized accounts suggest (see Abbasi, Alalouch, and Bramley 2016; Kallin and Slater 2014). When passing through an estate during my fieldwork, I was often struck by proximities characteristic rather than unusual: a pair of neatly dressed retirees walking home, laden with canvas shopping bags and enjoying a chat, while across the street a figure staggered and swayed, or slumped silently, in substance-induced oblivion. An entrenched trope in the study of the working classes invokes a binary, and often emic, distinction between respectable and unrespectable populations, while ethnographic study on council housing estates has conveyed a less easily categorizable diversity of experiences there, as well as other working-class locations (Evans 2012; Koch 2016; Miller 1988; Smith 2017). Such depictions of estate life have destabilized the council estate's negative reputation, conveying not merely the presence of "respectable" residents but also the complexity and irreducibility of residents' experiences and their engagements both within and without the estate (Hastings 2004; Jones 2012; Todd 2015).

The research on which this book is based has been conducted in an Edinburgh location that is doubly unexpected: a largely working-class neighborhood at the center of the Scottish city perhaps least associated with the working classes. As such, neither this setting, a neighborhood called the Canongate, nor its residents should be regarded as typical to urban Scotland. But the rather extraordinary combination of the Canongate's features—mostly white, working-class residents making their homes in council housing flats integrated into a built environment that has been designated a UNESCO World Heritage site and is situated adjacent to a royal palace, parliament, and city council headquarters—presents a blend that, though unique, touches on the experiences of residents in other Scottish cities that have also been shaped by processes of industry, decline, and tourism-courting redevelopment. The threat of the Canongate's redevelopment did not merely mobilize the neighborhood's residents; it also motivated many individuals and groups throughout Edinburgh to participate in and lend their support to the residents' campaign. Thus the following narrative weaves together a collection of related threads: women's roles in working-class political movements, community representation in municipal politics, the forging and negotiating of interclass alliances, and the interpenetration of urban and national politics.

This book does not attempt to convey a kind of representative study of Scottish working classes, and even less so of urban Scotland. The ten years over which I have studied with and learned from self-identified working-class political activists in Edinburgh have persuaded me that the experiences of working-class residents cannot be assessed solely through the marginalized locations of the peripheral estates and the social problems associated with their isolation. More often than not, my ethnographic research has traced relationships within the city center rather than around its margins. In fact, during the time I spent with Canongate residents, the most striking connection I observed between them and the council estates was the lack thereof—or, rather, the social distance between these locations identified by the resident campaigners with the working classes. The Canongate as a place was not closely tied through personal contacts to the peripheral estates, and though its residents navigated the city with the resource precarity that often characterizes working-class lives, social and political isolation did not typify their experience. Instead, as the following chapters show, more significant to the neighborhood residents was a shared sense of historical memory, which linked the Old Town as a place with associated social practices to the Canongate's working-class community life.

The conditions of urban life and the political engagements of Canongate residents negotiating for influence in a neoliberalizing urban development process have shaped these residents' national politics, even as the Scottish nationalist rhetoric, represented publicly by the Scottish National Party (SNP), has introduced concepts like multiculturalism that have been integrated into their political program (discussed in chap. 5). In its ten-year trajectory, from the self-organization of Canongate residents into a neighborhood campaign to the multiple national political engagements of the same residents, this book explores the convergence of urban and national imaginaries in what I identify as a political aesthetic. This political aesthetic recognizes a sense of place, belonging, and political accountability emergent in the neighborhood spaces of the Canongate and resonant with the national politics of Scottish independence. The pursuit of neoliberalizing urban development plans in Edinburgh has shaped the terms by which working-class residents in the Old Town identify with a multicultural, liberal democratic vision of Scotland. The popularity of this national vision among both working and middle classes in Scotland represents a significant divergence from patterns of national electoral politics across Europe, and given the social and economic stakes of such distinctions, ethnographic analyses that situate Scottish national politics within the solidarities, practices, and aesthetics of everyday life are urgently needed.

## Nationalism and the Working Classes

Throughout the European heartlands of liberal political philosophy, a resurgence of exclusivist ethnic nationalisms within apparently mature nation-states has exposed and shaken the progressive expectations of this region's intellectual and cultural elites. Whether or not such movements represent the triumph of ethnic or cultural identities over identities based in social contracts and the sharing of place, it is not difficult to see that they challenge the bases for inclusive political ideals of nationhood. These nationalisms have typically highlighted bounded traits, such as blood or culture, as the basis for national identity, and advocates expend much of their political energies on the fixing of boundaries around a centered set of such traits (Gullestad 2002; Miller-Idriss 2009). Homogeneity rather than difference is emphasized within that set that defines national belonging, and between that set and other groupings of traits, relations are construed primarily in terms of difference.

The turn of the millennium brought a magnification of anthropological attention to European nationalism. In 2002, Andre Gingrich and Marcus Banks published a discourse-orienting volume detailing the emergence of movements that they collectively designated "neo-nationalism," entailing the reconciliation of (or resistance by) "dethroned" global imperial powers (Gingrich 2002) to unsettling realities of decolonization and global migration flows (Gingrich and Banks 2006, 9; cf. Appadurai 1986). While Michael

Keating has noted that identifying contemporary nationalist movements as *neo*—the term *neonationalism* being applied to Scotland as early as 1977 (Nairn 1977)—misrepresents the recurrent nature of nationalism as a "perennial" question (Keating 2009, 205). The terminology of *neonationalism* and the general conviction that twenty-first-century nationalisms represented a new formation gained favor in political and social analyses. Ethnographic emphases on individual experiences and action within these movements have framed these movements as pursuits of "social agency" (Gingrich and Banks 2006, 11), and the Gingrich and Banks collection, though focusing on Europe, extends its examination to non-European contexts using a methodologically comparative lens. Searching for the global forces that animate the nationalist movements that anthropologists and others have identified, a diverse assemblage of social scientists have identified postcolonialism and the imposition of neoliberal political-economic measures on the former core states as stimulants for discontent in Europe and elsewhere (Friedman 2003; Giddens 1994; Peck and Tickell 2002; Rose 1999; Silverstein 2018). As the tide of this discontent rises (and indeed carries many politicians to power), attention has focused on the constituency most often courted by these neonationalist movements: the working classes. As Don Kalb states in the introduction to his and Gábor Halmai's edited volume *Headlines of Nation, Subtexts of Class*: "We make the anthropological case that working-class neo-nationalism is the somewhat traumatic expression of material and cultural experiences of dispossession and disenfranchisement in the neoliberal epoch. . . . We suggest that nationalist populism is a displacement of experiences of dispossession and disenfranchisement onto the imagined nation as a community of fate, crafted by new political entrepreneurs generating protest votes against neoliberal rule" (2011, 1).

This quote summarizes a link made in the analysis of (neo)nationalisms in Europe and the resurgence of anthropological interest in social class and economic anthropology more generally (Carrier and Kalb 2015; Carrier 2006; Hann 1998). There has been undeniable "downward pressure" on welfare provisions, on a broad conceptualization of social and community rights, and on the accessibility of (post)political processes faced by many residents in European countries that have adopted a variety of neoliberalizing policies, as part of "the agenda of the capitalist competition state" (Kalb 2011, 5). From these pressures has emerged a class-based politics—particularly centralized around working-class identity mobilized to populist-nationalist campaigns (Kalb and Halmai 2011). Such a narrative characterizes many European states, and it seems especially relevant, for instance, in England, where working-class Brexit voters appear to have been mobilized from frustrations with their own political and economic subordination and the breakdown of the political left (Evans 2017; Koch 2016). But this narrative does not apply as clearly to the context of Scotland as the "understated" nation in the United Kingdom (McCrone 2005), where recent electoral events demonstrate the resilience of left-of-center politics, carried by the SNP in the face of Labour's loss of credibility (Hassan 2009; Hassan and Barnett 2009; Henderson et al. 2020; Paterson 1997). Indeed, after Brexit, commitments to cosmopolitanism in the form of "ideals of freedom, tolerance, and social liberty" emerging via the "unusual channels" of Scottish nationalism have presented a disorienting choice of political futures for some English nationals in Scotland, as discussed in chapter 5 (Knight 2017).

The predominance of English case studies in studies of the British working classes amounts to an underrepresentation of Scottish people and places, which suggests a lacuna in our understanding of working-class politics precisely at the moment that Scottish electoral politics is underlining its departure from patterns across England. Such distinctiveness characterizes the electoral events surrounding Brexit, most notably the direct referendum for Brexit in 2016, in which every council district in Scotland voted "Remain" (62 percent against 38 percent overall), and the 2019 general UK election, in which the SNP gained thirteen seats, following a brief post-Brexit slump, to hold a total of forty-eight out of fifty-nine seats in Scotland. The Remain vote and the gains by the SNP contrast voting outcomes in England, which saw Brexit supported 53.4 percent against 46.6 percent, and the Conservative Party gaining a landslide majority of 80 percent. The English working-class politics identified with the populism of "the repressed" as described in Kalb and Halmai's (2011) volume has failed to gain popular purchase in Scotland, and as the case of the Canongate residents suggests, this failure reflects the fact that welfare-oriented political agendas continue to appear a viable, visible option through the SNP.

If recent Scottish electoral patterns have diverged from those associated with the English working classes and with working-class populism identified in many European countries, then to what extent are those electoral behaviors accompanied by appreciably different social contexts and public norms? Public political discourse in Scotland has long resisted the more virulently antiimmigrant, ethnic strains that have alarmed observers in Western Europe—the Netherlands (Mepschen 2017) and France (Art 2011; Grillo 1998; Silverstein 2018), and in Eastern and Central Europe—Austria (Krzyzanowski 2013; Wodak 2013) and Hungary (Bartha 2011; Halmai 2011). But as many social scientists have insisted, the rhetoric of political elites should not be taken as representative of the experiences of "black and brown Scots" (Davidson and Virdee 2018, 10). The proimmigrant rhetoric of the SNP can produce a self-congratulatory posture that obscures the need for critical recognition of the imperial history of Scotland (Devine 2003; Liinpää 2018) and the urgency of the cultivation of systematically antiracist policies across Scotland (Davidson et al. 2018). Antiimmigrant discrimination and racism against black and brown Scots are features of everyday life for many of Scotland's residents (Bonino 2019; Clark 2018; Goldie 2018; Grill 2012; Hunter and Meer 2018; Meer 2018; Mostafa 2018), creating vulnerabilities that have only been exacerbated by the COVID-19 pandemic (Loopstra 2020).

Concerning patterns in European nationalist politics, Scotland's distinctiveness must not be attributed to a lack of racism and discrimination. Instead, the degree to which "Scotland is different"[1] refers here to the nation constructed by political rhetoric, an image that, while influential, does not entail its own realization. Thus, while the dominant political rhetoric for national independence does not build on strategies for exclusion and isolation, exemplified in the refusal of its proindependence political party to proliferate discriminatory rhetoric in service of electoral success, as Davidson observes, the rhetoric alone guarantees nothing to black and brown Scots. Assessing the long-term impacts of such political platforms on the experiences of Scottish citizens and residents must therefore complement studies such as this one. For the activists discussed in this book, the SNP's promulticulturalism rhetoric has issued invitations into political discourses supportive of immigration, shaping their characterizations of the Scottish nation and their arguments for independence.

While such rhetoric should not and cannot be taken as the measure of racial discrimination in Scotland, the SNP statements and policies affirming "New Scots" have not been inconsequential for Scottish minority group members. Studies on immigrant experiences in Britain have found Scottish national identity to offer more broadly inclusive terms than its

English counterpart (Sigona and Godin 2019; Simpson and Smith 2014), and recent research among Scottish working classes in Glasgow has found support for this narrative of distinction (Gawlewicz 2020). Given these complexities, ethnographic accounts such as this one, which consider the relationship between elite rhetoric and the discourse of popular political mobilizations, offer important pieces of the puzzle of lived experiences of multicultural Scotland. The Scots introduced in this book are mostly white and working class, and so their perspective on the nation of Scotland, discussed in chapter 5, reflects the interaction between their personal histories and the public rhetoric of the SNP, but not their own experiences of racial discrimination.

The distinctively liberal quality of public political rhetoric among both elites and the Edinburgh community activists discussed in this book, with an attendant impact on the terms of identity and belonging for the black and brown people of Scotland, further raises the question of meaning regarding Scotland's recent electoral developments. The parliamentary election of an unprecedented SNP majority in 2015 broadly suggested an upsurge in Scottish nationalism, without specifying the interpretations of this election by the voters themselves (see Cohen 1996). Survey data on Scottish identity has suggested the rise of Scottish over British identity since at least 1979, so this most recent surge should be seen as an intensification of trends already underway rather than a course reversal or turn (Rosie and Bond 2008, 56). Research on identity in Scotland has long avoided the lumping together of national identity and constitutional preferences, as Scottish identity found its home in "unionist nationalism" through the nineteenth century (Morton 1999; see also Coleman 2018), accommodating from the postwar period a unionist Labour politics that prevailed until the rapid erosion of its base at the turn of the twenty-first century. The recent intensification of Scottish-first identification has accompanied an electoral shift toward nationalist politics, particularly among the working classes, Labour's former base, such that in analyses of Scottish identity, the prime constitutional question, independence, is always potentially in view.

As observed in the discussion of the independence marches' news coverage at the start of this chapter, the vocal participation of working-class Scots in the "Yes" campaign for Scottish independence in 2014 could lead an observer to construe this political activity and the electoral shift to the SNP as constituting one more example of working-class populism at play.

In fact, Kalb characterizes Scottish "working-class nationalism" as one of these populist movements (2011, 28), and a contributor to that volume, Paul Gilfillan, cites a 1996 study by David McCrone, Lindsay Paterson, and Alice Brown to suggest that the working classes represent the core nationalist constituency (Gilfillan 2011, 174). Yet in more recent analyses, nationalism in Scotland does not appear to be driven or monopolized by the working classes. In his analysis of the "Yes" campaign, Paterson found that it was led by politically leftist middle-class individuals, to the extent that, in 2014 polls, 47 percent of left-leaning middle-class people were planning to vote "Yes," compared to 42 percent of working classes as a whole (Paterson 1997). Strikingly, however, the working classes played an important part not only in this campaign but in the social imagination of these left-leaning middle classes. Paterson identified the two strongest intentions to vote "Yes" among left-leaning middle-class individuals *who identified with the working classes* and among working-class individuals who felt no strong class-based solidarity with the English working classes (Paterson 2015, 42–43 [emphasis mine]). The relationship of class to nationalism in Scotland has long been more complicated than a simple theory of displacement from class to nation would suggest, perhaps reflecting the fact that contemporary Scots continue to prefer to identify themselves as "working-class" over any other class identity (McCrone 2017, 238). As sociologist David McCrone has observed, there remains no straightforward translation of social class to politics in Scotland (2017, 241).

Such peculiarities in the relationships among class, national identity, and electoral politics demand a closer examination of the political activities of the working classes in Scotland, particularly regarding the connections between various instruments and scales of political expression. I suggest that the framework of political aesthetics offers a fruitful approach to these dynamics, traveling well between scales of engagement from neighborhood to national politics and conveying the sense of coherence expressed by Canongate residents. This coherence must be cultivated rather than presumed, resonating with the ongoing labor by which "activists and leaders . . . constantly reimagin[e] what the future civic and political world could look like," out of their own experiences of political mobilization (Baiocchi et al. 2014, 25). The following section elaborates this use of aesthetics and its application to the political life of urban Scots discussed in the rest of the book, which explores the links between the specific, everyday architecture of cities and structures of national political affect, or the political aesthetics of city and nation.

## Neoliberal Urbanism, Aesthetics, and Working-Class Cosmopolitanism

The aesthetic of nations refers to the cultivation of affect in response to particular aesthetic objects, on which the formation of public culture depends. National aesthetic has been linked by Nayanika Mookherjee to "the personal experience of a peculiar emotion, one's feelings for these aesthetic artefacts, as well as the social, political socializations of these feelings" (2011, sec. 5). I suggest that the Canongate residents discussed in this book cultivated an aesthetic, political in its affirmations and demands, through their campaign against the Caltongate development. This political aesthetic adapted to and remained evident within the activist trajectories of the campaigners as they appropriated Scottish nationalist rhetoric of equality, fairness, and multiculturalism in a distinctly Canongotian image. Applying an aesthetic perspective to the political mobilizations of the Canongate residents has captured both an underappreciated aspect of neoliberal urbanization and the coherence between the social and political visions articulated by the residents themselves.

Orienting a study of working-class politics to a neighborhood such as the Canongate not only offers a geographic scale handy for ethnographic study; it also suggests methodological advantages, over a lens of ethnic group or community, for the study of working-class life in Britain (Edwards, Evans, and Smith 2012, 6). In my research, this neighborhood lens has made visible the ongoing political activism of the Canongate residents, who have cultivated an interclass solidarity enabled by the density of connections that converged on their city-center neighborhood. As subsequent chapters show, for Canongate residents as well as for city councilors and private developers, aesthetic concerns related to urban development are inextricable from social and political imagination. The residents' initial focus on the appearance, shape, spaces, and functions of the proposed redevelopment conferred on their political vision and its frustrated critiques of neoliberal urbanization a material form. In the following chapters, I show that this material and political vision for which they claimed custodial responsibility, and which I came to understand as the Canongate aesthetic, has shaped their vision of the Scottish nation in the image of the idealized Canongate itself. In its close study of a neighborhood mobilizing to engage the mechanisms of urban development, this book contributes to an ongoing program in anthropological research of contextualizing neoliberal urbanism, the ascendant political economy of urban development in the North Atlantic (Harvey 1989, 2005; Peck and Theodore 2012), and examining its entanglements in social and political life. With attentiveness to the terms of the social and political vision cultivated by the Canongate residents, I argue for the significance of the aesthetic as a political field in which neoliberal urbanism is materialized and contested, though rarely assessed.

To elaborate the relationship between the political and the aesthetic, I have invoked Rancière's expanded definition of the aesthetic, by which he means the "sense of life" associated with the affective experience of "individual, community, physical and social life" (Rancière and Gage 2019, 5). This definition of aesthetics makes clear that the aesthetic is necessarily political, in that any specific sense of life consists in the evaluative ordering of such aspects in relation to one another. This conceptualization of aesthetics has been applied fruitfully by anthropologists to analysis of the affective resonances of political regimes and movements (Mookherjee 2011) and the processes and effects of art and design projects (Elinoff 2016; Sansi 2015, 2020; Yezbick 2020). As this book shows, the aesthetic as an analytic makes visible the coherence felt by Canongate campaigners between their everyday practice, the built environment and local historical narratives, and the aesthetic imported in the Caltongate master plan, with its own value-based neoliberal assumptions about relationships among urban space, economy, residents, the built environment, and political process. An aesthetic lens also directs attention to the materiality of urban contexts, discussed in chapter 4 through the theoretical framework of Hannah Arendt, as well as the relationship between the material and social memory, considered in chapter 3 through engagement with the work of Paul Connerton.

Most importantly, adopting an aesthetic lens centers the framings of the issue by the Canongate residents themselves, despite attempts to categorically minimize the gravity of aesthetic concerns by proponents of the Caltongate development, in chapter 3. Minimizing the aesthetic instruments of neoliberal urbanization and the sense of loss its transformations entail for affected residents only serves the rhetoric of neoliberal justification and obscures the very real and deeply felt impacts of such projects on vulnerable working classes in particular. I have observed in the Canongate a resonance cultivated between life and politics, producing a coherence of experience, place, and political vision that has been translated across scales of political activity. From city to nation, this book charts their creative efforts to cultivate a political aesthetic spatially and relationally articulated in practices of dwelling (Heidegger 1954), distinguished by embedded notions of urban heritage and strategies of interclass alliance, and to leverage this aesthetic as an ethical alternative to the values and practices of neoliberal urbanism. In their translation of these neighborhood political aesthetics to a national political scale, Canongate residents seek the realization of welfare state futures in Scotland.

The aesthetic coherence described in the following chapters reflects the historical, formative effects of material and social surroundings on the "sense" by which residents navigate material and social lives, in a matter somewhat suggestive of Bourdieu's habitus (1991). But rather than conveying an already-formed integration, I have observed cohering itself to be a creative, political act at the center of campaigners' justifications for their claims on the state, thus the emphasizing the cultivation of coherence and difference, of solidarities and the making of the world from the Canongate. I argue that political mobilizations, like that of the Canongate residents, can be illuminated when understood as "creative practice" in the sense described by Rancière, as an aesthetic discourse about the appropriate, moral relationships between related aspects of life (Rancière and Gage 2019, 5). Rancière suggests that a shared "sense of life" precedes and mediates such creative practice, and this analysis of the Canongate elaborates the mutuality of this support in an affective, evocative politics that is both intimate and public. As subsequent chapters show, knowing and advocating for the built heritage and current residents of the Canongate constituted a moral claim to political position rooted in place rather than an individual's genealogy or history, one open to Edinburgh's conservation professionals as much as the Canongate residents. The openness of this Canongate-based political aesthetic resonates with the liberal, place-based rhetoric of Scottish nationalism, indicating a shared well of political philosophy and cultural lore from which activists in both traditions have drunk deeply.

I characterize this Canongate aesthetic as a working-class cosmopolitanism, an idealized politics of national belonging that affirms the sharing of place, such as neighborhood or city, as an appropriate basis for leveraging claims to shared identity. But a cosmopolitan national identity may at first appear contradictory. The statement often cited as the original expression of cosmopolitanism, "I am a citizen of the World," was Diogenes's (412–323 BCE) answer to the question of his belonging. His reply declines to offer the political place name requested by his interrogators, and if we regard such a framing of identity as typifying a cosmopolitan perspective, we would be justified in wondering whether cosmopolitanism requires a refusal of place- or nation-based identity. But as contributions to a volume edited by Nina Schiller and Andrew Irving illustrate, the idea of citizenship in a generalized world, as opposed to citizenship tied to a place in the world, is an imaginative fiction. Irving and Schiller argue instead that, "citizens are not random individuals, but rather persons with rights and obligations to a system of government" (2015, 31). Cosmopolitans remain citizens obligated to one such system, and though they recognize identities based in, but not exhausted by, discrete characteristics like place, class, and religion, from these identities they act to affirm "times, moments and places of commonality," and achieve a kind of "coming together without disregarding disparate, multiple pasts and presents" (2015, 32). Such a cosmopolitanism resonates with Daniel Knight's uneasy musings about the migration of cosmopolitanism from the domain of British to Scottish national visions in the wake of the Brexit vote. He observes hopefully, "It is quite possible to express oneself through the trope of metamorphosed nationalism while behaving with civility and upholding the virtues of a social democracy" (2017, 240).

The Canongate activists discussed in the following chapters resisted the urge to frame the forces of neoliberal urbanism in terms of global interests crudely opposed to their own, local interests, and in fact they viewed international organizations as potential sources of authority to invoke over the urban development processes. These residents, who identified themselves as both local and global actors and sought political allies across Britain, Europe, and the North Atlantic (see Featherstone 2005), pursued a cosmopolitanism of resistance rather than accommodation to the expectations of the metabolic systems of neoliberal urbanism (cf. Muehlebach 2012). They cultivated crossclass alliances with Edinburgh-based conservationists, architects, and urban planners, not to mention anthropologists, and they contacted European Union officials as well as UNESCO in their search for support. Such alliances constitute the "intersections, interrelations, and interlocutions between those we identify, or who identify themselves, as working and middle class," which has been identified as one of the most pressing areas for study in the anthropology of Britain (Edwards 2017, 192). In these ways, the campaign itself reflected cosmopolitan postures toward place, class identities, international polities, and cultural organizations, and while initially mobilized by and dependent on working-class political actors, this campaign could not be characterized as exclusively working-class in its composition or in its resources.

The cosmopolitanism of the largely working-class Canongate campaigners came to incorporate a multicultural vision for Scotland and embrace a broadly inclusive reckoning of political citizenship and social belonging. While anthropological analyses have identified an eroded popular faith in the capacity of nation-states to deliver such visions across Europe (Silverstein 2018; Abélès 2017), as chapter 5 shows, this working-class cosmopolitanism is premised on hope in the future success of Scotland's social democratic welfare state, one promised by the SNP to be delivered as an independent Scotland. Rather than looking backward to a nostalgic national past, the affective power of the SNP's social democratic political vision lies in its orientation to the future: the hoped-for independent Scotland will depend on participation in international networks by cosmopolitan Scots of all classes. Such a vision appeals particularly to the Canongate residents, who through an ambitious slate of urban development projects in Edinburgh have found themselves increasingly marginalized and their concerns instrumentalized in service of the city's economic growth. In the section that follows, a summary of the city's growth-pursuant investment projects provides the background for the development proposals to come, and a brief timeline of the Canongate campaigners' mobilizations and political-aesthetic engagements orients the narrative of the subsequent chapters.

### Neoliberalizing Development in Edinburgh

Despite its boosterish discourse of jobs creation and opportunity, the urban growth coalition of private developers, local business leaders, and municipal government operationalizes a depoliticizing rhetoric of aesthetics as style, renewal, and growth in which working-class lives are characterized as an underrealized stage on a ladder toward middle-class actualization. In Edinburgh as elsewhere, the historic power of collective working-class political mobilization has been diffused in postindustrial urban economies that do not depend on spatially clustered laborers, at least not blue-collar laborers. Amenities for white-collar professionals have topped the priorities of urban development in Edinburgh since at least 1996, when the reorganization of local authorities with a strong economic remit granted more centralized, formal authority to act in pursuit of economic development (Fairley 1996). Edinburgh leadership identified its competitive advantages and directed resources into cultivating them further via industry clusters, some of the most successful of which have been in the fields of biotechnology, finance, and tourism: cloning Dolly the sheep, supporting Edinburgh in its prized place as the UK's second financial center, and marketing cultural events to portray the city as a year-round festival destination. While the clustering of industries represents a well-established economic strategy that long preceded this era of Edinburgh's economic development (McCrone 1999), the prioritization of these global projects in entrepreneurial urbanism has ambitiously remade the material and social life of the city. Urban development projects designed to provision the "new economy" have redeveloped the city center; the peripheral green belt locations that now surround business parks and the transport links that join them (Kerr 2005, 211); and, most recently, a city-center tram project constructed at the cost of £776 million.

When working-class city residents have complained about their neglect, as they did repeatedly during the period discussed in this book, it was suggested—by a prominent member of Edinburgh's city council and Labour Party—that they should not look to maintaining their working-class positions but rather to seeking upward class mobility. This vision of Edinburgh, turning over its built environment in service of the global mobility of white-collar workers and capital, and commending the moralized pursuit of class mobility as a means to obtain ever-ascending rents for both space and influence, has been difficult to reconcile with the everyday practices and values affirmed by the working-class residents with whom I have studied. Over the decade I have conducted research in Edinburgh, residents' claims that "there is no place for the working classes" in the city center—with the blame squarely placed on betrayals of local governance rather than on a scapegoated figure of the global—increased markedly.

The following chapters consider the claims, critiques, and actions that constituted Canongate residents' mobilizations in protest of these development plans and in pursuit of a more responsive state. As these chapters follow a thematic rather than chronological structure, a brief sketch of the timeline of that mobilization provides an orienting reference. Although the rest of this book shows that its origins lie much further back, the Canongate campaign was directly set into motion in the autumn of 2005 by the public presentation of a proposal for the largest development project in Edinburgh's city center since the construction of its New Town in the eighteenth century, a development project intended for the Canongate. This neighborhood, its foundations laid in the medieval settlement of Edinburgh, had over the last two centuries been profoundly reshaped through its participation in the city's second-largest industrial zone. Reflecting long-term working-class labor and residence, at the time of the development proposal, the neighborhood retained a concentration of council housing that continued to support one of the last remaining primarily residential areas of Edinburgh's Old Town. Immediately following the presentation of the redevelopment proposal, which was (confusingly and craftily) called Caltongate, residents in the Canongate formed a community campaign called Save Our Old Town (SOOT), warily regarding the proposal's enthusiastic support by city council leadership. One of several community mobilizations against development proposals around Edinburgh at the time, the SOOT campaign leveraged the Canongate's central location and the enormous personal labor of its leaders to secure coverage by local and national newspapers, which ran articles and editorials on the development almost every week (and often more frequently) during the initial period of my fieldwork.

I began attending campaign events in 2006 and over the next two years documented the work of the Canongate residents as they pursued formal engagement with the planning process. Although the Caltongate proposal was approved by Edinburgh's city council, despite the SOOT campaign, in 2008, a temporary reprieve granted by the economic recession of 2008–2009 enabled the residents to launch new strategies intended to pursue development in service of community welfare. By the time a new developer took up the council-approved plans in 2011, the residents had gained sufficient visibility, influence, and support so that some accommodations to their requests resulted in modifications to the development plan. This development, renamed New Waverley, has been under construction since that time, as observed through subsequent research trips in 2017 and 2018. Throughout this period, the (now-former) campaigners have addressed national politics and continued to challenge multiple aspects of neoliberal urbanism in ways that reflect the aesthetic concerns articulated in the

Canongate. Their adaptive political discourse makes common cause with the social democratic rhetoric of Scottish nationalism by appropriating its affective politics of hope and fashioning a national political vision in the moralized aesthetic of the Canongate.

The subsequent chapters show how Canongate residents drew on resources from their location in the Old Town, including a repertoire of local memory and national and international legal, professional, and community networks, to contest the application of the neoliberal development logics of depoliticization (chap. 2), aestheticization (chap. 3), and the framing of place as property (chap. 4). Such work required the development of an alternative social and political imaginary, an ethical order that would prioritize residents' everyday lives above short-term economic growth and be essentially identified with the aesthetic of the Canongate. Although the neighborhood campaign focused on immediate aims relating to a particular development proposal, in the aftermath of the campaign, Canongate residents invoked the rhetoric of an idealized Scottish welfare state to express this ethical order. The residents' political imaginaries of a compassionate and provision-oriented state, of the sort that *would have* recognized their moral and political claims as resident-custodians of the Canongate, resonated with the Europe-oriented social democratic rhetoric of the SNP. The idealistic SNP rhetoric called for social and political reforms that seemed to move in the direction of public accountability, conveying the image of a responsive state, belief in which many residents had come to abandon as futile at the end of the Canongate campaign (cf. Koch 2016).

While it can be observed that several of the former campaigners adapted their political engagement to a national stage, as political activists for independence, their vision of nation has also incorporated their experiences of frustration with an unresponsive, dispossessive neoliberal state. In this way, the Scottish nation is remade in the image of the Canongate. Through national rather than urban politics, the former resident campaigners have discovered that they can pursue political-economic alternatives to neoliberal urbanism that reject not its globalism or its multiculturalism but its competitive logics of dispossession and displacement. Their campaign experiences have validated a political aesthetic deeply concerned with places—as conveyers of belonging, access, and history—which aligns with official political rhetoric that construes the Scottish nation as a place-based rather than race-based identity.

In exploring the mobilization of these working-class Edinburgh residents from neighborhood to nation, this book contributes to a larger body of research on working-class politics, one especially relevant to understanding the resurgence of nationalisms across Europe, a narrative of resurgence that this mobilization complicates. The narrative of the Canongate residents places these working-class activists in unexpected, sometimes contradictory positions: in the heart of a historic city center but struggling for visibility, allying with middle-class professionals and defending the moral appropriateness of a working-class aesthetic, and ultimately asserting a national political imaginary that is broadly working-class and cosmopolitan.

### An Ethnographic Observation

In the autumn of 2007, I walked into the meeting hall of Old St. Paul's, a Canongate church with a history of women-led social reform work (Darling 2015, 117) just as the meeting was scheduled to begin. The hall was almost full, many people facing the front from rows of folding chairs, a few still standing and chatting in the back over cooling mugs of tea and Jaffa cakes. Nodding toward familiar faces in the crowd, I slid into a chair next to someone's lumpy canvas bag and drew out my notebook and pen. More than one year of meetings, and if anything, the attendance had increased; the core group of residents and early sympathizers dispersed among knots of dreadlocked, mohawked, and pierced visitors, shoulder to shoulder with prim cardigans, leather-buttoned blazers, and cuffed shirts. After a few more minutes of chatting, Catriona, a leader in SOOT, walked to the front of the room to signal that the meeting would begin. A long-term resident of the Canongate, Catriona lived in the flat passed down to her from her great-aunt. Employed as a part-time social service worker, by the end of the campaign she would be matriculating into a program to study law. In this room in the church hall, she knew many but not most, and so she began as she often did, with a call to action, acutely aware that she must always be working to persuade people to join the cause, that without reliable support from the city council, the campaign must be able, minimally, to invoke numbers and names.

Catriona began by introducing a well-known Edinburgh architect and an architectural conservationist, gesturing to them in their front-row seats. These men would talk to us about the Caltongate plans and tell us why the development did not need to look the way it did in those plans. "SOOT is not against development." She swept the room with her gaze. "We *do* oppose the Caltongate plans in their current form, because if the plans are put into effect, the Old Town will not be the Old Town anymore!" She paused for effect. "This is a 'stop the demolitions' meeting. So, you need to sign the petition that is going around the room. Otherwise, homes and historical buildings will be torn down, and the Canongate—and the Old Town—will never, ever be the same. We need to save it for the people of the world." Catriona opened her arms in an appeal to the already-sympathetic audience, and her voice hitched up a notch. "It is a *World* Heritage site, and it is not owned by the developers or by the city council. The Council are in fact custodians— who are meant to look after the city for *ourselves* and for the future."

The "homes and historical buildings" that Catriona invoked in that small speech signified an alliance crucial to the SOOT campaigners' political mobilization, an alliance that the next chapter traces to the historic activism that responded to dilapidation and overcrowding of the Old Town during Edinburgh's industrial era. But just as important, Catriona framed the significance of this neighborhood in terms emphasizing its global identity—as a "World Heritage site," identified by UNESCO as such since 1994. She also rejected the notion of the city council possessing property-based rights to the area, portraying instead a relationship between council and city residents much more reflective of welfare-oriented urbanism (cf. Harvey 1989). At this meeting, in October 2007, while I hastily scribbled Catriona's speech in my notebook, I was receiving a broad sampling of themes on which I would reflect for years to come, the outworkings of a working-class cosmopolitanism in, and against, a neoliberalizing city. The SOOT campaign and the organizations that have continued since its dissolution to pursue the work of community-led development in the Old Town have built on the alliances highlighted at this meeting. Examining their work through these organizations, the book shows how Catriona and her colleagues have mobilized a place-based cosmopolitan politics that coalesced in response to neoliberal threat, a politics that has subsequently maneuvered for expression through the broadly liberal democratic aesthetic of Scottish nationalism.

## FIELDWORK AND ORGANIZATION OF THE BOOK

The contentious debates over the Caltongate development proposal propelled coverage of the Canongate-based campaign to the headlines of the local newspaper, where it first crossed my path. The scale of the proposed development startled me into a close read: at six hectares, the plan would create the largest city-center development project since the construction of the New Town in the eighteenth century, within a UNESCO World Heritage site that was bounded at each end by the castle and the royal palace and included a working-class tenement neighborhood in between. Intrigued, I attended an advertised public meeting in a local church's halls, and then, for the next year and a half, I just continued attending. From 2006 to 2008, I went to campaign meetings and city council deliberations, eventually joined the community group in strategizing and planning events, and got a job working as a salesclerk in a women's clothing shop on Canongate Road (see interlude 2). The campaign organized by area residents to prevent the redevelopment of their neighborhood, which they called Save Our Old Town (SOOT), would feature in local and national media throughout the initial phase of my fieldwork, from 2006 to 2008. Both the development and the campaign to oppose it escalated the usual scales of such programs and movements in Edinburgh and provided a rich, if also contentious, field for study.

My relationships with group members were slow to grow, initially because although I attended meetings, introducing myself and making sure I got to the protest site before the advertised start time, I discovered that I was far from the only interested observer. At the first public meeting I attended, I noted with a little despair at least two other graduate students—after all, Edinburgh is home to several universities with faculty and academic programs invested in the process and outcome of development projects like this one. And though there were other areas of Edinburgh undergoing redevelopment, in truth there would be none quite like this one, promising to churn up acreage right in the middle of the city's Old Town. A distinctive characteristic of anthropological research methods, however, eventually worked in my favor: I literally outlasted the other interested academic types, and my persistent presence and engagement covered ground that my letter of introduction could not. Over time, in the halting progress that often characterizes ethnographic research, I was given the great privilege of knowing and being known by resident activists in the Canongate. Their graciousness and patience with an ever-present American anthropology student—and, subsequently, professor—made possible this project of understanding. Though many narrative accounts could be written about this community campaign—and I do not pretend to exhaust the possible interpretations of these events—I have written the one that has made the most sense to me, in light of my academic training and personal experience. A note on the transcriptions of interlocutors in this project: although ethnographic depictions of Scots' speech often use the Scots dialectical spellings, I have chosen not to do so. This choice reflects the fact that many of the people quoted in this book have published interviews, commentaries, and opinions in local media as well as public blogs, and in those pieces they have chosen not to use Scottish dialectical spellings to represent their language, which in practice often mixed both Scots and English phrases. I have followed their lead in using English spellings for their speech, except in situations in which Scots was used to emphasize a distinctive practice or idea, such as the doocots of the fourth interlude or the poem recited by a campaigner in chapter 3. This speech has been recorded via fieldnotes and interview transcripts, and throughout the book, all quotations of individuals from such sources are situated within their ethnographic contexts, offering situational rather than bibliographic citation. The individuals who consented to be interviewed are represented by a pseudonyms, and for the most high-profile individuals, among them campaign leaders, real names have been used when requested, as well as for officials who have been interviewed in their professional capacities.

The following chapters detail the development of a program of political activism in the Canongate and its translation into national political claims. The insights this narrative provides contribute to discussions of working-class politics, as noted in the previous section, and the final chapter elaborates their multiple relationships to nationalist movements, identifying the affective appeal and aesthetic resonance between the concerns and critiques of both the Canongate campaigners and the Scottish nationalists. The activist labor pursued by these residents is connected through a set of ethnographic interludes that alternate with the book's chapters, connecting them to adjacent places, communities, and social and political networks to provide an account of working-class urban politics that is contextualized within the web of relationships, history, and places that have given rise to this particular account of Scottish political life.

The first chapter introduces events in the Canongate residents' campaign and situates the concerns of the campaign within both a politicized history of neighborhood development and negotiations between the priorities of housing provision, conservation, and economic growth in the twentieth-century Scottish welfare state. The telling of Edinburgh's built history, through projects of demolition and reconstruction focused on the Old Town in particular, conveys the process by which urban development became the primary political field in which multiple groups negotiated for their priorities at given locations and across the city as a whole. The rise and influence of conservative surgery, a philosophy of the social reformer and planner Patrick Geddes, signaled an alliance between middle-class conservationists and working-class housing activists, which mitigated large-scale investment in projects aimed primarily at short-term economic growth for much of the twentieth century. The Canongate residents positioned their campaign firmly in this tradition of urban development negotiation in Edinburgh's Old Town, allying themselves with built heritage conservation organizations and claiming the expertise of Geddes for their cause. They soon found that the field for development decision-making had changed, however, and their bid for influence was thwarted by the ascendance of depoliticized neoliberal development priorities that foreclosed opportunities for public influence by privileging short-term economic growth as the more urgent objective.

A neoliberal aesthetic of urban development, which shaped the ascendant urban development practices introduced in chapter 1, is elaborated on in the second chapter. The introduction of neoliberalism to Scotland through Margaret Thatcher interrupted governance by the Scottish welfare state in which a meaningful degree of autonomy had allowed the exercise of more left-leaning policies in education, local governance, and the legal system. The forced deindustrialization, privatization, and imposition of austerity policies in Scotland under Thatcher animated popular interest in the devolution of more governmental powers to Scotland as a means of providing opportunities for Scots to pursue their own distinctive political priorities. This chapter shows that, following the devolution vote in 1997 and the subsequent reinstitution of Scottish Parliament, the supposedly "different" Scottish politics has reflected an awkward amalgamation of welfare-ist priorities and neoliberal economics. The urban development practices materialized in Edinburgh, in which political affect and moralized assessment of individual behavior cohere, are considered in the career and aspirations of an Edinburgh city politician from the Labour Party, who, while serving as the head of the city council, advocated for the acceptance of the Caltongate development project. The Caltongate master plan is presented as simultaneously a realization of neoliberal development ambitions for Edinburgh and a deferring of the historic priorities of conservation and working-class housing provision responsible for much of the Canongate's twentieth-century development.

In the third chapter, the Canongate campaign takes shape in response to the Caltongate proposal, insisting on the properly political nature of urban development decisions in the face of depoliticizing logics of technocratic and aesthetic expertise. Two primary strategies of depoliticization are levied by Caltongate development advocates, from city councilor to private developer and city business leader: firstly, management of community consultation, and secondly, deployment of aesthetic discourses of dispossession. In their management of community consultation projects, both the city council and private developers served to publicly exonerate themselves as carrying out best practices of urban planning, lacking any formal mandates to embrace the concerns and demands expressed at consultation events in the form of changes to the Caltongate master plan. Outside the formal processes of planning procedures, the advocates for the Caltongate proposal voiced their disgust for the aesthetics of the Canongate, introducing a competing aesthetic of social order that questioned the legitimacy and character of the place. This chapter follows the residents' array of adaptive responses as they rejected derisive interpretations of the Canongate implicit and explicit in the support for the Caltongate proposal. Through the reprieve on which they seized in an economic recession, Canongate residents' activities and alliances succeeded in somewhat modifying the realization of the Caltongate proposal, but they still failed to effectively challenge the logics of neoliberal urbanism that seem to necessitate the Canongate's redevelopment, along with other Edinburgh neighborhoods similarly identified by the council as underrealized.

Chapter 4 considers the ethical order that came to be elaborated through the Canongate campaign. The perspective for this reflection is gained from a tacking back and forth between the campaign, in 2005–2008, and the former campaigners' observations and activities in the subsequent years, through 2017. Through the former campaigners'—and, in most cases, now-former Canongate residents'—considerations of the changes in the Canongate neighborhood since the conclusion of the campaign and the progressive realization of the Caltongate redevelopment proposal, their rejections of the neoliberal aesthetic of that development continue to ring clearly. The idea of home, as a conceptualization of place that is singular and inalienable, has been invoked as a political claim to contest the commodification of place as property through the development proposal. The residents' assertion of belonging to this place through their performance of place-based social memory served to confirm their ties to the built-heritage conservationists and thus the alliance between these groups. I show that this politics of home can provide unexpected instruments of interclass solidarity, vital to a collective program of political mobilization.

Finally, chapter 5 explores the alignments between the social and political imaginaries developed by Canongate campaigners and those of Scottish nationalism, historic and contemporary. The chapter begins with an overview of Scottish politics and the currently ascendant nationalism, in comparative perspective with other European nationalisms, identifying themes of egalitarianism and cosmopolitanism that appealed to the campaigners' convictions and experiences. In addition to their shared experiences in the campaign, the residents negotiate with the content of Scottish nationalism in ways that reflect their backgrounds and priorities, affirming Cohen's (1996) characterization of nationalism as personal. The different orientations to Scottish nationalism expressed by three central campaigners illustrate the variety of interests obscured by a simplified binary vote of yes/no for Scottish independence, and I argue that the differences and commonalities in their social and political assessments help to illuminate the varied ways that neighborhood and nation interpenetrate in the production of multiscalar political agencies. The former Canongate campaigners have found more space for engagement with their social and political critiques at the level of national rather than municipal politics, but for these working-class Scots, the problem of opening up the reductive logic of urban development remains the central issue across these entangled political scales.

This narrative that begins in a working-class neighborhood of a European capital city conveys the mechanisms by which working-class appearance—and, by implication, presence—is obscured and marginalized via the processes and priorities of neoliberal urbanism. In this respect, the study contributes to a robust body of interdisciplinary research on the outworkings of neoliberalism in actual places, highlighting contradictions internal to neoliberal logic itself, alongside some unexpected instruments of dispossession in service of urban wealth accumulation. Tracing connections from their engagements with urban politics to a national scale, the book follows the working-class residents of the Canongate as they continue to seek opportunities for the political realization of a Canongate aesthetic. The rhetoric of Scottish social democracy brandished by an SNP ascendant in an era of imposed austerity measures offered a comfortable platform for their critiques of and concerns about a government's privileging of short-term economic gains and callous treatment of its working and poor classes, as well as familiar allies in the cause among Edinburgh's middle classes. Key to understanding their optimism regarding the SNP is its aesthetic resonance with the Canongate campaign in terms of their shared transformation orientation and vision of a moral reordering of individual, community, social, and economic life. Despite their misgivings, and protecting their own caveats and resistances, the campaign leaders chose to support the SNP and negotiate their personal positions on the independence question.

I show how these affirmations evidence a Scottish working-class cosmopolitanism, a moral stance the campaigners have cultivated between the shadows of neoliberal political economy on the one hand and ethnic nationalism on the other. But this posture must be understood not only in relation to their perspectives as subjects in the imagined community of the nation. A more intimate community life in the Canongate, through its crisis with neoliberal urbanization, has shaped the political agency of these residents in a locally familiar form, what I collectively indicate here as a Canongate aesthetic. This aesthetic, as the residents show, is portable and expandable, and when the former Canongate campaigners express critiques of neoliberalism and affirm socially democratic values through the idealized public rhetoric supporting an independent Scottish nation, the aesthetic order of their discourse is Canongotian. The following chapters explore the role of this urban location, a working-class neighborhood at the center of Edinburgh, in public contestation over the aesthetic materialization of competing social and political visions for the city and, ultimately, for Scotland.

NOTE

1. All uncited quotes from Anderson that follow are from that 2010 interview.

## CHAPTER 1

## HISTORY, HERITAGE, AND POLITICS IN THE OLD TOWN

ON JUNE 19, 2007, A rather small and inconspicuous part of Edinburgh's built environment mysteriously disappeared. Jock the Weathercock, a weather vane fixture atop a historically listed building in the Canongate neighborhood, had departed his roost. Affectionately regarded among the Canongate residents, Jock's public profile was heightened considerably in 2005 when the Caltongate redevelopment plan proposed the demolition of the historic Canongate Venture building, atop which he perched. When a group of area residents organized a campaign to protest this proposal, they kept watch over the Canongate Venture and other structures intended in the plan for demolition while that proposal was under consideration by the City of Edinburgh Council. By June 2007, the almost wholly favorable response of council members to this proposal was inclining the resident campaigners to eye with suspicion the apparently close relationship between commercial developers and several city councilors. That suspicion had coalesced throughout their (largely unsuccessful) campaign efforts to persuade the development management subcommittee to take seriously their concerns as residents of the neighborhood proposed for large-scale transformation (a campaign described in chap. 3). Jock's unannounced departure from a listed building under threat of demolition therefore spurred several residents into immediate action.

Residents noted Jock's absence one summer morning and marshaled volunteers to scour the surrounding area for clues. Though Jock was not found, wood from his bell tower perch was located in a nearby trash receptacle, and one of the campaign leaders, who was trained as a town planner, promptly phoned planning enforcement officers and a conservation officer from the executive body Historic Scotland. Historic Scotland confirmed that it had not received any notifications of plans to deal with Jock in its departments. Once the campaign leader obtained this communication, she contacted a member of the local press and gave the following public statement:

> Is this what we are to expect for the future of buildings which developers wish to buy from the council in order to redevelop the land? Have the council completely given up their responsibility to follow proper procedures? The council officer responsible for authorizing the work knew he needed planning consent, even if it were to be removed and replaced and had made the decision not to repair or restore this feature. Although the wood from the structure is chopped up, it is clearly *not* rotted in any way. Listed buildings are listed to protect them from unscrupulous developers. We have notified Historic Scotland, and we want the bell tower replaced and want Jock the Cock to be replaced. (Canongate Community Forum 2007)

The campaigners speculated as to whether distinctive "architectural features" were being removed or sanctioned for removal by city council members who supported the master plan for redevelopment in anticipation of the demolition of the Canongate Venture building. The idea was regarded as particularly repugnant to the leader with a background in planning, who cited planning code regulations and insisted on following "proper procedures" in dealing with historically listed buildings. Carrying out such undocumented work on a listed building was not only a violation of procedure, she claimed, but also a "criminal offence" (Canongate Community Forum 2007). Furious with the potential perpetrators of such an offense and convinced that these deceptions had been carried out under councilors' orders, she soon baited them in another public statement: "We fully expect a retrospective planning application in, as the council will panic because the community has caught them out. This is a corrupt way to circumvent their responsibilities to listed buildings. This is criminal damage and unless it is repaired we will be pursuing this in the justice system" (Canongate Community Forum 2007)

These statements emphasized the community's role as planning watchdog and characterized "the council" as corruptly implicated in a scheme to promote commercial development against the desires of the community and established planning protections. Levying these accusations, the resident campaigners continued to use council resources to pursue this mystery, contacting their local ward representative when their attempts to reach planning officers in the council failed to generate any response. Highlighting the futility of the residents' attempts, it was only through the ward representative pursuing the matter on their behalf that formal council replies began trickling in within four to ten days.

The news was rather unremarkable: the bell tower had been removed because a survey team deemed it to be damaged and therefore a public safety hazard. Jock was being stored inside the Canongate Venture until the belltower could be reconstructed. Just why the conservation officers responsible for vetting such requests had not received notification of this action was not addressed, apart from noting that the works constituted "emergency measures," so no planning consent was required (Canongate Community Forum 2007). Resident campaigners remained convinced that the explanation was merely retrospective and necessitated by the inquiries and accusations of corruption they levied.

This incident, though only a small event in the course of the campaign, was considered significant and symbolic by the working-class Canongate residents who challenged the depoliticized development process in which they were denied a substantive role, as indicated by the reluctance of municipal planning and council authorities to acknowledge their claims and requests. Although the issue of Jock the Cock's disappearance was raised many times by various residents and campaigners in the intervening ten years—and the Canongate Venture building was eventually saved from demolition by the residents' persistence and the onset of global economic recession—the weathercock and belltower have never been restored.

When we ignore its movements, the built environment can appear as the backdrop to life rather than as a dynamic process that is negotiated through conflict and consensus. The sheer scale of capital required for property ownership and modification and the formal permissions needed for projects of demolition or construction in a city obscure decision-making about the urban built environment behind the closed doors of economic and political elites. While the built fabric of the city more obviously manifests the will of such elites (Chesluk 2008; Fehérváry 2013; Rabinow 1989), the structures, blocks, and streets less obviously bear witness to the political, cultural, and economic activities of the working classes. At a time when attention has turned to the electoral activities of the working classes (Kalb and Halmai 2011; Walley 2017), works like this one, which convey the political mobilization of the working classes as an ongoing project, are needed to situate seemingly extraordinary political events within their ordinary and perhaps properly ordinal processes of social and political life. In this chapter, an overview of the politics of the built environment in Edinburgh's Old Town, and more narrowly the neighborhood known as the Canongate, forms a historical narrative of the production of that space that, following Lefebvre (1974), situates in both time and space the twenty-first-century political mobilization of Canongate residents.

This abbreviated retelling identifies agents and events key to the production—historical and ongoing—of the Canongate: alliances negotiated over shared interests and contested interpretations of social meaning, economic value, and the common good materialized in the metabolic rhythms of stone, steel, harl, and concrete. Concerns and practices that gained influence through the historical politics of the Canongate's built environment would be adapted through the Canongate residents' development campaign activism, as would their subsequent (and ongoing) political activities. Through examination of this Old Town neighborhood and the processes that gave form to its buildings and room to its inhabitants, working-class political mobilization proves not to be exceptional but rather characteristic of the processes by which Edinburgh has taken shape. The political processes of urban development, furthermore, though burdened by inefficiencies and conflicts, have maintained opportunities for Edinburgh's working-class residents to levy public claims on the state (Lefebvre 1974, 92). Through the negotiation between three primary development priorities—economic growth and modernization, built heritage conservation, and municipal provision for housing—each one advocated by networked local interests, Edinburgh's built forms have emerged through a productive (and at times destructive) tension.

As this chapter shows, the political nature of historical urban development in Edinburgh has provided opportunities for public influence that have largely been closed off following the city's adaptation to and eventual embrace of Thatcherite urbanism and its depoliticization of the processes of urban development (detailed in the following chapter). This reworking of development practice has produced a real and felt narrowing of state access for both middle and working-class development activists. Thus development protests like that of the Canongate campaigners cannot be reduced to ad hoc NIMBY (Not In My Backyard) reactions but can be read as more broadly challenging the politico-economic conditions of their disempowerment. While Lefebvre's assessment of space as essentially political describes the competing interests at play in the reckoning of urban space, the political economy of space operationalized under neoliberal urban governance greatly inhibits the viability of this political sphere as an instrument of access to the state. Thus the planning of urban space groans under impossible expectations: both political and politically inefficacious, apparently solicitous but actually opaque. Residents seeking to exercise their rights not only to indwell and make a particular urban space but also to bring their concerns to the view of representatives of the state must "chase after" these rights that, like answers regarding the fate of a lost weathercock, are not forthcoming (Holston 2009).

To understand the bewildered and frustrated reactions of those campaigners to the depoliticized development process they faced in 2005–2008, this chapter situates their campaign within a political practice that was shaped through the interdependent progression of the space known as the Canongate and Old Town. Excavating the social and material history of a local politics (Lefebvre 1974; Heidegger 2008), the following sections show the coherence of an aesthetic politics around the built environment, particularly, "what is seen and what can be said about it . . . who has the ability to see and the talent to speak" (Rancière 2004, 13). Political life in Edinburgh has long been shaped by these aesthetic concerns, and the Canongate itself has been shaped by opportunistic alliances formed between working and middle classes (Darling 2015) and their shared interests in conservation and housing provision, heroically represented in most accounts of Edinburgh by Patrick Geddes and his philosophy of conservative surgery (Johnson and Rosenburg 2010).

This chapter narrates the transformation of the Canongate's built environment from class-integrated burgh to Romantic symbol, industrial slum, and midcentury working-class community within the context of an emergent Scottish welfare state, conditions through which a distinctive platform for political activism cohered. The historical narrative highlights the transition from these conditions of political urban development to the increasingly depoliticized processes discussed in the following chapter. With the historical practices of development in view, this chapter concludes by arguing that the eventual mediation of the welfare state by Margaret Thatcher and New Labour–era neoliberal political and economic restructuring has

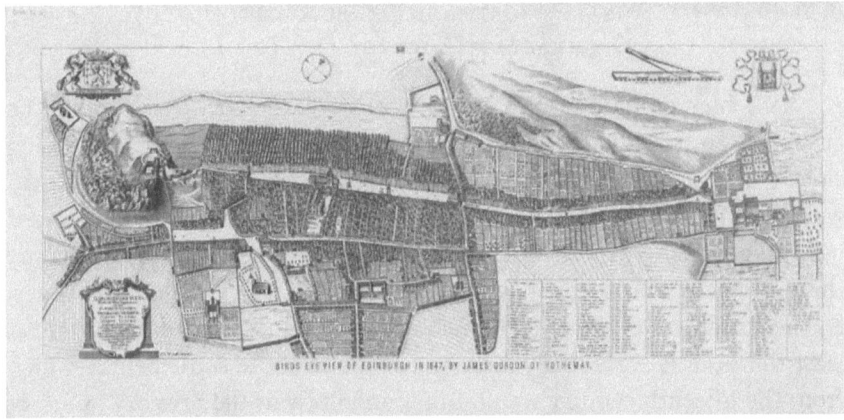

Fig. 1.1 Bird's-eye view of Edinburgh in 1647. By James Gordon of Rothiemay. Reproduced with the permission of the National Library of Scotland.

destabilized this mechanism for interclass political influence and therefore has diminished these groups' ability to contribute efficaciously to the shaping of a built environment. Since the aesthetic politics of the built environment offer the means for working classes in particular to levy claims on the state, this shift entails a strategic disempowerment of working-class politics.

The historical narrative begins by laying the early shape of the Canongate, originally an independent, medieval burgh adjacent to Edinburgh, and follows the growing-together of these burghs into the Old Town, simultaneously an object of antiquarian fascination and an overcrowded, dilapidated urban center needing repair. Inhabiting the tension between nostalgia and progress, Edinburgh quite literally took shape, and the Canongate's built forms indicated its mix of nobility, professionals such as doctors and lawyers, and an emergent class of literati, as well as laboring men and women, who lived in increasingly close quarters as the centuries progressed. The heterogeneity of this population suggests the potential for the intermittent interclass alliances that would form in the dual grip of the pressures of growth and industrialization. But in the mix of development influences were Scotland's changing relations with England, as the latter transitioned from a southern aggressor to a partner nation in Great Britain, as well as the social and cultural forces of the Scottish Enlightenment, which together transformed the original settlement into the Old Town of Edinburgh.

## The Canongate and Edinburgh: From Original Settlement to Old Town

At the center of Edinburgh's Old Town, its castle rock rises above the cityscape, and windy views from the top, when not obscured by low-lying clouds, or *haar*, present magnificent horizons: watery to the north and east, where the Firth of Forth and the North Sea lie, respectively, and embraced by arms of hills to the west and south. Archaeological evidence suggests that these protective prospects have attracted settlers since prehistoric times. As the structures of human habitation took more permanent form from at least the Middle Ages, the conditions of life in those settlements—which from the fifteenth century would function jointly as the primary burgh of Scotland—have required negotiation ever since (Dennison 2005, 71). The following paragraphs trace the development of medieval Edinburgh and its neighbor Canongate as central burghs for political, economic, and religious influence in Scotland, through the waning of their social and political significance following the union of the English and Scottish crowns in 1707 and to their configuration collectively as the Old Town of Edinburgh, with the construction of the New Town at the end of the eighteenth century and the onset of industrialization. The mutual transformation of social and spatial arrangements during this period saw a generalized movement from class-integrated tenements adjacent to the large homes of Scotland's peerage toward a pattern of increasing class segregation by neighborhood. Although spatial segregation of the classes would diminish their everyday interactions, the growing dilapidation of the city's older buildings in neighborhoods like the Canongate would eventually create new conditions for shared interests among middle-class antiquarians and working-class occupants.

While Edinburgh's significance may have been preordained by geologic movements, its neighboring burgh, the Canongate, perhaps depended on its proximity to the Scottish crown. In 1128, around the same time Edinburgh was founded, an Augustinian order established Holyrood Abbey at the base of the volcanic slope descending from the castle rock, and along the ridge of that slope, between the abbey and the castle, the Canongate burgh (from Canon's Gait or Canon's Way) was established. As a burgh serving the social and economic interests of this religious order, the Canongate also provided comparatively large plots of land on which Scotland's peerage could build their city houses, gaining proximity to the Scottish crown. The two

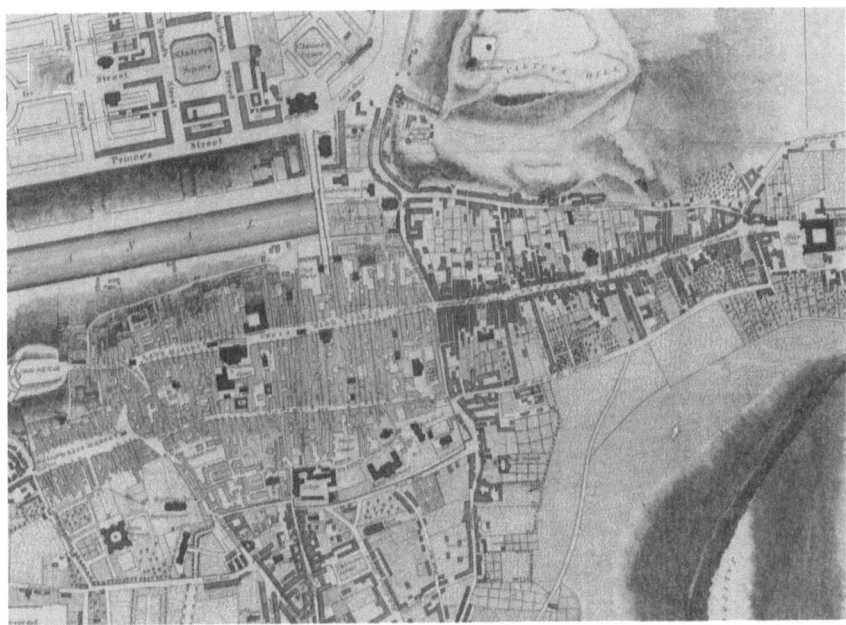

Fig. 1.2 City of Edinburgh, 1880. By John Ainslie. Reproduced with the permission of the National Library of Scotland.

burghs lay end-to-end along the ridge, their rows of tenements, with shops below and flatted houses above, lining two parallel roads that descended from the castle rock: the central High Street and the narrower Cowgate, along the lower, southern slope of the ridge. Dozens of smaller lanes and closes branched off from these primary arteries, creating pathways to back greens—many of which were large enough to be used as agricultural plots—and allowing for the main doors of houses to avoid the busiest thoroughfares (Campbell and Stewart 2005, 22–23). A pedestrian walking down the High Street from the castle would move from Edinburgh into the Canongate through the imposing Netherbow Port, the gate that controlled passage between the two burghs, and continue along the line of the High Street, which transitioned to the street called Canongate, as it sloped down to Holyrood Abbey and the Palace of Holyroodhouse. Although the Canongate was formally an independent burgh until 1856, by appearance and in daily life, the Canongate and Edinburgh were a contiguous settlement, one that would eventually be known as the Old Town of Edinburgh.

Fig. 1.3 The Canongate in 2017, looking up the hill toward the historic prison, the Tollbooth (see the clock on the right), and beyond toward the former boundary with Edinburgh. Photo by author.

From its earliest days, the Canongate's deep burgage plots provided respite from the density of tenement living. This was particularly evident in comparison to its neighbor Edinburgh, which from the fifteenth century functioned as the permanent seat of Scotland's governance and thus the primary burgh of Scotland (Dennison 2005, 71). This pattern of grand residences with architectural ties to continental Europe, across the street from multistory tenements inhabited by shoemakers, weavers, and bakers,[1] became characteristic of the Canongate neighborhood, where the "extremely wealthy and those of more humble professions" intermingled (Dennison 2005, 79). The walls that protected the settlements of Edinburgh and the Canongate from English invasion ensured that even in the less dense Canongate, the strains of population growth would by the late Middle Ages begin to be felt and by the seventeenth century would foster a widespread sense of a crisis of housing for the poor in particular.

This housing crisis followed a period of bounding population growth. Between 1329 and 1560, the population of Edinburgh and the Canongate increased from roughly two thousand to ten thousand and to twenty thousand in 1635 (Robinson 2005, 105), and yet for around four hundred years, the inhabitants of these two burghs were contained in approximately 130 acres (Robinson 2005, 113). Overcrowding brought with it the dangers of fire, plague, and the collapse of poorly maintained (and constructed) buildings. In response were the first attempts by municipal leadership to regulate and improve housing for the poor and working classes through town planning legislation (1621, 1624, 1625), as well as the first programs of large-scale slum clearances (Campbell and Stewart 2005, 32–33). New public buildings were also erected to care for the poor and sick, such as the Canongate Charity Workhouse, which opened in 1761 (Dennison 2005, 118). Despite these measures, the area continued to gain notoriety for its filth: excrement was piled on the streets below, and wastewater was flung from the windows above, accompanied by the plainly insufficient warning shout "Gardy loo!" (in Edinburgh lore and law, a corruption of the French *gardez l'eau* "watch out for the water").

The signing of the Acts of Union of 1707, part of which was conducted in the Canongate gardens of Moray House (Adamson, Kilpatrick, and McDonald 2016, 12), dissolved the Scottish Parliament and sent political decision-making for Scotland south to London, thus temporarily easing the pressures toward urban expansion. Many of Edinburgh's wealthier residents and nobility traded their Edinburgh homes for London residences, leaving their former homes vacant for rent and/or subdivision (Youngson 2002, 22). That departure, combined with a more general loss of confidence, stimulated an economic slump in Edinburgh and Scotland. Despite this double-fisted loss of political and economic capital, however, the intellectual fervor of the Scottish Enlightenment hardly dampened, with Edinburgh its undisputed center. As a comparison between the accomplishments of its intellectual community and the Athens of ancient Greece, Edinburgh gained its moniker "Athens of the North" during this period, distinguished by the Scottish literati who gathered in Edinburgh and produced a dazzling array of works in fields such as philosophy, literature, economics, and the natural sciences.[2] Suggesting the city's interpenetrating social and intellectual circles, one private club that met regularly in the Canongate gathered David Hume, Adam Smith, Alexander Carlyle, and Adam Ferguson among its members (Carlyle 1910, 288). The charms of the city's antiquity and natural beauty were decidedly compromised by the cramped and often squalid conditions of its primary settlement. In a letter written in the 1760s, Thomas Gray observed that Edinburgh was "that most picturesque (at a distance) and nastiest (when near) of all capital cities" (Andrews 1989, 207, in McKee 2018, 53). Inhabiting the "nasty" conditions of this city struck its illumined members as beneath their dignity and that of the city itself. They therefore joined their voices to publicly pressure the city leadership, encouraging them to invest in a new area for settlement directly to the north of the city, a purpose-built suburb for Scotland's peerage (McKean 2001).

It would be through the design and construction of that development, eventually known as Edinburgh's New Town, that the city's class divide would be spatialized in built form. The construction of the New Town, which began in 1759 with the preparatory work of draining the Nor' Loch and building North Bridge (1772) to connect Old and New Towns, was completed in 1830. Although it would take time for the in-process suburb to catch the imagination of the Old Town residents—not least because most of Scotland's nobles had already departed Edinburgh for London—the building of the New Town ultimately introduced the first patterns of firmly class-based spatial segregation in Edinburgh. Before the construction of the New Town, the Old Town had been a "mixed-income community with 23,000 people of all classes living within vertical sandstone tenements" (Johnson and Rosenburg 2010, 34), but the New Town (as well as the construction of some middle-class suburbs to the south) drew away the wealthier residents, leaving behind the poorest and least resourced. From the 1780s, middle-class professionals began vacating the Old Town in earnest (McKean 2001, 43). By 1830, the completion of the New Town construction, only one in twenty residents of the Old Town and Canongate could be identified as middle class (Rodger 2004, 18). The result for Edinburgh "irrevocably" diminished the "sense of shared interest between rich and poor" by transforming the "traditional pattern of class contact" (Johnson and Rosenburg 2010, 34).

While the construction of the New Town was admired by continental Europe and enabled the continued expansion of the city's population, the decision to direct city resources to resettling its wealthier classes, rather than addressing the (equally expensive) problems of housing in the existing settlement, resulted in the reframing of Edinburgh's original settlement as the "Old Town." This area became an object of antiquarian fascination replete with grand old houses and a broad and impressive High Street, winged by stair-stepped closes and increasingly shabby tenements. Addressing the tension between these two aspects of the Old Town proved to be the fundamental challenge for Edinburgh's planning and development throughout the twentieth century. In large part, this challenge speaks to the segregation facilitated by the New Town, which had profound impacts on social stratification among Edinburgh's population, lasting throughout and beyond the era of industrialization. The Old Town in general and the Canongate in particular, due to its participation in a major industrial zone, were thereafter shaped by ongoing conflicts between municipal authorities' priorities relating to modernization, preserving an antiquarian aesthetic, and improving the everyday realities of working-class life. In broad strokes, it could be said that the city's efforts to modernize initially emphasized industrial investment became derivatively and intermittently concerned with working-class infrastructure, and provoked concerns among the city's elites and professional classes that the ancient buildings of the Old Town were being demolished. The social and economic restructuring pursued through industrialization has presented cities throughout Britain with similar quandaries, but as the following section shows, the joining of conservation and housing provision interests in Edinburgh produced a planning strategy with enduring influence.

### Industrialization and the Old Town: Slums, Schemes, and Conservative Surgery

In 2004, the BBC aired a television series called *North & South*, based on an 1885 novel by Elizabeth Gaskell. This series, like the novel, highlighted the differences between an idealized rural life in the south of England and the entrepreneurial, hard-edged world of industrial Manchester, which was represented by the fictional town of Milton, in Darkshire. Seeking filming locations to convey the class-divided urban architecture of industrial Britain, the producers decided to film the Milton scenes on the pavements, stairs, and hilltops of Edinburgh. Noteworthy for this chapter is how the Old and New Town built environments were incorporated into the plot of

*North & South* to elaborate architecturally on, respectively, working-class and genteel social life. As the visual frames for two sides of Milton, Borthwick's Close in Edinburgh's Old Town set the scene for "Rag Alley," while Moray Place in New Town offered a wide pavement for conversation between an industrialist and a professor. The choice of Edinburgh to represent a quintessentially industrial town is, from most perspectives, surprising. Most academic accounts of Edinburgh, both historical and contemporary, have tended to downplay the city's industrial investment in favor of an emphasis on more middle-class professions (Madgin and Rodger 2013). The ability of the city's built environment to convey its industrial signifiers, even in the twenty-first century, however, may suggest the visual power of class symbols written into the built environment, leaving an enduring stamp of social and economic hierarchies despite the histories told.

Indeed, as Richard Rodger has argued, narratives depicting Edinburgh as a city of professional occupations contribute to the erasure of working-class residents from both the city's histories and modern portraits. In fact, Edinburgh depended on a powerful and diversified industrial economy throughout the nineteenth and much of the twentieth century (2004, 22), but unlike the Scottish cities of Glasgow or Dundee or the English cities of Manchester or Sheffield, the city relied on no single industry. From 1841 to 1911, three in five men and two of five women in Edinburgh were employed in various industries, including brewing, printing, glassmaking, and textiles (Rodger 2004, 21). Given that much of this industrial development took place along Edinburgh's east-west axis, including large areas of the Old Town, this industrial era, according to then-resident Patrick Geddes, contributed many "disasters" and "vandalisms" to Edinburgh's urban development (Geddes 1915, 349–50). Such vandalisms were committed on an unprecedented scale: a remarkable 40 percent of Edinburgh's present-day built environment was constructed during this period, as Edinburgh councilors sought to facilitate industrial expansion and accommodate population growth (Edwards and Jenkins 2005, 83).

While industrial work had initially been confined to the closes and back lanes of the Old and New Towns, by the mid-nineteenth century, the securing of national markets and technological innovations enabled construction on greenfield sites around the city's peripheries (Rodger 2004, 91). As a result, in 1860, the Canongate became embedded within an industrial conglomeration on the eastern edge of the city, which included a distillery, foundry, brewery, and engineworks, the second-largest industrial complex in the city (Rodger 2004, 96). The pressures of Edinburgh's aging building stock to accommodate the commercial and domestic demands of modern industry provoked a second crisis in housing that inspired a growing movement in working-class politics to agitate for housing improvements.

In the late nineteenth and early twentieth centuries, it was often the politics of housing rather than labor that succeeded in generating class consciousness in urban Scotland (McCrone and Elliott 1989, 225). In Glasgow, working-class activism was profoundly shaped by the women leading rent strikes, which gave rise to a broader platform of working-class concerns, resulting in the radicalization of the political vision popularly associated with Red Clydeside (Hughes 2010; Melling 1989). In Edinburgh, by contrast, the appeal of socialism as a response to similar housing concerns was mitigated from the early twentieth century by a combination of state pressures on local landlords and the repression of socialist groups (McCrone and Elliott 1989, 227). There the interests of the middle classes in preserving the historic buildings of the Old Town joined with the concerns of the working classes in the pursuit of habitable, safe housing. In the political field of urban development, this interclass alliance, while fragile and often frayed, has continued to converge at multiple points in the city's history of urban development, including the 2005–2008 campaign against the Caltongate development plan.

To consider its influence, it is instructive to compare this planning compromise with Glasgow, where pressures to modernize the city in service of industrialization resulted in large-scale demolition of the historic built environment (Smyth 2019, 108). To the industrial complexes in both cities came waves of workers, many of them migrants from the Highlands or Ireland. The effects of this population growth among the tenements of the Canongate, as well as in Glasgow's districts of worker housing, rapidly evidenced the problem faced by industrializing cities throughout Europe: the deterioration of existing housing under conditions of overpopulation and under-attention from municipal leadership. The first solutions pursued by leadership in Europe's industrial cities emphasized the removal of the unfit housing but paid little attention to the rehoming of the displaced population of residents. In Paris, these so-called slum clearances were used to make way for Georges-Eugène Haussmann's construction of imperial, tree-lined boulevards (Saalman 1971), and similar clearances were a major instrument of social and spatial change in Glasgow and Dundee (Devine 1999, 345).

Edinburgh's municipal leadership also initially embraced this strategy, and under the provisions of the Edinburgh Improvement Act of 1867, Lord Provost William Chambers obtained support for what became known as the Chambers Scheme. This sanitary plan targeted thirty-four areas designated as "unhealthy" around the Old Town, comprising more than three thousand properties on fifty acres of land, in which the most densely populated areas contained as many as six hundred persons per acre (Smith 1989, 103). Nearly one-third of the Old Town's housing was demolished and 8 percent of Edinburgh's entire population displaced (Rodger 2001, 437). The displaced residents were not provided new homes, as it was expected that they would find their own housing in other neighborhoods (Johnson and Rosenburg 2010, 42). The result was both increased overcrowding in the surrounding neighborhoods, where existing housing was subdivided by private landlords to make spaces small enough for the displaced households to afford (Johnson and Rosenburg 2010, 46), and the replacement of many demolished residences with the construction of new roads and nonresidential buildings (44). In the Canongate, three new roads cut through the former housing areas: Blackfriars Street, St. Mary's Street, and New Street. In the end, both the city's middle classes and working classes objected: the middle classes determined the Chambers Scheme to have used an enormous amount of resources at public expense, and wielded "questionable" authority to do so, while the displaced population took the matter "personally," claiming their rights to rehoming and compensation (43).

The need to provide housing for Scottish working classes continued to press on the country's municipalities, producing incentives in the form of the Housing of the Working Classes Act 1890 (Rodger 1989, 8). In Edinburgh, the mutual dissatisfaction of the middle and working classes with the Chambers Scheme prompted city leadership to consider an alternative, offered by a young biology lecturer at Edinburgh University named Patrick Geddes, who had recently taken a flat in a depressed tenement block in the city's Old Town. A Scot who had moved south to Edinburgh as an adult, Geddes and his wife, Anna, had quickly grown to love this city, with its unique heritage of medieval and Enlightenment-era planning (Geddes 1915, 209), which Geddes saw as under threat equally from industrial expansion and the sweeping demolitions of sanitary improvement schemes.

By this time, voluntary and civic organizations in Edinburgh, including a working-class cooperative movement, were advocating for municipal improvements by way of a slate of concerns, two of which included purpose-built housing for working classes (Rodger 2001, 364) and the preservation of ancient buildings, particularly in the Old Town (Johnson and Rosenburg 2010, 59). Geddes joined these concerns in his campaigning reform work for improvement of Old Town housing, which sought to retain existing structures where possible, refurbishing and regenerating them to provide reliable, sanitary homes within the existing network of streets, an innovative city planning approach that he termed "conservative surgery." Unlike the strict preservationists such as Lord Cockburn, Geddes did not support the retention of long-standing structures at any cost but rather desired that "old buildings [be] conserved and yet renewed to vital uses" (Geddes 1915, 262). This philosophy of urban development, connecting a concern with welfare to the conservation of the historic built environment, aptly characterized turn-of-the-century middle-class urbanism in Edinburgh (Morris 2013, 121).

The response of city leadership to Geddes's proposed methods was markedly positive, as redevelopment via conservative surgery addressed the amalgamation of philanthropic and economic priorities particular to industrial Edinburgh and promised to provide housing and conserve the city's architectural heritage (Morris 2013, 102). Geddes's completion of his early projects in the Old Town proved to be so persuasive that when the second phase of the Sanitary Improvement Scheme was embarked on in 1893, the primary approach taken by the city council evinced their adoption of conservative surgery methods (Johnson and Rosenburg 2010, 89), although their execution revealed unanticipated challenges to this approach. The undertaking of the 1893 scheme involved the compulsory purchase powers of the city council and the financial contributions of multiple voluntary organizations of civil society and private companies such as the North British Railway Company (Johnson and Rosenburg 2010, 98; Morris 2013). The most contentious issue negotiated by the public and private bodies under this scheme was the rehousing of displaced households, particularly providing affordable housing for the poorest families. The council financed some new tenements on sites throughout the Old Town, and Geddes was offered the right to buy and refurbish additional sites. The results of these projects increased the available housing for skilled artisans, but most of the displaced poor were forced, again, to seek housing in the subdivided flats of neighboring areas. The 1893 renewal scheme did provide comparably superior low-income housing, though contemporary criticism suggests that the state of these homes left room for improvement (Johnson and Rosenburg 2010, 133). Because the scheme did not address all of the Old Town, leaving parts of the Canongate in particular in stubbornly slum-like conditions, the housing needs of this area would be revisited in a 1927 improvement scheme. That scheme, due to its contributions to the built environment of the Canongate, would retain an enduring influence on the imaginations of the Canongate campaigners almost a century later.

Following the 1893 development project, Geddes's conservative surgery methods were viewed largely positively, but lack of financial resources for this expensive strategy—and the recognized need for much more work on the provision of sanitary housing in particular—forced Edinburgh leadership to temporarily halt further building projects. A virtual moratorium on wartime housing construction owed to high material and labor costs but only compounded overcrowding and inadequate housing throughout urban Britain. In the 1920s, therefore, most British cities applied themselves to the provision of housing for the general population rather than addressing the persistent problem of their slum areas. The local authorities of Glasgow and Edinburgh, however, opted against this trend to invest in the improvement of slum conditions, but with varying approaches: Glasgow returned to sweeping slum clearances, whereas Edinburgh invested again in Geddes's methods of conservative surgery, combining the provision of housing with concern for the conservation of the built environment (Johnson and Rosenburg 2010, 145).

The location of this project, launched in 1927, addressed an area omitted from the 1893 scheme, which was suffering from renewed pressures of overcrowding. Called the Canongate–Corstorphine Scheme, this plan designated seventeen sites across Edinburgh, including eight in the Canongate, for remediation. With concern specifically for the "sensitive" nature of the Canongate's built environment, the strategy adopted for this area sought to deliver both preservation of older buildings and their conversion to new uses where possible, with an emphasis on the provision of homes for working-class residents. In doing so, this scheme put into practice Geddes's small-scale principles of conservative surgery, resisting pressures to redevelop the Old Town according to the comprehensive plan popularized by the emergent profession of modern town planning (Johnson and Rosenburg 2010, 162). The scheme also preserved the Old Town's pattern of high-density living against trends more popular throughout England, which inclined toward modified Garden City developments on the edges of the city.

Geddes's philosophies thus informed the most intensive period of working-class housing development in the Canongate, from 1927 to 1937, although Geddes had moved on by this point to work in Palestine and India. A key figure in the adaptation of Geddes's methods was City Architect Ebenezer MacRae, whose preference for infill construction and the adaptation of building scale and materials to the immediate context has meant that his buildings tend to blend into the cityscape rather than attract attention in their own right. At Numbers 221–223 Canongate Road, MacRae replaced dilapidated slum housing with new four-story tenements, carefully inserted into a historic city block, to provide local authority housing for low-income residents. Fronted with stone, the buildings continued the imposing cliff-like line of tenements along Canongate Road. Tenants shared a common interior stair, and behind the tenement buildings opened up the backlands, or back gardens, whose relatively generous size was enabled by the formerly large burgage plots of the medieval Canongate.

Tenements like this one initially housed residents displaced by slum demolitions, as the local authorities learned that centrally located residents were reluctant to relocate to the emerging low-density, working-class housing estates around the city's peripheries, a theme repeated in 2008 interviews with Canongate residents. The reasons for this reluctance were identified at the time as residents' desires to remain close to their workplaces and their "traditional amusements," as well as their concerns about incurring greater costs of travel and rent in the new estates (Johnson and Rosenburg 2010, 161). Such reasoning would ensure that these Canongate tenements would house a working-class residential community in the area for another eighty years.

These investments in the Canongate's built environment were accompanied by ongoing projects in social reform dedicated to the needs of the residents in that neighborhood. This work also contributed to the development of interclass relationships through philanthropic partnerships pursuing progressive educational and social philosophies, which represented part of a "wave of women-originated and women-centered work" in the Old Town at the turn of the century (Darling 2015, 120; cf. Morris 2013). The Free

Kindergarten, which operated from 1906 to 1977 out of a property of Old St Paul's Church, adopted as its practice the building of relationships between home and school. The largely middle-class women who served as teachers and headmistresses created their own working groups with parents and siblings, made common practice of home visitations and social gatherings like picnics, and often acted as advocates on behalf of students and their families (Darling 2015, 122). Though their work—and their public personas—was less visible than that of Patrick Geddes, the circles of these social reformers in Edinburgh overlapped considerably. Their mutual efforts in providing for the city's Old Town residents, especially the poorest, created lines of visibility and channels of communication across the defining geography of class segregation. The practices of working together, particularly among working- and middle-class women in the Old Town, should be viewed alongside affirmations of conservative surgery as important contributions to the development of an Old Town–based social welfarist imaginary of the built and social environment.

The outcomes of both social reformist projects and building projects of conservative surgery in the Canongate achieved a compromise between the tensions of modernization, conservation, and the provision for the working classes, secured through the activities of its residents as well as allies invested in a vision of the Old Town that married social and architectural reforms. As a result, the Canongate by midcentury had become a working-class neighborhood sustained by low-cost housing from the local authority, nearby sources of mostly industrial work, and an assortment of small shops serving the needs of this particular population. The primacy of the breweries, which persisted until the final closures in the late 1980s, supported a variety of entertainments, including public houses, dance halls, picture shows, and sports fields, as well as Catholic and Protestant churches, which together constituted a virtually self-sustaining, though mostly class-segregated, area. The efforts of City Architects MacRae and, later, Robert Hurd (Coleman 2018), as well as architectural firm Gordon & Dey (Adamson, Kilpatrick, and McDonald 2016, 24), in balancing care for the historic built environment and provisions for the working-class residents in their development schemes meant that for this Canongate community, the priorities of protecting the built urban heritage and attending to the contemporary community's needs were not experienced as competing interests but rather as complementary strategies for urban development. In fact, then as

Fig. 1.4 Blackfriars Street, added through the 1867 Chambers Scheme for slum clearance, provided a continuous edifice of tenement-and-shop buildings. These Victorian-era tenements were on average one to two stories shorter than the tenements along the main artery of Canongate Road and provided housing primarily for the managerial working classes, but they could not accommodate the hundreds of families that the scheme eventually displaced. Photo by author.

today, it is the modernization priority that has proven least compatible with these two development strategies.

### Modernization: Problems of Scale and Solidarity

The built legacy of Geddes and his methods of conservative surgery has shaped a local public imagination about what kinds of development are both possible and desirable, an imagination that has enabled a shared platform for activism among conservationists and Old Town residents in particular. From the second half of the twentieth century onward, however, these activists have often found themselves advocating conservative surgery ideals in negotiations with city leaders more inclined toward large-scale projects. Such projects sometimes pit the planning priorities of housing provision and modernization against conservation, but the conservation movement, which had been gathering steam since the turn of the twentieth century (Glendenning 2013) gained sufficient support in Edinburgh to influence development decisions through most of that century. As this section shows, following an early wave of large city development proposals, coalitions of residents and conservationists succeeded in staving off city-center development for a few decades, but since the 1990s, the challenge of projects pursuing modernization at the expense of low-income family housing and conservation concerns has returned in force.

During the postwar era, the inadequacy of housing supply for Britain's working families motivated slates of ambitious housing projects across the country. The conservative surgery methods in city centers required high investment and produced relatively modest numbers of refurbished homes, and the postwar period emphasized the need for a large quantity of new houses over other development concerns (Rodger 1989, 5). This wave of house building thus tended to focus on new developments in the peripheries of the city; in Scotland the "new towns" in the central belt; and on the outskirts of the four major cities of Glasgow, Edinburgh, Aberdeen, and Dundee (Gibb 2004). This period thus emphasized the importance of housing provision and modernization at the scale of regional planning, though a jostling for responsibility over those provisions generated debate among local authorities, the Scottish Office, and politicians at Westminster, who each sought influence over the Scottish Special Housing Association, an organization created in the 1930s to address Scotland's particular problem with urban overcrowding (Rodger and Al-Qaddo 1989). Attention to the conservation of the old urban fabric of the city temporarily waned by comparison, though concerns about aging housing stock in Scottish city centers continued to motivate smaller projects of investment in the rehabilitation of the existing stock (204).

Peripheral council estate construction in Edinburgh, including the Inch, Craigmillar, and Wester Hailes, intensified efforts to provide working-class housing but did so largely at a distance from the middle classes. Edinburgh's long tradition of tenement living, now associated by "garden city" planning advocates with city-center slums, appeared to lose ground in favor of a modified English pattern of suburban development, sorted by social class into neighborhoods of either private bungalows or tenement housing rented from the council (Rosenburg 2016). Desiring to protect the distinctive form of their city, Edinburgh's postwar local authority determined to stem the flow of suburban development and in 1950 designated a development-free green belt around the city. This green belt prompted the infill of council housing among the partially developed garden suburbs, somewhat softening the trend toward spatial segregation by class (Glendenning 2005, 155). The imposition of the green belt forced developers and the city council to look back toward the city center, but their interests in designing large-scale projects had been stimulated by advocates of the new profession of town planning on a scale that posed problems of realization in areas already built up over centuries.

In the 1960s, the movement of architects toward new styles and away from traditional materials and designs produced a litany of modern developments requiring multibuilding demolitions in central Edinburgh (Adamson, Kilpatrick, and McDonald 2016, 24). Two projects attracted the greatest public concern at the time: the construction of a new university library, requiring the destruction of a square of Georgian houses to the south of the Old Town, and the destruction of tenements and shops on Leith Street to make way for the new shopping complex called the St. James Centre—the latter of which would come to epitomize "bad development" to all sides of Edinburgh's twenty-first-century development debates. The scale and location of these projects collectively remobilized interest in the conservation of the built environment of the city. Built heritage conservation organizations and neighborhood street associations provided the institutional structures that brought together middle-class and working-class residents over their shared interests in small-scale, sensitive redevelopment and resistance to relocating residents to the city's margins (Smith and Luque-Azcona 2012, 406). Because this activism coincided with a wave of professional advocacy for public consultation among city and town planners, joint conservation and neighborhood efforts gained steam from the 1970s in particular. For a time, investment continued in both large-scale development and small-scale restoration, even within the portfolio of individual architectural firms (Adamson, Kilpatrick, and McDonald 2016, 25). The protection of architectural heritage achieved further support in the form of acts and policies introduced to require municipal permissions for demolitions in newly designated conservation areas (Smith and Luque-Azcona 2012, 406). The conservationists, through formal organizations like the Scottish Georgian Society, gained through this advocacy and their common cause with professional planners a legitimacy that enabled them to obtain consultative rights and formal invitation to the planning process.

Through this professionalization, as well as the waning of city interest in ambitious development proposals in the 1970s due to economic recession and the added protections of successful conservation area designations, the ties between conservationists and residents, originally wrought in response to external threats, began to relax (Jenkins and Holder 2005). The construction of the peripheral housing estates for Edinburgh's working classes had separated work and home life, failing to provide onsite community facilities, particularly when compared with the proximate amenities of the working-class neighborhoods in the city center (Rodger 1989, 13). These factors, along with the structure of the high-rise council flats, greatly diminished the public associational roles played by working-class women, who had historically taken leadership in neighborhood-based participatory politics (Melling 1989). When home was removed from the public associational spaces in which waged labor was embedded, the workplace came to bear the burden of political organization. But city-center investment in industry was dwindling throughout this period in central Scotland, and so city centers like Edinburgh offered fewer spaces conducive to working-class mobilization. It is noteworthy that, despite these challenges, some women did organize effectively from the peripheral estates, with one such campaign laying the groundwork for the Craigmillar Festival Society, discussed in Interlude 3.

The redirection of working-class residences to the city margins appeared to be addressing large-scale needs of housing provision in Edinburgh as in other Scottish cities where, throughout the twentieth century, councils and local authorities provided homes at a rate of typically twice that of English municipalities (Rodger 1989, 11). The causes that had united working-class and middle-class activists over shared interests in the restoration of the built environment and addressing the needs of local residents also appeared to be gaining some traction in local initiatives. In the 1970s and 1980s, Edinburgh's Housing Department supported the regeneration of housing stock in small areas of older construction, and the leaders in these undertakings were local housing associations and cooperatives, which not only designed tenement housing for families but also, in the case of the Grassmarket Area Housing Association, provided hostel accommodations for homeless people and, in the case of the Mushroom Trust, created small parks and gardens (Johnson and Rosenburg 2010, 229–30). To some limited degree, then, stimulated by conditions of economic recession, the city leadership supported a locally led version of conservative surgery (221), effecting in the Old Town the short-term resuscitation of a declining residential population (229). The small-scale regeneration projects conducted in the Old Town during this era are too numerous to detail here; for more on the various plans, advocates, and critics, an attentive and expansive account is presented by Jim Johnson and Lou Rosenburg (2010). As interest in Old Town renewal gained a broad base of support, a high-water mark of the mutual investment in such projects is found in the formation and work of the Edinburgh Old Town Conservation Committee, formed in 1985 and restructured in 1991 as the Edinburgh Old Town Renewal Trust, an organization that loomed large in the memories of several Canongate activists. Created by the District Council though not formally a statutory organization, the committee consisted of six councilors and six elected community representatives, who along with officers of several statutory bodies, monitored planning applications and proposals for the Old Town, distributing available funds and grants as they saw fit (238).

Even as the Old Town Renewal Trust facilitated the exercise of considerable influence by its residents in the development of the Old Town, the replacement of instruments for a vigorous, unruly politics of the built environment by a streamlined and increasingly centralized planning process focused on short-term economic growth was being pursued through local governance practices (Nadin and Stead 2014, 208). The introduction of neoliberalizing policies from the Conservative government out of Westminster emphasized development as projects of economic modernization for places and individuals, mitigating collective interest logics and advocating market deregulation and private sector investment in their stead. Such policies did not, as this chapter has shown, introduce a new and unfamiliar logic of urban development but rather enabled the ascendance of economic modernization priorities over those other priorities with which it had long negotiated. Advocates of those "minoritized" priorities; namely, conservationists and working-class residents, would not disappear but would find the access to the state that they had enjoyed under more open development consultations thwarted through the closure of this political sphere. As chapter 3 shows, the planning system continues, confusingly, to bear the traces of multiple value systems, from social democratic to neoliberal and thus at times contradicts itself, "inconsistencies" that Nadin and Stead identify with "continuing interaction between collectivist social welfare and individualist liberal principles" (191).

Thatcher's restriction of state funding, introduction of the right to buy council properties, and advocacy of private corporations for the delivery of formerly state-supplied services, a process described in the next chapter, encouraged the investment of large development firms in the redevelopment of Edinburgh's built environment, particularly in the form of large projects that promised higher rates of return. Although this wave of development focused on the margins of the city and even the greenbelt itself, by the late 1990s, developers were turning to the city center. These neoliberalizing processes further undermined the old alliance, hastening the loss of long-term residents from Edinburgh's city center, especially the Old Town. By the first decade of the twenty-first century, the working-class residents in the Canongate could be identified as one of the last remaining pockets of long-term residents in the Old Town. A 2016 architectural survey conducted by Historic Environment Scotland observed about the southern Canongate neighborhood along Holyrood Road that "almost no plot has remained untouched" by ongoing development projects since the late 1990s (Adamson, Kilpatrick, and McDonald 2016, 118).

The Canongate residents who remained throughout this intensification of development observed their neighborhood, only recently supported by local industry and shops for everyday living, transitioning rapidly through these piecemeal projects. The most comprehensive of these projects is discussed in the following chapters: the Caltongate proposal, a redevelopment plan devised on the largest scale faced by the city center since the eighteenth century. The fact that one of MacRae's most successful applications of the conservative surgery methodology, the MacRae tenement at 221–223 Canongate Road, would be proposed for demolition in this development foreshadows changing perspectives within the local authority on the appropriate balance between modernization, conservation, and housing provisions, discussed in the following chapter.

### The Enduring Relevance of Conservative Surgery

Whereas slum clearances provided the impetus for sweeping demolitions and displacements in the late nineteenth century, today the perceived need to compete internationally for accommodations and activities for tourists and mobile professionals motivates an industry of "regeneration" for aesthetic-economic ends (Zukin 2010). In this context, Geddes has been injected with new and urgent relevance by development activists—and not only for his conservationist designs but for his concern for the everyday lives of the working classes as well. Geddes emphasized the importance of providing sunlight, air, and green spaces for the working classes, and he sought and worked with their input in his projects, noting that these residents took an "intense public interest" in the planning of city spaces (1915, 293). Campaigners in 2005, like their industrial-era predecessors, allied themselves with middle-class conservation professionals in the intellectual and practical heritage of Patrick Geddes, building from his ideas to advocate for their communities in the twenty-first-century Old Town. From activists naming their community garden group the Patrick Geddes Gardening Club in 2015, to publishing a trilogy of books by local authors on the Old Town from 2014 to 2017 titled *The Evergreen*—the title used for a quarterly publication of Geddes from 1895 to 1897—Geddes continues to feature boldly in their imagination of another way to develop the city and a more active role for themselves in this process.

As the fourth chapter and the following interlude indicate, the solidarities that supported conservative surgery can be restored in view of an external threat, but the space for this coalition to engage and meaningfully contribute to the shape of a development has been significantly reconfigured by the tension-filled accommodations to entrepreneurial urbanism in the Scottish welfare state. This, then, is the context in which a historic piece of the built environment and local character, Jock the Cock, could be removed without consideration of residents or conservationists, in support of a not-yet but presumed-approved development in the Old Town of Edinburgh.

The Canongate residents who fought so determinedly for the retrieval of their affectionately regarded weathercock found themselves at a transition in the dominant municipal regime of urban development. Geddes's conservative surgery methods and ideals that had united many neighborhood organizations and advocates for Edinburgh's built heritage in common cause through the 1960s had fostered an urban social ecology that softened spatial segregation of social classes by maintaining a working-class Old Town presence through small-scale infill projects providing affordable housing. In the proposal for the Caltongate redevelopment plan, residents faced the transition of large-scale urban development practices from the city's greenbelt peripheries to the built-up and densely populated city center, as well as the city council's decision to prioritize short-term economic growth via investments in cultural tourism, a manifestation of Edinburgh's maturing regime of neoliberal urban development. The social geography produced by these development practices tends toward the organization of de facto socioeconomic zones, as neighborhoods, throughout the city. In this spatialized class map, the Canongate of 2005 stood as an anomaly in the city center: marked by its exceptionalism according to working-class residents who maintained their lives there and by aggravation according to city leaders who have found its working-class aesthetic undesirable by city-center development standards.

Similar to the built environment's capacity to retain artifacts of Edinburgh's industrial heritage, despite the erasure of its industrialization in most historical narratives, I have shown that the built legacy of conservative surgery preserved in the Canongate, and in the Old Town more generally, recalls alliances between middle-class protectors of architectural heritage and the working-class residents of these neighborhoods, united against the large-scale modernization projects, which have been proposed for Edinburgh's city center in various forms since the second half of the nineteenth century. The next chapter delves into the neoliberal logic that has motivated the Caltongate development proposal, as perhaps the most ambitious recent modernization project. The rise to dominance of this logic in urban development is explored with reference to the leadership of a Labour city councilor instrumental in its advocacy, indicating the popularization of this strategy beyond its Conservative Party origins and the circles of its presently enduring appeal. The Caltongate proposal, as an outworking of this logic, stimulated once again an alliance between the Canongate residents and leaders of local heritage organizations, in which the legacy of Patrick Geddes has continued to be invoked as an exemplar by both groups. The rise of neoliberal development in postindustrial Edinburgh, however, indicates the adaptability of development advocates and their evolving methods for mitigating these challenges, to disempowering effect for the groups invested in the old alliances.

## Notes

1. See Edinburgh Post Office Directory 1799–1800, cited in Adamson, Kilpatrick, and McDonald (2016, 182).

2. The ascription of this title to Edinburgh's topographical and architectural features occurred later, in the early nineteenth century, and then often with mocking or sarcastic overtones (McKee 2018, 91).

INTERLUDE 1

# ON CONSERVATION, COMMUNITY, AND CLASS

> Caltongate won't work. I don't understand why they're putting in a public square there, and they're telling us it will be so successful—it will be like Hunter Square. And nobody believes that Hunter Square is successful. Public squares are not indigenous to Edinburgh, and the only public squares are: Hunter Square, full of drugs; Bristo Square, full of skateboarders; Festival Square, full of nobody at all.
> —*Conservationist 1*

> What do you do in that situation? Do you say "No, just let it keep deteriorating"...? Or do you say, "This is kind of a once-in-a-generation opportunity to do something here, and hey, it's going to bring in folks to the city center and more tourists and bigger events, and all this is for the benefit of the city? And what's not to like?" It creates these kind of dilemmas. And it kind of intrinsically marginalizes the conservation campaigners because they're left saying, "Well, we really don't want that kind of thing. It's really not appropriate." It sounds rather precious, it sounds rather elitist.
> —*Conservationist 2*

THE PLACEMENT OF THESE TWO statements juxtaposes quotes from two of my conversations with members of Edinburgh's longest-standing built heritage conservation organization, the Cockburn Association, which took place ten years apart. Conservationist 1 was responding to the then-active planning proposal for the Caltongate development, and Conservationist 2 was reflecting on the now-characteristic struggle for conservationists to gain political and popular support for critiques just like that one. In the face of simplified, sunny public rhetoric in support of projects like Caltongate, which skims the surface of economic and aesthetic arguments just enough to cannily invoke "creating jobs," "dynamic modern architecture," and "convenient lifestyle" references, the arguments left to conservationists—"the wrong scale," "inappropriate," "not indigenous"—appear dim and dusty by comparison. As Conservationist 2 suggests, the conservationists active in Edinburgh through the Cockburn Association, as well as similar organizations such as the Architectural Heritage Society, feel the frustrations of this position keenly.

In my discussions with these conservationists, I found that a strategy of outreach to community activists, who were often their copursuers of common cause against a coalition of developers and supportive city councilors, injected their cause with a sense of morality or justice; even as for the community members, the conservationists lent the heft of professional expertise to their protests. Through these alliances, middle- and working-class urban residents formed temporary ties of solidarity and mutual support, which, though tenuous and fraught with class-based tensions, have offered the primary public challenge to fast-paced and large-scale urban redevelopment. Such alliances have, in their responses to the Caltongate and New Waverley developments, affirmed the values and ethos of a left-leaning social democracy, the rhetoric of which has been appropriated by the Scottish National Party (SNP), as discussed in chapter 5. The conservationist-community alliances that have periodically formed, faded, and reformed in tandem with development projects across Edinburgh over the past two decades have thus supported conditions favorable to a positive mixed-class response to the rhetoric, at least, of Scottish independence.

Conservationists and community activists have, as described in chapter 1, negotiated roles of significant though inconsistent influence in the history of Edinburgh's built environment, particularly since the turn of the twentieth century. In the first two decades of the twenty-first century, that relationship has continued to adapt to social and economic pressures felt, though experienced differently, by both groups. The following pages relay some of those pressures, as shared with me by both conservationists and community activists, and consider some frustrations of navigating political partnerships that attempt to span geographic and social divides.

## Coming Together: Airbnb, Tourism, and the Year-Round Festival City

> They say, oh, you can make some extra money, but then you find yourself renting out your bedroom to strangers for £100 a night, and suddenly you realize you can't do without the income.
> —*Former Canongate resident*

> The Airbnb thing has moved beyond the original conception of somebody just taking somebody in for a couple of nights, to a situation where properties are being purchased with the intention of operating them as a B and B. At the moment, there's very little regulation that can address that issue.
> —*Conservation professional*

When I visited in 2017 and 2018, virtually everyone I met with worried about the rapidly unfolding, but as-yet poorly understood, impacts of Airbnb and similar property-booking platforms on Edinburgh's built and social environment. The brightly colored key boxes clustered around ground-floor tenement entrances provided a visual cue to the transformation, pointed out to me on many walks through the Old Town. Anecdotal evidence is discussed widely among Edinburgh's planning and conservation professionals, and those with whom I spoke called for systematic analysis capable of reaching more deeply than the critical news pieces that circulate occasionally in Edinburgh's popular press. But few commentators have yet discussed the lived experiences of the Airbnb property letters themselves—not the multiproperty owners who rent out entire flats but those who, as the quote indicates, rent out one of the rooms in their daily living space and navigate the sharing of these spaces with tourists.

When Diane, one of my long-time interlocutors and a former Canongate campaigner, invited me to dinner at her home in July 2017, two of her friends joined us. After introductions and appetizers, we began to talk about what was happening in Edinburgh these days, and short-term letting—including but not limited to Airbnb—soon came up. Two out of the three, one woman and one man, had their rooms posted on at least one short-term letting site, and they compared notes of their experiences and those of their friends. Diane brought up her friend Kevin, who rents his

Canongate bedroom on Airbnb. In the beginning, she recalled, he would go down to the pub with his guests and chat with them, genuinely interested in getting to know them. By now, she shrugged, he just does not care; he checks them in and leaves them alone. Diane attributed this change to his experiences with a disinterested international clientele that have left him bewildered and jaded. As an example, she relayed the story of one woman who had traveled across the continent to visit Edinburgh and rented Kevin's flat for two nights. Having initially written to him about how excited she was to come to Edinburgh, according to Kevin she only left the flat for a total of about six hours during her stay, and when he asked her whether she would like to go out and see Edinburgh, she assured him, "Oh, I've already seen the Golden Mile and the castle!" Diane and her friends scoffed at the superficiality of this tourism practice. She told me about books she had seen in the tourism section of a popular bookstore, a series instructing readers in thirty-six-hour tourism in various locations. She was incredulous—"What can you see? What experience do you have? Ticked that box! Right, ticked that box!" In Edinburgh, she speculated, tourists rarely make it out of the Royal Mile, or possibly Princes Street.

Diane and her friends had embarked on the letting of their rooms with an ideal not only of making a bit of money but also of meeting new people and sharing some of their culture and history. Instead, they found that the tourism supported by an industry focusing on place images and cultural consumption enabled a very superficial engagement with places and people. The result they all reported was a growing sense of alienation from both those guests and that tourism industry, while at the same time their household budgets grew increasingly dependent on that income. No longer the entrepreneurial-sounding "side hustle," renting out their rooms had become part of the grocery and heating budget. The place marketing scheme so central to developments like Caltongate had in these ways intruded on the spaces of their homes and their private lives, and so became yet more repugnant to them, even as they struggled to extricate themselves.

In their desire to curb the reach of Airbnb and other online rental companies, these residents have allied themselves with Edinburgh's conservation professionals, even if the impacts of short-term letting intersect with their lives in different ways. Although I have not carried out a systematic analysis of letting practices among conservation professionals, of the half dozen with whom I spoke in 2017–2018, none rented their rooms, by comparison to half, four out of eight, of the residents in largely working-class neighborhoods with whom I spoke in the same period. Closer analysis of this phenomenon and any class-based distribution of effects appears warranted, but despite their differentiated experiences of it, the two groups share concerns that Airbnb is hollowing out the formerly residential city center, accelerating trends toward transience in as-yet unrestrained trajectories. For some of the residents sharing their homes with short-term tourists, proximity has produced the added effect of shaping a distaste for certain kinds of tourism practices, strengthening their sense of Edinburgh's development priorities having discounted its residents. Concerns about Airbnb thus unite these residents and conservationists, whose doubled voice insistently asks, "Who is the city for?" to the city council and the Edinburgh public.

For Diane and her friends, however, this critique of short-term tourism refused to reject tourism and tourists in one stroke. Tourism, as they had experienced it, could be done differently. They offered their own practices as exemplars. Discounted airlines like Ryanair and British Midland had provided them access to the European continent, and low-cost hostels and holiday rentals had allowed them to practice a kind of slowed-down tourism, in which they behaved much as they would at home: they walked most places, they took local buses, they cooked for themselves with local food and made a point of meeting and making friends on their visits. All of these practices they contrasted with the short-term consumption-oriented tourism they identified in Edinburgh. In their narratives of tourism as with urban development more generally, these working-class residents found common cause with middle-class conservation professionals, and they adopted a working-class cosmopolitan posture from which they criticized the easy, superficial internationalism of consumption instrumentalized in neoliberal development practices. As with the residents' political activism, the welfarist values of Scottish nationalism's Scotland in Europe seemed to align with these experience-based critiques, and yet the limitations of their tourism practices suggest some tensions between them and national aspirations of Scottish economic development. Depending as they did on relatively cheap air travel, Diane and her friends admitted that they could not travel much in Scotland; the price of train travel, bed and breakfast accommodations, and even food was prohibitive. As tourists, they took up their role as "Scots abroad" by necessity, finding freedom through those links with Europe that their own national economy did not provide.

In their political activism, at the level of both city and nation, these Canongate and Old Town residents sought to make living more viable for the working classes, and they found ready allies among Edinburgh-based middle-class professionals toward this end. As these working-class activists have taken an interest in the conservation of Edinburgh's built environment, so the conservationists have been making further moves to affirm the embeddedness of this built environment in communities and the necessity of attending to these communities' needs. In 2017, the Cockburn Association produced a document titled "A Civic Agenda for Edinburgh," in which only one out of nine action items focused on the conservation of historic architecture, and the remaining eight items addressed the built and social environment as integrally related, advocating partnership with neighborhoods and communities, the provision of housing for families, devolution of budgets to residential organizations and responsiveness to their needs. My interactions with representatives of residential and conservation organizations attest to the networks of public activism between them; when I have been meeting with someone in a conservation organization, that person would often recommend that I meet with a residential activist whom I already knew, and vice versa. As the conservation agenda in Edinburgh has elaborated its commitments to civic concerns, the ideological agreements between conservationists and residential activists like those in the Canongate have focused on the role of communities in innovative projects with a conservative surgery ethos. In their shared concerns over Edinburgh's trajectory of development projects, conservationists and community development activists in Edinburgh are coming together in a public agenda that is broadly critical of many projects and processes key to neoliberal urbanism. Given that neoliberalism is most often associated with the Conservative and Labour Parties in Scotland (though, as chap. 5 shows, the SNP is far from antineoliberal), further research is needed to understand how this mixed-class coalition of built environment and community activists interacts with the rhetoric of cosmopolitanism, egalitarianism, and fairness associated with Scottish nationalism.

### Coming Apart: Class and Muted Conflict

> There is no place for the working class in the city center anymore.
> —Catriona

Despite the ideological agreements and affirmations, stitching together interclass political coalitions has left some seams raw and gaping. As the preceding section indicates, although the respective groups share significant commitments to conservation and even desires for community empowerment, they do not share an equal stake in the outcomes. This inequality is readily observable in the differentiated impacts of the approval of the Caltongate master plan on the various actors allied against it: for the external allies of the Save Our Old Town (SOOT) campaign, that large section of the Canongate became a disappointing and anodyne place, which they regret when they think about or pass by it. But the Canongate residents weighed their everyday lives in that balance, and, as shown in chapter 3, because the place promised to become disorienting and alienating, they moved to new neighborhoods and lost the community life that had depended on it. Such risks have continued to cast a heavier burden on the working-class residents in the years following the Caltongate master plan, with costs for the coalition itself.

The Edinburgh Old Town Development Trust (EOTDT), formed in 2009 as the organizational community successor to the Canongate's SOOT, inherited the unenviable responsibility for a kind of social alchemy: transforming the fervor of community activism stirred up by the SOOT campaign into long-term social and political investment in the neighborhood. The meager resources designated to this endeavor communicated that any success would require further alliances and the securing of additional resources: the funding made available by Development Trusts Association Scotland provided £30,000 for one year, funding one full-time job but none of the supporting work. The most likely source of any resources, the leaders determined, lay in the gaining of an asset, most likely an older, underutilized building. To that end, the leaders of the EOTDT wrote an extensive conservation statement about the Canongate Venture building, following the 2008 failure of the bank loan to the original Caltongate developer. That statement was created with the support of local conservation organization members, and though it seemed a promising project for some months, as described in chapter 3, the arrival of new developer Artisan meant that despite the enormous amount of work that EOTDT members had committed to this process, the organization was not able to gain use of the building. The EOTDT members, whose numbers have continued to dwindle as the embers of the SOOT campaign cool, searched for a replacement building asset for another ten years. Reflecting on the length of that process and its result—a designated community building—the then-leader of the EOTDT resigned himself to a rather sunny take: "That's not bad for the Old Town!"

He was still in the process of raising money for the refurbishment of that building when we last met in 2018.

As one community leader explained to me, while community groups collaborate with conservation organizations, the scarcity of available resources for such groups has meant that groups, especially those who share the geographic area of the Old Town, tend to compete with one another. This competition sometimes works to generate resentment for the outsiders whose contribution can confer advantage to a given group. Given the typically middle-class professional position of allies such as the conservationists alongside the preponderance of working-class residents in the community groups, the presumption of class identity attributed to the external allies has in some cases fomented criticism from Old Town community members. In a 2017 meeting with a community organizer whom I'll call Richard, he shared his frustration that residents in the housing estate of Dumbiedykes continued to resist his overtures to join in community work, a resistance he attributed to their "class-based suspicion." Richard explained that some residents saw him as a middle-class interloper who had come in from the outside to solve the community's problems. Given his long-term work in Old Town community development, he found those characterizations tiresome and frustrating. Not only had Richard lived in the Old Town for more than a decade; he also emphatically rejected the middle-class label. "If they knew my upbringing, knew what I'm about . . . I am really working-class. It's who I am," he exclaimed, shaking his head.

Richard speculated that his middle-class label mostly reflected a popular identification of his cultural activities in writing and art as "middle-class priorities," a characterization he dismissed out of hand, pointing to the Craigmillar Festival Society and its working-class cultural accomplishments. That organization had shown what good could be done when the middle and working classes collaborate, he concluded wistfully. The long-term activities of a Dumbiedykes-based writing group, with whom I had met previously, suggests that even if Richard's speculations are true of some Dumbiedykes residents, a suspicion of such cultural activities still cannot be widely attributed to that neighborhood of the Old Town. Nevertheless, Richard's frustrations should not be dismissed as idiosyncrasies of personality; his frustrations echoed some quietly dropped comments made by local conservationists as well, who also saw themselves being bracketed out as middle-class and therefore held by some residents at arms' length in local development work.

While my own interactions with and observations of residents in the Canongate would not corroborate accusations of their hostility toward the middle classes, the narrative of the Canongate residents' campaign framed their story as a story of the working class, as Catriona's quote at the start of this section indicates. Negotiating the right to a place for the working classes in the city center may have produced new alliances and expanded social and political networks, but the project from the outset foregrounded a class identity, and so the success of any outcome—of community development work, planning or activism—will also be evaluated in terms of its impacts on those groups. That this class-based lens continues to persist despite real growth in mutually beneficial interclass alliances may ultimately frustrate the idealism of middle-class allies most of all. Despite such tensions, shared opposition to the ascendant neoliberal urban development practices promises to continue providing a substantial, if unfortunate, base for common cause between conservationists and community activists in Edinburgh. Their recent and ongoing activities indicate that these groups continue to grow together in their shared interests and public voice, even while navigating the uncertain terrain of class identity and practice highlighted by the class-differentiated experiences of development in the city's Old Town.

CHAPTER 2

# DEPOLITICIZING DEVELOPMENT
## Neoliberal Urbanism and Caltongate

OF THE THREE OFTEN-COMPETING DEVELOPMENT priorities discussed in the previous chapter, the Caltongate development proposal reflects the ascendance of economic growth over concerns for provisioning working-class life or conserving the city's built heritage. This chapter explores the proposal of Caltongate and the arguments offered by its many supporters in municipal governance in the context of Edinburgh's historical patterns of urban development. These supporters of Caltongate emphasized neighborhood aesthetics, grounding the argument for this development in a de-politicizing, economic assessment of public benefit. This rhetorical move is especially significant given that advocacy by working-class groups has historically obtained success through the arena of politics rather than attaining access to the professional practices of economic counsel. In the Old Town in particular, political advocacy for the conservation of the historic built environment has been joined with demands for retention of residents in the city center, thus facilitating the joining of working-class and middle-class interests in urban development throughout most of the twentieth century.

This chapter situates the shift in urban development logic in Edinburgh as part of the broader neoliberalization of Britain and the transformation of municipal political economies that have followed. The logic behind the Caltongate development is presented, with minimal interjection from the Canongate residents, to highlight the arguments, ambitions, and expectations that made sense of this particular political-economic arrangement, as a locally distinct outworking of neoliberal urbanism. This approach reflects insights from architectural history in Edinburgh, which has shown that contemporary constructs of national political economy are necessary to interpret the aesthetic of a given development and the concerns it is designed to address (Brown, McCrone, and Paterson 1996; Coleman 2018; McKean 2001; McKee 2018). This book expands the relationship between the aesthetics and politics of the built environment further into the politics "from below," showing how in Edinburgh, urban development has constituted a field in which aesthetic political subjectivities have been cultivated across and between urban and national scales. Regarding the neoliberal development logic that recommended Caltongate to the Old Town, the depoliticization of the terms of development stimulated the identification and elaboration of a "community of sense," in Rancière's (2004) meaning, a project taken up by the Save Our Old Town (SOOT) campaign discussed in the following chapter. In this chapter, the Caltongate master plan is presented as a materialization of Edinburgh's accommodations to neoliberal urbanism, following the British state's imposition of this political-economic strategy. That the Caltongate-style development trends derive from values endorsed by former British prime minister Margaret Thatcher traces a genealogy both highlighted and reviled by the Canongate residents, as discussed in the following chapter. The design, functions, and placement of the Caltongate development all signaled to them an alignment between political rule from Westminster and the development priorities of Edinburgh's Labour city leadership. Thus, while development proposals like Caltongate constitute an aesthetic and moral project sanctioned by Edinburgh's municipal leadership, the profound implications for working-class geographies and lives that are entailed in the reorganization of the built environment simultaneously gesture toward capacities for influence within the politics of Britain.

## Neoliberalism and Devolution

To understand the senses in which the Caltongate proposal seemed to the members of Edinburgh's city council planning committee a self-evidently positive step for the Canongate neighborhood, our discussion must walk backward a bit through history, beyond the devolution of governmental powers from Westminster and reformation of Scottish Parliament, past the policies of Thatcher and the global recession to which they responded, to consider the post–World War II consolidation of the British welfare state. The political-economic model of the welfare state, and especially its promises of provision for the population's needs, featured prominently in the political imaginations and social critiques of the Canongate residents who campaigned against the Caltongate proposal. Analyses of contemporary Scottish politics show that the promises of the welfare state continue to be invoked in the rhetoric of the Scottish National Party (SNP) and that parliamentary devolution was seen as enabling the realization of such intentions (Paterson 1997; cf. Stewart 2004). So this turn to (a reformist version of) the midcentury welfare state has been prompted by a combination of the continued political relevance of the Scottish welfare state as a political-social ideal (discussed in the final chapter) and by the critical nostalgia for that political-social era that emerged among the Canongate campaigners themselves (discussed in the subsequent chapter). It is with reference to these political and social visions that the Canongate residents' support for Scottish independence must be understood.

Even before parliamentary devolution, Scotland experienced considerable autonomy within its civil society, which has been historically defined as having three parts: a separate legal system, local governance, and the presbyterian church (Paterson 1997, 56). Under these conditions, the Scottish welfare state operated with considerable room under the federal UK system to navigate its own cultural, philosophical, and political convictions in areas such as housing, education, and health (Paterson 1997, 59). Those convictions produced policy outcomes to the left of those coming from Westminster, even as the institutions of Scottish welfare policy, primarily the Scottish Office (Brown, McCrone, and Paterson 1996), came under critique in Scotland for their centralization and therefore distance from directly democratic processes.

The degree of Scottish autonomy allowed under the welfare state model served the rhetoric of Scottish distinctiveness well, while for a time maintaining the viability of a "difference within the Union" perspective, which Gilfillan (2011) found to typify the views of his working-class Scottish interlocutors from that postwar generation. But the national economy that supported the welfare state foundered during the global recession of the 1970s, which ultimately provided the impetus for a docket of economic privatization and the "rolling back" of the state on which the Conservative Party was elected to power, by a largely English vote, in 1979. On her ascent to the position of prime minister, Margaret Thatcher embarked on the operationalizing of a political-economic logic of neoliberalism across the United Kingdom throughout the 1980s, implementing cuts to the financial and material bases for working-class labor and community life, which notably included council housing (Harvey 2005). In 1980, more than half the population of Scotland lived in homes rented from council or housing associations, but following almost twenty years of Thatcherite policies, this percentage fell to one quarter (Matthews 2015, 24). In Gilfillan's working-class mining town and elsewhere across Scotland, Thatcher was popularly vilified, consistently failing to gain support relative to her popularity in England. In Scotland throughout Thatcher's tenure as prime minister, resentment was expressed through majority Labour votes, and it would eventually be a misstep in Scotland—the imposition of a flat-rate tax on every individual a full year before implementation in England or Wales—that provided proof for many that the nation was treated as merely a policy guinea pig by their own Prime Minister. The political disaster that ensued brought Thatcher's tenure as Prime Minister to an end.

Thatcher's agenda, however, outlasted her occupation of that singular office, and by the time the Conservative Party was voted out in 1997 in favor of the self-proclaimed "New Labour" Party, across Britain, her neoliberalizing regime had dealt powerful blows to Scottish economic strongholds like heavy industry and manufacturing and diluted the provision of public welfare and services, against the resistance of Scottish voters. Key to Labour's election campaign "manifesto" was a promise that the frustrated Scottish voters would be given an opportunity for a devolution referendum to direct some significant economic and political powers of self-determination to a reinstated Scottish Parliament. This parliament had been dissolved in 1707 by the Acts of Union, which had united the English and Scottish Parliaments in a single British Parliament, at Westminster. Although a similar Labour-led devolution referendum in 1979 had failed to gain majority support, the intervening decade of English-led policies, from a Conservative Party that had comparatively little support in Scotland, propelled 74.3 percent of Scottish voters, at a turnout rate of 60 percent, to vote in 1999 for the reinstating of a Scottish Parliament.

The vote was charged with expectations for political and social change, and in particular for a restoration of the welfare state at which the English-led government had been so steadily chipping away (Stewart 2004). At the opening of the Scottish Parliament, then-First Minister of Scotland Donald Dewar cast a vision for the newly restored political body: "We are fallible.

We will make mistakes. But we will never lose sight of what brought us here: the striving to do right by the people of Scotland, to respect their priorities, to better their lot and to contribute to the common weal."

In practice, however, Scottish governance after devolution has reflected tensions between the dominant rhetorics of value, which express social democratic leanings, and the realities of economic influence and decision-making. The result has been policies awkwardly shaped by a combination of "social-welfarism" and "neo-liberal economic policy" (MacLennan 2016, 63). A decade of economic structural reforms initiated under Thatcher's leadership have established an enduring influence (Torrance 2009), which not only found their place in the Labour government that followed (1997–2010); they also continue to shape postdevolution Scotland (Paterson, Bechhoffer, and McCrone 2004). In particular, the central role played by the finance sector throughout Britain has been sustained from Conservative to Labour Party leadership in England, and in Scotland, from the graduated transition of Labour to SNP leadership in the Scottish Parliament (Hearn 2017, 29). The finance sector's centrality has coexisted with long-standing political "aspirations" to "do things differently" than England (Hearn 2017, 29), and, as Gerry Hassan has shown in his commentary on the Scottish government's (2013) white paper on independence, the Scottish Parliament largely view its work as "the embodiment of pre-devolution hopes and the so-called 'new politics'" (Hassan 2018, 39).

But social-welfarism and neoliberal economics make a strange brew. Indeed, Thatcher introduced neoliberal political-economic policies to hollow out, if not dismantle, the British welfare state, so how can a Scottish welfare state sustain both? Many commentators in and on Scotland have queried the sustainability of these two components of Scottish policy and practice, observing that the state of Scottish democracy reflects "obvious failings," evident in its accommodations to the corporate finance sector, tendencies toward centralization, and social justice policy, as well as the empowerment of local governance over and against communities (Hassan 2018, 39; see also Blackburn and Keating 2012; Hearn 2017; MacLennan 2016). This book lacks the scope to adequately and appropriately address the Scottish democracy question, but it seeks to contribute to the discussion by highlighting the incongruities apparent in the Scottish outworking of a "'broad tent' alliance of social democracy and good business sense" (Hassan 2009, 4). In this chapter and the next, the tensions between a welfare state ideology and urban planning governed by neoliberal logic and relationships of influence are explored through the Caltongate proposal and its rejoinder by the residents of the Canongate neighborhood.

In Edinburgh as elsewhere, urban development has become an instrument by which neoliberal logics manifest an idealized aesthetic of social relations in material form. Such aesthetics are essentially political, in the sense of determining the conditions for appearance and presence (Rancière 2004), and yet the processes of development mask the conditions of its own production, creating an alienable product, the city, that is ripe for appropriation. This chapter unmasks those conditions, charting the affect of competitive anxiety driving the depoliticizing of development by tracing the political trajectory of a primary proponent of such development in Edinburgh, then a Labour city councilor. As the following chapter explains, attempts to depoliticize these properly political debates on affective and aesthetic grounds have set into motion an aesthetic politics, in which residents in the city's Old Town have leveraged a case for their own political authority. This authority coheres in a sense of place that opposes the designs of Caltongate and authorizes in its stead a neighborhood aesthetic freighted with claims to morality. These residents critically assess the drift of the Labour Party, from a party inviting public debate about the public good to one that has accepted the foreclosure of such debates on behalf of presumed social and economic gains, which are often indexed by neoliberal keywords like *leadership, flexibility,* and *innovation* (Leary 2018).

NEOLIBERALIZING DEVELOPMENT IN EDINBURGH

To begin a discussion of neoliberalism requires a delimiting introduction. As Jonathan Hearn and many others have pointed out, neoliberalism is often overappropriated and underelaborated precisely because its realities are always adapted to its contexts, the navigating of which may produce internal contradictions and locally distinct forms (Hearn 2017, 16; Collier 2012). For this reason, Hearn prefers to focus on the mechanisms and logics specific to his particular field of inquiry, or what others have called "actually-existing neoliberalism" (Brenner and Theodore 2002). Some authors prefer to avoid the term in an explanatory capacity in favor of locally derived vocabulary where possible (Kipnis 2007). While I share a skepticism for flippantly causal claims made about neoliberalism, I do find comparative value in retaining the concept, particularly regarding urban political economy in Scotland and Britain. While the recent rise of the SNP has suggested a widespread dissatisfaction with the political status quo, Scottish national economic decision-making continues to indicate the stubborn persistence of "insider Scotland," for whom neoliberalism works quite well (Hassan 2016). Indeed, despite declarations of its demise in the economic recession of 2008–2009 (see Hassan 2009), neoliberalism as political-economic ideology has proven adaptable and resilient, from Conservative to Labour to Scottish National Party policies. This section thus elaborates the processes, expectations, and aesthetics of Edinburgh's neoliberalizing development, in which the Caltongate development proposal made sense to its proponents among the city's municipal and business elites. Given the centrality of the finance sector to neoliberal political-economic arrangements in Edinburgh, the logic emerging from that sector is considered first.

In one of the few ethnographies of the finance sector, and the only ethnography to date on a Scottish financial institution, Jonathan Hearn conducted fieldwork in the Edinburgh-based Bank of Scotland during the 2001–2002 period of its merger with the English bank Halifax, during which he observed the decline of an older Scottish culture of banking, to be replaced with an English banking culture that emphasized competition as an institutional virtue. While competition was already one of the values guiding Scottish banking, Hearn found that competition in the larger bank culture at Halifax occupied a more central place. Because of the bank merger, he observed through the Bank of Scotland's transition to Halifax Bank of Scotland (HBOS) the importation of a moralized affect of "reflexive competition," in which competition is "deliberately harness[ed] and organize[d]" as "a preferred way to decide who gains what." This logic, he noted, is not confined to the operations of financial institutions but has extended throughout social, economic, and political life, with effects of "legitimating distributive outcomes in a way that often appears very natural, obscuring the human hand in when, where and how it operates" (Hearn 2017, 16).

The proliferating virtues of competition to which Hearn observed Scottish finance practices being converted typify "neoliberal agency," a mode of meaningful practice that pervades individual and institutional action and generates its own moral frameworks of human value (Gershon 2011; Muehlebach 2012; Leary 2018). The case of the Caltongate development illuminates the formative effects that neoliberal conceptualizations of virtuous competition—for space, influence, and presence—have on the public sphere, specifically on deliberative political processes by which residents levy claims on the state. The close tracking of designs for the redevelopment of the working-class Canongate neighborhood, interpreted through an interview with the municipal leader who cleared a path for the development of this area, explores the constellations of value and desire that manifest themselves in the materiality, intentions, and people that would aggregate as the Caltongate development.

ON THE CUSP OF CALTONGATE: DEPOLITICIZING DEVELOPMENT

Edinburgh has particularly strong associations with the emotional, romantic Scottish nationalism expressed in the novels of Sir Walter Scott and the contemporary Scottish national movement (Hearn 2000) while also serving as the hub of Scottish finance. The overlay of these two centers of influence has generated a complicated history of divergence and interdependence, which the SNP leadership has in the last decade sought to reconcile, as Edinburgh-based finance is an essential resource in the independent Scottish economy that it has outlined. The 1999 decision to site the Scottish Parliament in Edinburgh affirmed the historical continuity of Edinburgh as Scotland's political capital, and this location continues to facilitate the national government's proximity to the Scottish engines of global finance. The centrality of finance to national and municipal programs of economic growth was firmly established under Thatcher, and it has never been dislodged or even genuinely threatened from its prime position.

The competitive urbanism endorsed by Thatcher resonated with the interests of a well-established corporate sector in Edinburgh, which has thrived through close relationships with Thatcher's fellow Conservatives and subsequent Labour leadership. As this section shows, Labour council leadership in Edinburgh embraced neoliberalism's moral arrangement of persons, property, and revenues. From shared presumptions that the framework of internationally competitive urbanism should dictate the assemblages of such people and places in the city, this leadership has derived an affect of urgency, which thus envelops projects and processes of urban development. The public processes by which interests in Edinburgh's built environment have been negotiated in the twentieth century have been transformed by Labour's characterization of development according to this moralized affect. As the imperative to offer competitive assemblages of the built, social, and economic environment has come to press especially firmly on the largest projects of urban development, Labour-led projects have foreclosed public debate over the social and material costs of such developments, as well as alternative calculations of public benefit.

The material and social transformations of neoliberal urban development are readily apparent in its aesthetic arrangements, consumption clusters, and class segregation. As the Caltongate planning process indicates, the neoliberal affect of competitive urgency has powerfully shaped the political sphere in the pressure it applies to contain and limit unwieldy, inefficient processes of political representation and negotiation. Affect, as the emotive "priming" of agents to act in specific ways (Barnett 2008, 189) may characterize urban spaces as well as politics, and I suggest that the neoliberal processes of development in entrepreneurial urbanism produce and sustain a sense of critical imperative and necessity attached to the delivery of development of a predetermined kind. For a darkly humorous commentary on the affective dimensions of urban development, one might look to Italo Calvino's prescient surrealist novel *Invisible Cities*. In the voice of his narrator Marco Polo, Calvino writes, "If you ask, 'Why is [the city] Thekla's construction taking such a long time?' the inhabitants continue hoisting sacks, lowering leaded strings, moving long brushes up and down, as they answer, 'So that its destruction cannot begin.' And if asked whether they fear that, once the scaffoldings are removed, the city may begin to crumble and fall to pieces, they add hastily, in a whisper, 'Not only the city.'" (1972, 127)

That among Edinburgh's development drivers the construction of any large-scale development, such as Caltongate, is viewed as a bellwether for the city's economic fortunes can be observed from the newspaper editorial columns to city council chambers and many conversations in between. As in Calvino's fictional city of Thekla, the material, social, and economic fortunes of the city are tangled in a skein of hopes and fears that generate real affective power.

The effect on political discourse around development has been the stymieing of debate about the social good because the good is represented as a deferred objective: obtainable indirectly by urban residents engaging in moral economic behavior, such as obtaining jobs that a new development brings, and as an urban consumer benefiting from the hypothetically increased revenues of municipal budgets. But the developments directly seek economic gain and only indirectly social good; they do not address family housing shortages, local space for artists, or fruit and vegetable markets. For urban residents to partake in the benefits of urban development requires first their submission to the discipline of neoliberal norming.

In discussions around the Caltongate development, its proponents considered the question of social good to have been settled by presumed consensus: contingent on short-term economic growth and derivative of moral behavior. In the Canongate campaign presented in the following chapter, the development process foreclosed space for genuinely open-ended debate between alternative calculations of the good, as represented by the Caltongate development aesthetic and Canongate neighborhood aesthetic. As the following sections of this chapter show, neoliberal urbanism operates according to presumptions of consensus, a consensus that is achieved by submission rather than debate. Foreclosures of debate, as refusals of competing values, are themselves moralized as a kind of efficiency, and the resulting depoliticization of development processes has contributed to a stripping-down of the public sphere, which reflexively deflects dissenting claims from a neoliberal moral order.

This section explores how the depoliticization of development played out in the lead-up to the Caltongate proposal by following the role played in this process by one individual in Edinburgh's municipal leadership, erstwhile city councilor Donald Anderson. Anderson's trajectory—from council estate resident, to Labour representative, to city council leader, and ultimately settling in as a consultant for private development firms—charts the changing political and economic priorities of Labour in Scotland. Anderson is a pro-development Edinburgh councilor par excellence: he took a leading role in bringing multiple major projects to Edinburgh, solicited plans for the redevelopment of the Canongate area, and secured funding for the city's branding. His record as Edinburgh's city council leader reads like an urban development portfolio, and he frames these ambitious projects in terms of economic growth, jobs, and choices for the working classes. Additionally, Anderson's proeconomic development career spans a period over which his political party suffered a significant loss of public trust, derived from its handling of the economy in particular (Henderson et al. 2020). I suggest that a consideration of Anderson's trajectory of support for development in Edinburgh offers insights into the logics and affect operationalized by individuals in neoliberal urban governance, who presume but defer public benefit of the sort sought by the Canongate campaigners. Given the largest development project he *almost* brought to Edinburgh, Anderson's narrative opens up the thinking and values behind such projects and situates them within a larger social and political vision, which differs from that of the Canongate residents on several significant points.

Donald Anderson was raised on a midcentury council housing estate in south Edinburgh. This development had been designed, according to the prevailing urban planning wisdom of the day, by garden city principles, with low-rise housing for families and single adults, adjacent to a green park and provisioned by a single street of shops, gathered between two local primary schools. Like many of the Canongate residents, Anderson's education and career trajectory have never taken him far from Edinburgh; even as he has pursued and achieved social mobility, the horizon of his achievements traces the skyline of the city's Old and New Towns. After completing all of his education in Edinburgh, Anderson worked as a scientist in his early career and entered politics in 1986, when he was elected as a Labour representative to the Lothian Regional Council.

The Labour Party during this period had consolidated the greatest share of political power in Scotland, with the district and regional councils acting as the power base for the party and effectively managing a collective image of public Scottish representation. When Anderson joined the Labour Party, he entered a political organization at its peak: Scottish Labour won the largest portion of Scottish votes in every UK general election between 1964 and 2010. His interests and activities, from the earliest years of his political career, preview the party-wide shift in Labour priorities toward optimism about markets as delivery systems for social goods, as Anderson pursued business and economic development from his most minor roles through his election as Chair of Economic Development in 1990. When the regional councils were reorganized into local authorities across Scotland in 1994, he was elected as the councilor for Kaimes, a South Edinburgh neighborhood of middle-class bungalows and semidetached houses only a mile from the housing estate on which he was raised. In my 2010 interview with Anderson, he affirmed that his primary interests throughout his council career lay in promoting economic growth in Edinburgh, an interest demonstrated in his convening of the economic development groups in both regional and city councils, and no less in his successful bid for the position of city council leader in 1999.

Anderson's political career parallels the twilight era of Labour's dominance in Scotland, from the vantage point of 2020. Reflecting on that career, Anderson's greatest appreciation has come from Edinburgh's leaders in business, while critical political commentators have claimed that Anderson leveraged his working-class background to establish an authority to speak on issues related to council housing and working-class life, on occasion against the cause of current council housing tenants (Swanson 2016). The trajectory of this career, interpreted through Anderson's narration in our 2010 interview, reveals the encroachment of neoliberal terms of judgment, commending deferred public benefit for morally economic actors, and animated by an affect of urgency. This encroachment has riven the Scottish Labour party with factions, the effects written not only on Edinburgh's built environment, as discussed in this and the following chapter, but on the national political discourse, discussed in chapter 5.

In his work as city council leader, Anderson has described himself as "obsessed" with promoting Edinburgh's international reputation (Baker 2006), a compulsion that motivated him to pursue the redevelopment of an area of Edinburgh's city center that he considered an unfortunate blight: the Canongate. For almost a decade, Anderson cleared obstacles to the redevelopment of that area, and when the Caltongate master plan was proposed, he spoke publicly of his admiration for it while officially recusing himself from consideration of the plan in his capacity as council leader. In the fateful parliamentary election of 2007, the first of many "unprecedented moments" in the turning of the Scottish electoral tide toward the SNP, Anderson ran for office as a Labour MP and lost to the incumbent Liberal Democrat. He soon found his feet in the private sector, working for PPS, the public relations firm that had lobbied for Caltongate, and remained there until he launched his own organization in 2016, offering consultancy to development firms seeking to present their proposals favorably to local government, media, and the public.

In his trajectory from Labour political representation to unabashedly "prodevelopment" consultancy work in Edinburgh, Anderson has advocated for a neoliberal vision of Scotland's future, a vision closely keyed to the success of large-scale financial investments, tourism, and property transformations. When describing his contributions, Anderson has maintained

Labour's lens of public benefit, but his reckoning of the distribution of that benefit illustrates the turn from managerial to entrepreneurial politics described by Harvey (1989). As effective as any single policy or plan, the affect of urgency that Anderson has contributed to the city's development process has been embraced even by his formerly critical political competitors. In agreeing to the affective terms of the urban development process, such leadership has foreclosed the deliberative politics of the built environment, which has historically provided an instrument for working-class political claim-staking. This loss indicates the shifting political grounds navigated by Edinburgh residents like the Canongate campaigners discussed in the next chapter and experienced as the drift of Labour from working-class interests (Johns, Mitchell, and Carman 2013).

I interviewed Anderson in the New Town offices of PPS, a handsome example of the rehabilitation of historic Georgian architecture to the purposes of a commercial firm. A secretary around my age, but much better dressed, buzzed me in, then walked me through the building to a conference room lit by a wall of tall, street-facing windows and offered me tea or coffee. After she left, I waited for a few minutes in silence until Anderson, a tall, confident, smiling man in a gray suit, joined me. In his postpolitical role, Anderson spoke freely of his perspectives on the Caltongate development, on development in Edinburgh more broadly, and on the Canongate campaigners. Because these perspectives have proven consequential for the Canongate neighborhood and its ongoing redevelopment, I allow Anderson's narrative to introduce the Caltongate development, replicating how the master plan first came to the Canongate.

The origins of the Caltongate master plan harken back to a document titled the Waverley Valley Redevelopment Strategy, which focused on the overlapping Canongate and Holyrood neighborhoods and was completed in 2001. Anderson had campaigned among Edinburgh's councilors for the formulation of such a strategy since at least 1995 as a solution to the primary problems that he had identified in Edinburgh: competitive loss of retail to Glasgow, underrealized tourism revenues, and the city's too-distant relationships between private corporate actors and local governance. Development, he explained, should serve the larger project of attracting investment to Edinburgh. Complementing this pursuit of the Canongate area's redevelopment, Anderson's upward trajectory in positions of municipal leadership facilitated access to expanded resources that could be marshaled to the cause of attracting investment to Edinburgh. In 2004, he secured funding (£950,000) from the Scottish Executive for a citywide branding project to raise Edinburgh's profile as a location for investment, an achievement he spoke of with great satisfaction. The brand selected, "Inspiring Capital," makes this investment focus baldly, if playfully, visible. An extended quote from our 2010 interview below illustrates the connections Anderson perceived between investment and development.

> I was instrumental in driving the whole [branding] thing forward, and I make no apology for that. I think it's helped to position Edinburgh as a location for investment. We did phenomenally well in Edinburgh because of the fact that Edinburgh was seen as a very attractive place, but also because it had West Lothian beside it, which was really the inward investment driver for central Scotland, and they got huge amounts of investment in West Lothian. It was called Silicon Glen at the time. You know, high-tech companies, Motorola and many others, came to West Lothian, but we got some of that in Edinburgh as well. Hewlett Packard are out at Queensferry.
>
> That kind of thinking, that approach of trying to attract investment, it just came naturally when I came to be involved in Economic Development in Edinburgh City Council. And then when I became leader, it was a huge part of what I wanted to do as well. I was able to use more of the tools of the council, to gear things towards bringing jobs and investment to the city. That's what I saw as my primary role and function.

Anderson's political vision privileges short-term economic growth, with the expectation that such growth leads to long-term public benefit. The primary attention to growth focuses the efforts of the council on the perceived growth instruments, identified above as large international technology firms (although at other points in the interview Anderson identifies high-end tourism and retail as other sources of growth). The supposed beneficiaries of that growth, the residents of Edinburgh, are presumed but not foregrounded in a logical succession of public benefit that, two decades previous, would have seemed like a priority reversal from a Labour councilor. Technology firms in particular typify the global mobility of investment that urgently necessitates an urban leadership committed to providing internationally competitive clusters of the resources such firms and their employees demand. As Anderson observed, international investment anticipates the aesthetic-economic judgments of these actors: "Edinburgh was seen as an attractive place."

Because interurban competition is the game that never sleeps, and success at this game is presumed to be the means to ensure public benefit, success mandates favorable arrangements of the built and social environments of the city, with employees and their lifestyles in mind (cf. Plotnicov 1990). This connection suggests Anderson's trajectory, from economic development-focused politician to private consultant for property developers: the economic growth models that the commercial and financial firms courted in entrepreneurial urban governance strategies require the redevelopment of the urban built environment in their own image, a destructive and reconstitutive process usually coded as "regeneration." The Caltongate proposal for redeveloping six hectares of the city center was designed to address the urgent demands of internationally mobile lifestyles, from residences to restaurants and retail. Notably, directly aesthetic discourse—such as a public statement on the desirable "look" for the area—was not part of either the developer's promotional material for Caltongate or the public documents from the city council. Instead, the language of "regeneration" offered coded promises of aesthetic transformation.

Even before the Caltongate proposal, convictions about the immediate need for such regeneration had led to a narrowing of the decision-making processes relating to development, to privilege private partners with the greatest capacity to influence investment decisions. Anderson described the priorities of development as formulated through "very, very close working on economic development-related issues" between the council and the city's chamber of commerce. The chamber of commerce however offered too blunt an instrument for the efficiency required to satisfy this urgent demand—in its inclusivity, open to all of Edinburgh's businesses, the chamber constituted a large and variable group, prone to debate over conflicting interests and investments. Foreshadowing the closure of development debates in the public sphere, opportunities for engagement in the private sphere shrank to a privileged few, when in 2005 city councilors collaborated with the city's biggest commercial firms to form the Edinburgh Business Assembly. The Business Assembly was an elite group of fifteen to twenty business leaders with a remit specifically related (though not confined) to shaping city planning processes. The Business Assembly's launch document notes, "Over the last two years, there has been an *increased imperative* for a *more focused engagement* as community planning has developed and as the profile of all Scotland's cities has been raised" (City of Edinburgh Council

2005, 2 [emphasis mine]). The affect of urgency characteristic of neoliberal urbanism displays itself in the language of the "imperative" and the call for "focus" toward the ends of competitive advantage between cities. The redevelopment of the city center is identified as one of seven "key issues of strategic concern" the Business Assembly planned to address, the first being "finance and advocacy," and the fifth being "the City Center," elaborated below. In support of redevelopment, the Business Assembly document offered a generalized aesthetic critique, noting the city center's "major problems in . . . its physical presentation," and prefiguring a discourse to come. "The City Center is crucial to the success of the entire Edinburgh city region. As the most accessible business location in south east Scotland, it is a national and regional center for the office, finance and retail sectors. It faces major problems in, for instance, its physical presentation, in dealing with through traffic and in its retail offering" (City of Edinburgh Council 2005, 3).

The Business Assembly was organized with the intent of focusing business engagement on city planning, particularly in light of trends toward more robust community engagement processes, as advocated in the first National Planning Framework for Scotland, published in 2004 (Nadin and Stead 2014, 203). Proposed planning reforms would increase public participation in planning, making it a more deliberative—and therefore, in the eyes of neoliberal development proponents, inefficient—process. The conflict between public participation processes and the urgency of development delivery was highlighted in the Business Assembly's founding document, but this conflict also featured in anxieties expressed by municipal leaders about the loss of firms to Glasgow, where, they fantasized, development decisions were arranged "over a cup of tea" with the council's head of planning (Blackley 2007).

Close working arrangements between Edinburgh's municipal government and its lead commercial firms managed many development projects around the city in the first decade of the twenty-first century. The Bank of Scotland took a direct role in the oversight of several projects, including a climbing center, and financed several more, including Caltongate. This book lacks the scope for a detailed study of the partnerships involved in development projects across Edinburgh, a worthy vehicle for the study of neoliberal state entanglements in itself. The discussion below focuses on Caltongate and the projects that prepared its path, presenting with Anderson's interjections the logical succession that led to its council approval and, as detailed in the following chapter, its protest by neighborhood residents. Caltongate is the highest-profile development in a litany of projects that have proceeded with an affect of urgency and deferred expectations of public benefit, characteristic of neoliberal development and yet out of step with historic expectations in Edinburgh of urban development decisions belonging properly to a deliberative public sphere.

### Preparing the Path for Development

Regarding the two projects discussed in this section, the location of new government buildings—one national and one municipal—was determined by Edinburgh's Labour-led council to offer a stimulus for economic and social "regeneration." Regeneration strategies have come to signify real estate instruments for those urban places in which nostalgia for an imagined social, cultural, and economic past can be hitched to aspirations of economic benefit and through the magic of urban development be made to realize new profits in real estate and a new zone of retail consumption. A premise of such strategies is aesthetic; to seek an area's regeneration indicates a current state of dereliction or underrealization. While the council's arguments for redevelopment did not dwell on aesthetic judgments, the language of regeneration stood in conveniently for aesthetic judgments that had already been made.

At this stage, when the council sought a willing developer and proposal, city councilors limited their aesthetic discourse to the language of regeneration, highlighting the need for development. The style and design of a development proposal remained firmly in the purview of the private developer, at least in public, owing largely to the fact that the proliferation of urban development regeneration projects over the last twenty years has conveyed a sense of generalized aesthetic expectation to these projects. In committing to the location of these government buildings, the city council signaled its sufficient support for the regenerative redevelopment of the surrounding area, with the intent that their project of construction would attract partners from the private sector. This hope would be realized with the Caltongate proposal, the occasion of which simultaneously justified the siting of the governmental construction projects. The close relationship between the city council and private developers, which Anderson has described and which is evident in the discussion of the following projects, typify entrepreneurial schemes for urban regeneration as a strategy for capital accumulation (Goodwin 1993; Hall and Hubbard 1998; Harvey 1989).

The devolution referendum prompted the decision that a new parliament would be sited in Edinburgh, which spurred intense debates over the location of the building. An early favorite among some traditionalists was the reappropriation of the historic Old Royal High School building on Calton Hill (overlooking the Canongate), primarily for reasons of its longstanding national symbolism. This location also appealed to Anderson but due to its lofty position in Edinburgh's topography rather than symbolic value; the scenic location of the hill offered an opportunity to use the parliamentary building as a lever for increasing property values and retail and investment opportunities in the Canongate area. He thus campaigned energetically to have the building located on Calton Hill, where he felt it could produce the maximum effects for "city center regeneration," but he reported with some frustration being thwarted by then-Secretary of State Donald Dewar, whose interest in locating the new parliament across from Holyrood Palace, at the foot of the Canongate, was driven by more nationally representational concerns. "Dewar had a very fixed view. He wanted a new building, and he wanted it to be a statement about Scotland, the new Scotland—all that kind of stuff. And we could have had a new building on Calton Hill, but he just wasn't for shifting."

Looking back with ambivalence a decade after the building's construction, Anderson felt that the results had proved less than satisfactory. Although he acknowledged that there had been some "fantastic" regeneration brought by the siting of the new parliament building in the Holyrood/Canongate area, the building had not produced the same effect on the city center that it would have had, he insisted, if located on Calton Hill.

But Anderson had not left the matter entirely to the influence of the parliament building. When construction on the new parliament began, he continued to push for projects to regenerate what he called the "east end of the city center." Where his influence had collapsed against the desires of the Labour secretary of state, his council position enabled him to advocate powerfully for the relocation of the council headquarters. By 2005, construction had begun on a site on New Street, a road that had been cut through a block of dilapidated tenement houses as part of the Canongate–Corstorphine Scheme of 1927. This relocation was accomplished, remarkably, without consultation of neighboring tenants and property owners, who observed with dismay as the steel frame of the building climbed higher than any other building in the neighborhood. When I asked Anderson about the reason for the relocation to the Canongate, Anderson emphasized that the site was chosen "with the *express purpose* of trying to regenerate the east end of Edinburgh, that area [Canongate] in particular."

Ultimately, the council's investment in the site did attract the kind of development Anderson had in mind, as the London-based development firm Mountgrange approached the council with an ambitious plan for area redevelopment and, in Anderson's words, after all that planning and investment of public funds, "We weren't going to say no!" This remark evokes Anderson's relief and exasperation—a private firm with the means to accomplish the hoped-for redevelopment had finally appeared, promising fulfillment of the necessity he perceived in regenerative redevelopment. Guided by his conviction about the urgency of the development issues, Anderson did not seek directly democratic ratification of these plans, and planning practice did not strictly require it. As MacLennan has noted, in postdevolutionary Scotland, the empowerment of local government has often come at the expense of neighborhood communities (Blackburn and Keating 2012, 104). The development processes that ushered in the Caltongate proposal, animated by the affect of urgency, likewise pursued expediency in achieving designated development priorities with the result of narrowing the public space for political negotiation by area residents. As chapter 5 explains, the reduction of opportunities for communities to make effective claims on the state is mismatched to a flourishing sphere for public discourse and debate (Hassan 2018).

The proposal for the Caltongate redevelopment project therefore arrived, unbeknownst to the residents of the intended area, on the heels of significant municipal investment so ordered to designate the development proposal as a largely economic instrument to promote investment in Edinburgh. While the residents would perceive the proposal as an issue for open political debate, councilors like Anderson had framed the development instead as an issue of economic, and therefore only derivatively public, benefit. By this logic, to ensure the deferred benefit of the public, the development decisions were better left to the expertise of technocrats, not deliberated through the democratic will of the people or open to negotiation via the historic politics of development.

Fig. 2.1 View of the Old Town, framed by the omnipresent construction cones and traffic barriers. Photo by author.

### Caltongate Revealed

On September 30 and October 1, 2005, plans for the most expansive redevelopment in Edinburgh's city center since the eighteenth century were displayed in the St. James Centre, across the Waverley Valley in Edinburgh's New Town. As the above section has shown, this plan fulfilled the aspirations of councilors like Anderson, as well as local business leaders like chamber of commerce chair Ron Hewitt, who supported the plan's promise to transform a "dingy" part of the city center. The name of the development, "Caltongate," even played to the natural feature that Anderson had wanted to highlight in his vision for parliament-led area regeneration, Calton Hill. By retaining the *gate* suffix of the Canongate, the new nomenclature retained an aura of historicity and "fit," without invoking the constraints of

Fig. 2.2 The public square as envisioned in the Caltongate master plan. From www.caltongate.com, accessed 2009.

the neighborhood's population and, more recently, its working-class history. Strikingly, in my discussions with supporters of the development like Anderson, the neighborhood area was usually referred to as "Caltongate," avoiding the historical Canongate place name in both present and future accounts.

Caltongate promised an ambitious, total scene change, and the new scene it projected conveyed an aestheticized landscape of consumption opportunities accessible by the global-mobile elite. Such scenes had already been familiarized through the proliferation of place-marketing images across Europe (Bianchini and Parkinson 1993; Kearns and Philo 1993; McDonogh 1999), and Caltongate was positioned for maximum impact as a "flagship" development (Loftman and Nevin 2003), with exclusive French hotel chain Sofitel to run a five-star hotel at its coveted Royal Mile street address. The promotional materials for the proposed development promised "a prestigious new signature office building," "a new public space with exceptional surroundings," "a substantial residential sector featuring a broad range of innovative and desirable homes," "a flagship five-star hotel with comprehensive leisure amenities," "a new fully equipped conference centre with state-of-the-art facilities," "an exciting new arts quarter," and "a new street, Parliament Way, destined to become the major route between Princes Street and the Parliament area" (Caltongate 2006). Taken from the developer's website, the statement below casts an ambitious vision for the Caltongate development:

> Very rarely, a development changes the entire dynamic of a major city. The breadth of vision behind the Caltongate project is stunning. Bold and contemporary, it is in total harmony with the commercial life and history of Scotland's capital.
> 
> Caltongate is right in the heart of Edinburgh, just yards from Waverley Railway Station and Edinburgh's financial district. It will create a new concourse between the old town and the eastern quarter of the new town.
> 
> **CALTONGATE. STUNNING. BOLD. CONTEMPORARY.**
> Caltongate will raise urban living to new standards of luxury and convenience. Running from the Canongate down towards the foot of Calton Hill, in precisely the way that Edinburgh's first houses grew up and formed the historic shape [sic]. (Caltongate 2006)

The materials emphasize the centrality of finance and "commercial life" to "urban living," In fact, they make no mention of the urban life that was already happening "right in the heart of Edinburgh" and specifically right in the Canongate area targeted for redevelopment. Most controversially, the master plan required the demolition of two historically listed (Class C) buildings, the Canongate Venture and the Sailor's Ark (City of Edinburgh Council 2006a, 34–35). Additionally, the demolition of an early twentieth-century tenement building contributed by City Architect Ebenezer MacRae for the Canongate–Corstorphine Scheme was required to make way for the hotel's main entrance onto the Royal Mile, and its inhabitants were approached by city representatives who bought the building's eighteen flats so that the building was vacant from January 2008.

The Caltongate development thus sought to accomplish the priorities that Donald Anderson had pursued throughout his political career: to increase the attractiveness of Edinburgh's city center to the lifestyles of those employed in the city's "financial district," as well as those of the tourists seeking five-star accommodations. Caltongate would provide a central location for this global-mobile elite to sleep, shop, and dine only blocks away from the high-end London-based department store Harvey Nichols, which Anderson had been instrumental in bringing to Edinburgh. As such, the Caltongate development represents a physical product of the "reflexive competition" logic of neoliberalism: the framing of persons as potential customers and the city, including all the places nested within it, as potentially marketable products.

The aim of these projects of urgent urban development, and therefore the motivation of actors like Anderson, are not amoral or cynical, despite the suspicions of their critics. Instead, these motivations should be recognized as moralized calculations of the content and distribution of public benefit: more city revenues and more jobs, accessible by individuals who adopt morally economic behavior. As Gisa Weszkalnys has shown, differences in urban planning priorities tend to reflect differences in the perception and calculation of the good (2010). Anderson's view of the Caltongate master plan certainly reflected his convictions not only about what constitutes good development but also about the political processes by which public benefit is attained. When I questioned the development's impact on the neighborhood residents, he pointed out that 25 percent of the housing in the Caltongate development would be designated affordable housing, per city requirements. That the assignment of a reduced rate to those units would only last until the property was sold, freeing the unit to uncontrolled market rates—in Edinburgh, these rates were far out of the reach of any working-class family—or that the houses were assigned to a location at the perimeter of the development rather than dispersed across it—were details that only muddied the clarity of that claim and were regarded as inconsequential to it.

The logic by which Caltongate presented a compelling route to public benefit, including benefit of the Canongate residents, required the designation of correct economic practice and moral behavior. The necessity of neighborhood improvement thus implied an instrumental narrative of individual improvement, as illustrated by Anderson's answer to one of my questions relating to social class and belonging. Nearing the end of the interview, I presented the concerns of the Canongate residents about the exclusionary impacts of this development and asked him whether his vision of Edinburgh included a place for the working classes within the city center. In an exasperated tone, Anderson responded flatly that my question was "just wrong." "The idea that somehow the working-class areas should be preserved as working-class areas because it has merit in its own right, to me is incredibly defeatist and patronizing. When I grew up in a council estate, I wanted to make myself a better person. I wanted to achieve more with my life.... It's not about not valuing the role that the poor or the working class have in the city. It's about trying to make their lives better by making jobs available and helping them get into those jobs."

Anderson's argument, invoking his own exemplary life trajectory, implicitly identified improvement as an individual's mobility from working to middle class. The securing of higher-paying jobs represented the routes to making oneself a better person. Such a construal of a life represents well the "neoliberal agency" described by Gershon (2011) and implies not a few "keywords" of neoliberal discourse (Leary 2018).[1] Most notably, this negative framing of working-class identity marks a departure from historical representations in Scotland of the "respectable working class" as a core Scottish constituency (for examples, see Smyth 2019, 120; see also Jones 2012). As he explained, Anderson framed the Caltongate development as offering "choices" that the Canongate did not provide, lamenting that "for kids on the Royal Mile, if all they see are kids who are like them, who are [from] relatively low-income families, they don't get exposed to the full range, and they don't actually raise their aspirations." Setting aside for the moment the mismatch between this characterization of socioeconomic seclusion and the residents' descriptions of their easy access throughout the city center from the Canongate, this construal of choice as the means (and presumed desire) to participate in a social climb marks another distinctive of neoliberal discourse, and one with which the campaigners fundamentally disagreed. In representing the moralizing semantics from which Anderson's statements derive, John Patrick Leary has observed that "in a society structured around the wisdom of individual consumer choices, there is no such thing as the people, the community, or as Thatcher famously said, society—there are only individuals, whose responsibility is to themselves" (2018, 37). The dismissal of collective responsibility identified by Leary and entailed in Anderson's remarks generated some heat when I shared them with the resident campaigners a few days later.

Having gathered for dinner with four of the Canongate campaigners at an Indian restaurant just down the road, I read aloud a few of Anderson's remarks from my notes. Although they had heard plenty of his public comments on development, they had not had the opportunity (or, in truth, the desire) for a personal meeting with him. I thought they would find his frank interpretations illuminating to their processing of what exactly had happened regarding the council's reception of their concerns.

Exclamations of disbelief and anger cut across the final words as I read. Interrupting each other in their aggravation, they pronounced him a "class traitor" and rejected the moralizing narrative of improvement, countering that an individual who "betters" herself without making life better for her community is merely selfish. Sally scoffed scornfully that "some people who are born working-class just can't wait to go and leave their roots behind," dusting off her shoulder dismissively. That the Caltongate proposal disregarded the appeal of life in this largely working-class neighborhood; that it did not seek to improve the living conditions of the current residents but assumed instead, as Anderson indicated, that the residents should change made this vision of the future both irrelevant to their experiences and hostile to their hopes for future city-center living. As the moral terms of Anderson's expectations suggest, however, in their very refusal to "aspire," they are marked as those who reject improvement, a rhetorical dismissal with moral teeth. Such is the power of arguments that purport to obtain public benefit, according to the individualizing semantics of neoliberalism, those who disbelieve the claims are represented as opposed to the objectives of public benefit, or even moral behavior.

In these ways, a five-star hotel and conference center, office buildings, leisure facilities, and a continental-style open-air square came to stand for public benefit in the Old Town of Edinburgh. The leadership that ushered in this logic, while supported by representatives in Conservative and Liberal Democrat Parties, was centralized in Edinburgh in the Labour Party, ascendant at the time on its delivery of devolution. Tensions between Labour priorities are evident in Anderson's career; within a party that has traditionally represented collective benefit to working classes, he advocated the distribution of benefit via economic mobility of working-class individuals. That Scottish Labour has struggled to devise a unified economic plan or even a convincing political posture following devolution reflects these tensions; conditions of postindustrial and postdevolution political economy have compounded its confusion. As the following section shows, the neoliberal logics that have pervaded careers like Anderson's and contributed to the unraveling of Scottish Labour have left few corners of genuine refusal in Edinburgh politics. The reception of the Caltongate proposal among Edinburgh's city councilors, discussed below, shows how compelling this logic had become in municipal governance by the end of the first decade of the twenty-first century. The neoliberalization of both development affect and moral economic behavior, especially in the Labour Party, was read by the Canongate campaigners as a betrayal of working-class interests. As the following chapter shows, however, acceptance of the terms of neoliberal judgments has been far from complete, and its opposition has created opportunities for new alliances and solidarities to form. That the logic has been so broadly embraced in local city politics, even in the city that centralizes governance for a Scottish welfare state, suggests the difficulties faced by this opposition.

### Caltongate's Reception

[Caltongate] is becoming an exemplar case for the future of Edinburgh's city center. Edinburgh needs to be more assertive in what it wants.... If this development doesn't go through, then it will send a message to the rest of the world that Edinburgh city center is off-limits.
—*Deputation from Edinburgh Chamber of Commerce,
February 6, 2008*

Tourism is responsible for 31,000 jobs in Edinburgh [and] is a critical part of the city's economy. It has been quite clear in studies carried out that around 4,000 new hotel rooms will be needed by 2015.
—*Deputation from Visit Scotland,
February 6, 2008*

The Old Town Community Council has made every effort to engage the developers. Housing in the [Caltongate] plans will predominantly be occupied by transients, and families will be priced out of the area. The Canongate has always been home to the workers of the city, along with royalty and gentry, and it has been this mix of people which has made it unique.
—*Deputation from Old Town Community Council,
February 6, 2008*

> The buildings have been decapitated; they are flat and boxed in a passé 1960s cubist way. There is no response to the natural topography of the Royal Mile or to the steep-pitched slated roofs of the Canongate buildings. There will be light blazing out from huge windows at night, mismatched to the neighboring tenement windows. The wonderful cliff of masonry stones which characterizes the shape of the area now will be completely changed. These are thoroughly second-rate, unworthy proposals, and they have failed to match our expectations.
> —*Deputation from Royal Park Terrace and Spring Gardens Residents Associations, February 6, 2008*

The patterns of reception to the Caltongate proposal that emerged across Edinburgh indicated the larger social and political transformations that had shaped the city over recent decades. In particular, for the municipal leadership of Edinburgh, addressing the capital city of Scotland and navigating its first decade postdevolution (and prerecession) shaped an economically and politically optimistic outlook, seasoned by the desire to prove the city competitive on a global stage. For the city councilors considering the development proposal, a sense of urgency and of a tantalizing opportunity for economic gains for the city led all but one representative to support its approval.

The Caltongate proposal was sent to the city council chambers as a raft of individual proposals for each building included in the master plan, seeking planning permission from the Development Management subcommittee, in February 2008. A full day's program, open to the public from the viewing gallery, included statements from professional architectural heritage organizations and residents' associations, as well as the lone SNP councilor of the central district, which were critical of the proposal. These challenges to Caltongate were followed by supportive statements from the chamber of commerce and tourism representatives from Visit Scotland and the Convention Bureau.

I arrived early and sat in the gallery with Canongate residents, who heckled, advised, and commented freely throughout. When the time came for consideration of each individual proposal, the committee councilors made remarks and asked questions of the developer representatives seated in the front row. With the exception of one councilor, Steve Burgess of the

Green Party, who challenged the proposal components in each instance, questions were notably tentative, and the developer was treated as the primary authority on the impact of the development. On each proposal, Burgess alone objected, along lines relating primarily to the lack of fit with current buildings and the need for councilors to support local residents' concerns. The Caltongate master plan met with approval across Labour, Conservatives, Liberal Democrats, and one member of the SNP, with the exception of one building, intended to be a landmark restaurant. The design of that building attracted aesthetic concerns because of its unusual shape (a "shoebox," it was deemed by one councilor), and thus it was voted down as too "ugly" by a majority of councilors.

The council vote for Caltongate came in amid a protracted, contentious public debate over the rightness of development for the Canongate area. Dozens of articles, newspaper editorials, blogs, and radio spots had covered the residents' campaign, heritage professionals' concerns, business and political leaders' perspectives, and many meetings of various groups organized along the way. The council organized and hosted a community planning day, which drew more than seventy participants and resulted in the design of alternative development plans for the area, but at the end of that 2008 council meeting, the only objection that carried weight concerned the aesthetic of a restaurant. All indications suggest that the urgency of short-term economic development via urban "regeneration" in the sense Anderson advocated had become the common wisdom within the Edinburgh city council, a pressure that, Burgess later told me in an interview at his council office, he had recognized and rejected.

The pressures toward that perspective appear to have been considerable. Although the Labour Party had cultivated the economic and affective conditions for market-led development in Edinburgh, the persistence of both conditions following Labour's loss of leadership in the 2007 council elections attests to their persuasive power. The affective climate to which the close working between the council and local elite business leaders contributed did not dissipate with the transfer of leadership but rather assimilated the new party leaders to its framing of the urgency in urban development toward critical objectives in interurban competition.

In March 2007, after Anderson had stepped down as council leader to run for a parliamentary position, popular disapproval of Labour, interpreted in Edinburgh at least in part as a public commentary on the party's highly publicized acceptance of a £4,000 campaign donation by the Caltongate developer Mountgrange, resulted in council elections ushering in a Liberal Democrat–led coalition. Among her press statements in the weeks after her selection, new council leader Jenny Dawe delivered a strongly worded critique of the Caltongate plans to a reporter for national newspaper the *Scotsman*, dubbing the plans "grotesque and hideous" (Ferguson 2007). As she began her work as council leader, there was no further commentary on the development until one year later, when in May 2008 she praised the council's February approval of the Caltongate plans for indicating their ability to make "tough" decisions, for the good of the city.

Within a year of taking on council leadership, Dawe's initial assessment of this development that had been championed by erstwhile political competitor Anderson had been disciplined through the compelling urgency of a neoliberal logic that framed Edinburgh's public benefit in terms of short-term economic growth. In Hearn's (2017) words, the "distributive outcomes," in this case relating to the right to shape an urban place, had achieved their legitimation. Dawe's about-face in her assessment of the development's impacts indicates the challenge of political persuasion to an alternative arrangement. If the example of nineteenth-century development of working-class housing in the Canongate might suggest an example, such an alternative would indeed be costly: requiring the ideological commitment of capitalist investors, in conjunction with the state, to take on financial risks and incur opportunity costs of not pursuing other, more lucrative types of property investment (Morris 2013). As MacLennan has observed, a contemporary social-cum-political alternative vision is markedly absent from contributions by the corporate sector and its "affluent individuals" to the broader discussions of the social good in Scotland (Blackburn and Keating 2012). Instead, as in Anderson's reckoning, the short-term economic growth itself came to stand for the social good (cf. Bloch and Parry 1989). It was in these terms that the Caltongate development promised to justify itself, but as the following chapters show, while neoliberal affect and political-economic arrangements have pervaded Edinburgh's local government, some voices within the city have not only resisted but also affirmed their alternative practices, rooted in habits of indwelling the Canongate. That SNP and Green councilors offered the lone voices of support for the community's activism against Caltongate would also be remembered by the residents in their search for a positive political-cum-social vision.

The power of the neoliberal logic to persuade would-be critics like Dawe lies in its seeming matter-of-factness once the link between economic growth and public benefit is accepted along with the crucial delimitation of moral behavior. Development projects like Caltongate promise to distribute public benefit to the city's deserving, upwardly mobile residents and internationally mobile professionals. By situating the supports for the Caltongate development in the language of economics, the issue of redevelopment has been carefully depoliticized and placed in the sterile domain of technocratic decision-making rather than the messy public forum of political debate (Nadin and Stead 2014, 208).

James Ferguson (2006) has shown how African economic arguments have been strategically remoralized by actors questioning the apparently indifferent, technocratic posture of Western economic advisors. As Anderson's commentary on the prehistory of the Caltongate development has shown, the apparently amoral, technical rationale for development in Edinburgh in reality reflects moralized calculations of appropriate economic behavior, which brackets out the legitimacy of claims on the state to defend and sustain the urban spaces of working-class lives. The Canongate residents were thus faced with the project not of remoralizing an amoral sphere but of challenging the implicitly moral expectations of urban development themselves. As the following chapters show, they pursued this task by claiming a special role in the development process as "the community" and by recasting the aesthetic language used to describe the Canongate and the Caltongate redevelopment. Ultimately, these aesthetic claims would appropriate the image of the Scottish welfare state, which they would translate from an idealized component of postwar Britain to a vision of independence cast through the political rhetoric of the SNP.

NOTE

1. For instance: Excellence, Meritocracy, Resilience (see Leary 2018 for excellent historical analyses of the use of these terms).

## INTERLUDE 2

# A SHOP IN THE CANONGATE

An arterial narrative of the Canongate's recent history, shared with me by its residents, former residents, and other campaign participants, recounted the seemingly inexorable disappearance of their neighborhood shops. Fishmongers and bakers, secondhand shops and grocers, the shops dedicated to everyday existence—or, as one resident put it, "shops that could survive if all the planes stopped worldwide for a month"—locked their doors somewhere in the fifteen years bookending the turn of the millennium. When storefronts reopened under new leases, their windows were hung with graphic T-shirts and clan tartans, their doorways lined with revolving wire postcard stands advertising the Highland scenes accessible by buses idling at the depot just blocks away. Fresh produce, household supplies, and neighborly chat became more scarce as the neighborhood shops turned toward the capture of tourists ambling downhill from Edinburgh Castle toward the Palace of Holyroodhouse and Scottish Parliament. The shops that resisted this turnover to tourism presented an unexpectedly wide and seemingly random variety of goods of the sort found only in unplanned development; they sold wares ranging from records to druid and faery art, whiskies, books, men's custom kilts and dresswear, and women's clothing.

These shops garnered fresh respect from the Canongate resident protesters as a bulwark against the rising tide of tartan tat, no longer merely present but *re*presenting the local as a newly significant alternative to both low-end tartan tourism and high-end business tourism. As is often the case, however, what is considered "local" is a construction more fluid than it may seem. Does "local" indicate the origins of goods or ownership, the origins of clientele, the location of the shop, or some combination of these factors?

In the Canongate, I found that a shop's local quality reflected the imputation of its clientele belonging in some generalized sense to the surrounding neighborhoods. While a record shop cannot strictly be regarded as providing an essential neighborhood service, perhaps even less so the selling of druid and faery art, these shops were judged to address the interests of individuals in a proximate population, and for that, the residents embraced it as a welcome alternative to tourism-based commerce. The way these shops belonged to the Canongate came to matter particularly in exception to the trends of shop loss. One of the local shops, a retailer of high-end women's clothing that I'll call Vista, employed me as a salesclerk for a few months in 2008. Through this experience, I observed the making of this belonging in the complicated ways Canongate residents and shop owners loosely but carefully bound themselves together through a mutual construction of locality in neighborhood commerce during the era of the Caltongate proposal.

### Vista: Caught between the Canongate and the West End

I first heard of Vista from my contacts among residents invested in the campaign against Caltongate: it was a very nice shop, and the owner was lovely. At the time, I was hoping to find a way to participate in regular life in the Canongate, outside the rhythms of the campaign events and scheduled interviews. When I learned from residents that Vista was looking to hire a new salesclerk, I presented myself and my decidedly academic resume to the owner, Elsa, for her consideration. Both the resume and, it seemed to me, my appearance as someone evidently unskilled in the art of fashion were met with gentle skepticism, but my promises of hard work and my commitment to learning allowed me to address both shortcomings. Throughout my tenure as a salesclerk, I was instructed in a varied list of duties, from guiding customers in accessorizing, to placing the A-board sign on the pavement so as to manage the biting spring winds that raced along Canongate Road even on the sunniest days, to making my peace with the ghost that seemed to move around in the underground office of the shop. (Almost all the buildings in the Old Town have ghosts, I was assured; this one seemed pleasant enough.)

Following my introduction to the rhythms and responsibilities of retail in this unusual location, the care of the shop was entrusted to me from

9:00 to 4:00 p.m. for three or four days a week, according to a schedule that divided the weeks between me, Elsa's daughter Ava, and one other clerk. The daily efforts of this position reflect a gendered division of working-class labor, differing significantly from some accounts of masculine labor experiences such as the numbingly repetitive motions of ringing up groceries under the glow of fluorescent lighting described by Ben Chappell in his 2012 study of Mexican American working classes in Austin, Texas. Instead, my paid work more closely resembled feminine domestic labor in a small and ancient home: cleaning shelves and floors, arranging racks of dresses and refolding sweaters along straight lines, and presenting myself as an unobtrusive but willing attendant to middle- and upper-class women browsing the objects within. The historic character of the Canongate's built environment presented constraints that had been cast as charming by the aesthetic efforts of Elsa and Ava. Two bow windows, the exteriors of which had been painted a deep and glossy shade of eggplant, provided seasonal displays of carefully accessorized clothes to the street and filled the shop with light, as long as the sun was willing. The ceilings were not high, and the interior space was long and narrow, but the shop's decoration—from the white painted trim to the porcelain vase filled with fresh flowers on the round white kitchen table at the center of the shop, which also served to display the latest order of cardigan sets—conveyed the charming cottage aesthetic often associated with habitation of (and reconciliation to) historic architecture in Britain. In this way, decoration of the shop space, located on the ground floor of a characteristic and otherwise unremarkable sandstone tenement building, highlighted the literal proximity between shop and home.

Elsa, joined in more recent years by her daughter Ava, had built an impressive reputation for independent label fashion in Edinburgh out of this historic and somewhat quirky space. While I was going through the hiring process in the winter of 2008, a newspaper feature highlighted Scottish fashion in a piece that was illustrated by a large color photo of Elsa in the Canongate shop. The particulars of the shop's layout and location had always offered both charm and inconvenience, which owner and customers had navigated as necessity. Elsa noted that her faithful customers had always struggled with the lack of parking in the neighborhood, but they had managed it somehow; more than once, I greeted a customer dashing into the shop, explaining that she had parked in the street with the hazard lights flashing, to pick up an item quickly—with apologies.

When the West End shopping district, that exemplar of neighborhood redevelopment in the estimation of then-council leader Donald Anderson, had offered newly renovated shops for lease, Elsa's profitable business in the Canongate allowed her to take up one of these shops in a prime corner location. Unlike the Canongate shop, the ceilings in the new space took advantage of the Georgian dimensions of New Town architecture, reaching upward of twelve feet, and the storefront boasted the floor-to-ceiling plate glass windows typical of department store displays. Once I began working in the Canongate shop, Elsa was able to spend more of her time in the West End location, for which she often expressed admiration, encouraging me to come by and have a look around. She and Ava found my request to work exclusively in the Canongate shop a curiosity, which I attempted to explain by reminding them of the location of my research project in that neighborhood.

The characteristics of the Canongate location that had stimulated my interest in that research project—its architectural and social history, its present inhabitants—would make my duties as salesclerk more difficult. Such difficulties for Canongate retail had been stimulated by fresh competition—not from another city such as Glasgow or Manchester, as the development boosters like Councilor Anderson and business leader Ron Hewitt warned in their statements to local media, but from their single-minded investment in redeveloping another location within Edinburgh for high-end retail, business, and leisure. The formerly integrated model of multiclass residents among a diverse assortment of retailers, by which Elsa and Ava had achieved financial and popular success in their Canongate shop—just doors down from a shop identifying itself as "Scotland's oldest occult store"—was giving way in those months of my employment to a rearrangement of retail and residence in Edinburgh that privileged a consumer-based clustering according to social class. The emergence of the latter arrangement, with all the advantages it appeared to offer for the retail of high-end women's clothing, as well as the disadvantages it not merely *reflected* but actively *created* for the Canongate shop, was beginning to foster an uncomfortable dynamic between Elsa and the resident campaigners, despite their mutual, neighborly affirmations of one another.

Although I tried my best to manage the shop's soundtrack, watered the flowers, dusted the shelves, straightened the clothing racks after each customer sorted through them, and offered carefully cultivated suggestions to the browsing women, business was never booming. For long stretches of the afternoon, I would sit behind the front desk and try to come up with tasks for myself; after tidying the shop, I would research new lines of the clothing labels that Elsa suggested for me, and once I had completed those tasks, I might look up sites related to the Caltongate planning process. I would check in over phone calls with the salesclerk at the West End shop, embarrassed to find almost every day that my sales tallies compared dismally to hers. My self-consciousness at not living up to expectations as a salesclerk was eased somewhat by Elsa's disappointed observation that the Canongate shop never sold as much as the West End shop, no matter who staffed the shops or the strategic differentiation of goods between them. (A line of Shetland wool clothing had been stocked only in the Canongate shop as a nod to the browsing of curious tourists there, while the most rarefied wares were reserved for the West End shop.) Elsa and Ava regularly exclaimed in dismay over this comparison as we perused the records of the week's sales.

Despite its reputation and former successes, by the spring of 2008, the revenues of the Canongate shop had taken an unsustainable downward turn, and by 2010, the shop would be shuttered for good. Pinched between anticipations of a mixed-class residential and commercial quarter that never quite materialized, and the diversion of Edinburgh shoppers to a high-end consumption district in the West End, the viability of a women's clothing shop selling small-batch European labels at prices far above those of the British chain stores in a neighborhood with a shrinking residential population and growing array of low-end tourist shops, dwindled to insignificance. The attractions of the West End initially concentrated on its spatial provisions for expansion and display and its proximity to purpose-built professional offices, parading throngs of would-be customers by their plate glass storefronts. (It is not by happenstance that Vista in the West End now sells men's clothing too.) The West End shopping district ultimately diverted customers from shops located elsewhere, including Elsa's Canongate shop, thus making such shops less financially viable. The city scale by which development supporters are prone to measure success and loss renders such intra-Edinburgh trajectories invisible. This shop-level fieldwork, however, revealed that the West End redevelopment project did not merely image an ideal that development supporters like Anderson would elevate as progress; instead, it made already-existing alternative arrangements in the city less viable, and so, as a model for development in Edinburgh, class-based consumption clusters accrued an air of inevitability.

The Canongate at the edge of the twenty-first century offered one such alternative arrangement, a combination of mixed-class residence and minimally planned retail that facilitated interaction between residents and shop owners in a neighborhood of shared though disparate spaces. Without romanticizing the relationships that grew from such contact, it is worth noting the respect and good feeling that was mutually expressed by these neighbors, even in the face of an issue, the Caltongate proposal, which held the potential to divide them and degrade that feeling. As I spent time among both groups, instead of a neighborhood divided, I observed in these relationships—particularly between the campaign leaders and Elsa—the deliberate minimizing of opposed views, navigated with restraint. I found such restraint remarkable among the resident campaigners in particular, whose opposition to the Caltongate development was otherwise as freely expressed in personal relationships as in their public pronouncements. Throughout the twilight months of the Canongate shop, even as Elsa and Ava were privately discussing the probability of signing over their lease, and long since the residential campaign against the Caltongate development had been well established, the shop maintained its appeal as a local institution to residents in the Canongate neighborhood. Both residents and retailers delicately danced around their incompatible views on the Caltongate development.

### Neighbors and Strangers in Neoliberalizing Edinburgh

One unusually sunny afternoon, when the bell on the door chimed, I looked up as usual to greet the incoming customer. It was no stranger, however. The woman making her way into the shop was happily familiar, a resident campaigner seeking me out for a chat. Pleased to find temporary release from stultifying retail boredom and hoping for some news on the campaign, I joined her on the shop floor. As we began to discuss the good weather, I realized that this was no business visit but a social call that afforded my friend the indulgence of perusing the shop's clothing racks. We strolled slowly around the shop, and she took a fancy to a sundress in bright floral print. While holding the hanger up to her shoulders before the mirror admiringly, she lifted the price tag and burst into good-natured laughter:

the high-end price required no deliberation; the dress might as well have been on the moon. The dress went back to the rack, and as she placed it, my friend directed an approving gaze around the shop. "She stocks such lovely things, doesn't she?"

This approving remark, a token of the warm regard that passed between Elsa and the resident campaigners, covered over some striking differences of opinion of which I suspected my campaigner friend was aware. Both Elsa and Ava held a rather different view of the Caltongate development than that expressed in the Canongate residents' campaign. The financial difficulties experienced by the shop, as a retailer increasingly out of place along a street overdetermined by the commerce of low-end tourism, led Elsa to hear possibility in the Caltongate proposal's promise of a new residential and commercial quarter centered on the Canongate. When I discussed the development with her and Ava, both immediately noted that they get along well with the residents organizing the campaign, distancing themselves from any of the derogatory judgments expressed by Caltongate supporters in the local media. Notwithstanding these personal feelings, Elsa and Ava observed that the Caltongate development could benefit the neighborhood and especially local businesses like theirs. Elsa framed her support in mildly optimistic terms, with a glance for my reaction, "If it increases footfall, then it could be really good." Indeed, to the owner of a successful neighborhood shop that had found itself newly struggling in the face of the council-led diversion of city-center consumption to a new shopping district in the West End, a development model like Caltongate that construed its value in the language of competitive neighborhood advantage resonated clearly. That this awareness remained unspoken among the campaigners, and that Elsa refrained from publicly expressing those opinions, perhaps suggests the felt constraints of those neighborly ties—and their acceptance—by both parties.

By 2010, the Canongate shop had closed and the resident campaigners were moving out. In my subsequent research trips and visits, I have made a point to visit the West End Vista shop and catch up with Elsa and Ava. They have no more contact with their former Canongate neighbors, who in the absence of neighborly proximity do not continue to stop by and chat with Elsa. Although those residents do pass her West End shop in their traversing of the city center (I joined one of them in an indifferent stroll past that shop), their homes are now situated in primarily working-class neighborhoods elsewhere. In Edinburgh's geography of increasingly class-based clusters, the fragile strands that once connected working-class residents in the Canongate with a retailer of high-end women's clothing have withered and dissolved entirely. That those threads once subsisted on the most banal, everyday interactions—greetings and conversation conducted in humble public spaces—suggests that the grounds for such ties do not require a total reconceptualization of the built environment. The experience of these former participants in Canongate neighborhood life indicates that conditions for relations built on in-person, in-place interactions—in short, for the mutual construction of locality—by a new generation of working-class urban residents and small business owners, however, require a reversal of current development trends toward social and economic segregation.

## CHAPTER 3

# SAVING THE OLD TOWN, ONE MORE TIME
## Ancient Concerns for Neoliberal Times

> Oh we're no awa' tae bide awa'
> We're no' awa' tae le'e ye,
> We're no' awa' tae bide awa',
> We'll aye come back an' see ye.
> As ah was walkin doun the Canongate
> Ah met wee Sandy Stobie
> Said he tae me, 'Can ye go a hauf?'
> Said I, 'Man that's just ma hobby!'
> So we had a hauf and another hauf
> And then we had another.
> Said he tae me, 'Am gan awa'
> But mind, come back an' see me.'
> —From *"We're No Awa' Tae Bide Awa',"* by Andy Stewart
> Adapted by Margaret, SOOT campaigner

IT WOULD BE A MISTAKE to romanticize the much-loved tenement houses of the Canongate. Often drafty, these flats projected sounds from the stairwell and thinly muffled movements from floors above and below, including the maddening, recent additions of daylong bagpipe serenades broadcast from shops with names like "I Love Scotland." Flats rented from landlords were often maintained in worse condition than the council flats, which, despite their spare furnishings, benefited from renovation on a rotational schedule. One such privately rented flat, in which a campaigner named Agnes and her two children lived, had been bought from the council under Margaret Thatcher's Right to Buy program and transferred later to one of the private landlords who managed properties in the neighborhood. It lacked central heating or properly insulated windows, both of which had been added to council properties in the interim years. When I visited Agnes, I kept my coat on, and she often did too. In fact, she drew some moral satisfaction from the chilliness of the flat: "If you don't wear a jumper in your house in the winter, you're just being wasteful!"

Yet these tenement flats, both council-rented and privately rented, anchored a working-class community life that tied them to a tradition of "working people" in the Canongate. The residents' positive association between the tenements and the provision of council-rented housing their community depended on often gestured reflexively to the twentieth-century welfare state that had supplied them. As the primary built environment contribution of that welfare state, the tenements of the Canongate staged the inconveniences described above, inextricably bound to residents' social and political lives and invoked in their resistance to the property-development mechanisms of neoliberal urbanism.

Their connections to the Canongate of the past were often performed in the spontaneous telling of its oral histories. One such performance was cobbled together by an unlikely pair of storytellers in the days of the campaign discussed in this chapter. The public indoor spaces of the Canongate, such as the People's Story Museum or Storytelling Center, would often draw passing residents to drop in for an update or conversation. In the spring of 2008, the awarding of a community grant pursued by Catriona provided one such temporary space in the form of a vacant storefront on St. Mary's Street; the space functioned as a hub not only for events organized by the Canongate campaigners but also for residents seeking company and a chat. One April afternoon, I was writing up field notes in the sunlight streaming through the wall of west-facing windows, when a conversation started up between Agnes and Margaret. In some respects, the women appeared a study in contrasts. Agnes, a passionate activist and single mother, sported a T-shirt, faded jeans, and lugged boots as she regaled Margaret, a retired and vigorous campaigner dressed in a trim turtleneck, belted trousers, and sensible shoes, with a story from her day. They chatted animatedly over mugs of tea and a plate of biscuits at one of the plastic tables, while I sat in a chair nearby and agonized over the wording for an invitation to a community event. The drift of the conversation was lost to me until both women exclaimed delightedly, at which point I glanced up to hear that they had just discovered they had been born in the same hospital, the Elsie Inglis Maternity Hospital. Although it had closed in 1988, Elsie's, as it was known, had long served the Old Town from a location adjacent to the Canongate. Agnes drew me back into the conversation, pleased to explain to me one of her favorite local figures.

"Elsie Inglis was Scotland's Florence Nightingale," Agnes began. "She fought to help out in the Crimean War, as a woman trained in nursing, but she was turned aside and told to go home and make someone's tea. But she just went, 'Oh fuck it!' and went anyway." "Aye," Margaret nodded, "the woman was a saint." "Yes!" Agnes enthused, "she was *insane!*" Margaret hesitated, with a small frown at Agnes's mishearing of her more sober praise, but as Agnes turned her grin to me, Margaret hid her expression in a quick sip from her mug, letting any awkwardness of the moment pass unaddressed .

While we returned to our former tasks, I mused over the network of space and practice through which Elsie's maternity hospital had drawn together the narratives of Agnes and Margaret, a generation (and more) apart. Agnes's framing of the actions of Elsie Inglis, a nineteenth-century nurse, in the contemporary language of passionate idealism and defiance of oppressive patriarchal leadership illustrates the campaigners' perceptions of the close relationships between projects of social and political activism in the Canongate's past and present. Not only the historical narratives but also the practice of their telling stitched ties between the Canongate residents and campaigners, and through the performance of knowing and telling the area's history, the campaigners vested themselves with the moral responsibilities of the community. Later, Agnes would explain to me how she came to know the Canongate's stories. "When [my child] was wee, you'd go, 'Shit, it's raining; what'll we do? Oh, let's go down to the People's Story [museum]. Oh, let's go up to the museum or whatever. So you're just constantly absorbing that. But you also had the neighbors telling you, you know—it was more that oral history. So people would tell stories about—you kind of knew the stories."

In this way, Agnes had been introduced to and socialized into historical narratives of the Canongate, as a relief from the limitations of parenting in a council housing flat in a wet country, and as a means of forging relationships with her neighbors. Agnes's description was echoed in the accounts of other mothers raising children in the Canongate, as well as my own experiences of accompanying them to local museums for a casual wander and conversation. The limited space of the council flat and its proximity to museums depicting the neighborhood's history thus framed the practices of neighborly social life. The aesthetic of the Canongate produced through these interactions privileged history and the built environment, as well as the role of the community who had inherited both. As the conversation between Agnes and Margaret illustrates, although the museums provided valued historical information, the telling of the Canongate's "stories" did not rely solely on the official museum accounts but freely improvised and drew those stories into the present day. Agnes had learned the story of Elsie Inglis, and she retold it as an affirmation of her connection with Margaret and as a means of drawing in an American anthropology student to the communal practice of listening and sharing the stories. No dry or dusty history lessons; the stories shared in and about the Canongate oriented its residents to each other and to the place, and, as this chapter shows, residents would hold any proposed development up to scrutiny according to the aesthetic cultivated in the process.

The distribution of responsibility and moral authority without accessible pathways for influence produced a political disorientation of the kind that is well documented among working-class communities in the neoliberal era. For the Canongate residents, the changing shape of the built environment reflected the movements of a state that effectively buffered itself from their demands, its attention focused on development projects marked as economically urgent. Compelled by a sense of having lost a means of political agency to which they should rightfully have recourse, the Canongate campaigners looked to the past to claim their moral justification and strategies for development. Throughout their campaign, residents strove to redefine themselves as political subjects, cultivating a form of knowledge rooted in the sensible qualities of the Canongate and entailing an ethic of care, which is moralized as essential to the Canongate aesthetic (Sansi 2015, 79). In the following pages, the campaigners wrestle with the state against the depoliticization of urban space, contesting the terms of their deferral and dispossession in an exhausting though ultimately mobilizing process.

By the end of the campaign, their inability to effectively influence the state had left these idealistic activists at such a loss for viable strategies that they welcomed economic recession as one of the few agents capable of imposing limits on growth-oriented urban development. At this moment, they appeared to stand at the edge of a political subjectivity much like their working-class English compatriots, who had abandoned traditional politics in favor of the disruption of a crushing system (Evans 2017; Koch 2016; see also Abélès 2017). In only a few short years, however, some of them would be jubilantly waving saltire flags at independence demonstrations, while the majority contributed their votes to usher the Scottish National Party (SNP) into a phase of as-yet unprecedented political influence on a platform even its skeptics identify with "hope" (see Scothorne 2020). In the crucible of the Save Our Old Town (SOOT) campaign, a political aesthetic took shape in the Canongate that would, in the following years, sympathetically resonate with the rhetoric of the SNP and the cause of national independence, linking up campaigners' resistance against neoliberal urbanism with the SNP's liberal democratic rhetoric. This chapter details the labors, accomplishments, and failures of that campaign and its effects on the Canongate residents who would take that political journey.

### Rising Activists: Repoliticizing Development

"Mortals dwell in that they save the earth—taking the word in the old sense still known to Lessing. Saving does not only snatch something from a danger. To save really means to set something free into its own presencing. To save the earth is more than to exploit it or even wear it out. Saving the earth does not master the earth and does not subjugate it, which is merely one step from spoliation" (Heidegger 1954).

Heidegger's reflection on the relationship between dwelling and saving resonates powerfully with the activities of the Canongate residents as discussed in this chapter, in the work they identified as a project to Save Our Old Town. By 2005, residents of the Canongate had been primed to expect the proposal of redevelopment plans for a plot of land in their neighborhood. Since the 1990s, Edinburgh's city-center redevelopment had been quickening pace, and the construction of the Scottish Parliament building at the end of Canongate Road had already stimulated multiple projects along Holyrood Road along the Canongate's southern edge. The northern backs of the Canongate, moreover, presented arresting views across Waverley Valley toward Calton Hill, as well as a large, vacant bus depot site, which was regarded by virtually unanimous opinion as an opportunity for new construction with only moderate demolition required. (There had been, I heard, one group particularly keen to preserve brick bus depot buildings like this one, but they found few supporters among residents or built heritage enthusiasts, and so this objection sank quietly and quickly.)

Anticipation circulated through neighborly conversation just before the Caltongate proposal, as it was recalled to me later, by residents who had initially adopted a guarded, but not unhopeful, wait-and-see posture. Perceptions of neglect by the city council and city services, responsible for leaving waste uncollected and obstructing sidewalk signage unmonitored, as well as frustration at the encroachment of derided "tartan tat" shops selling the most egregious examples of commodified Scottish Highland heritage along Canongate Road (cf. Trevor-Roper 1983), prompted genuine interest in community-oriented development. "Could we get some new shops in?" "Maybe a fruit and veg market?" "How about some places for local businesses?" "Affordable spaces for local artists would be amazing."

But during the wait, the city's Council Headquarters was unexpectedly relocated from the upper Royal Mile to a location adjacent to the bus depot lot. Residents observed the progress of its construction with growing alarm, watching its steel skeleton climb higher into the sky, soon outstripping surrounding buildings. "They can't be going any higher than *that*," "Surely it's not allowed to go higher than *this*," "There're supposed to be regulations about how high things are here!" A Canongate resident recounted standing around the pavement gawking at the site with her neighbors. The building site observed by these residents suggested an aesthetic and economic frame for development decisions that would become clearer later, but at the time it fed a shared sense of unease and growing anxiety about the plans that might be coming next. Notably, both Canongate campaigners and then-council leader Donald Anderson identified the construction of the new Council Headquarters as a pivotal moment—for the campaigners, prompting realization of the type of development that would follow, and for Anderson's interests, attracting a suitable developer to propose a project for the adjacent site.

While the construction of the new Council Headquarters checked many of the residents' hopes about a community orientation for the new development, by the accounts of campaign leadership, the proposal of the Caltongate master plan, in October 2005, still astounded them. The first public display was held in the St. James Centre, in New Town, over the September 30–October 1 weekend, a rather unfortunate location for a development display, because this retail center had obtained special notoriety in Edinburgh as the epitome of insensitive and ill-conceived massive development of the 1960s. Two of the visitors who would wander through that display were women who were each raising children in council housing in the Canongate. Though their neighborly circles had not yet overlapped, they shared a conviction that the display at the St. James Centre that autumn weekend should be accountable to both the Canongate's community and history, the locally resonant aesthetic into which they had been socialized.

The two mothers, Sally and Janet, stared at the mocked-up development scenes before them. Everything from the breathtaking scale of the plans to the suggested demolitions of historic buildings and dramatically reconfigured city blocks in a sleekly commercial aesthetic proclaimed this project's dissonance with the built environment that they had come to cherish. Sharing their dismayed impressions with other visitors, Sally and Janet made their introductions to one another, and they committed to seeking and organizing any willing opposition. This encounter at the St. James Centre between the two young mothers set residents along the path to community mobilization, through the formation of the Canongate Community Forum (CCF) and its "action arm," SOOT. The following pages relay in brief the intensification of political engagement with the development process that this mobilization delivered, a messy and disorienting tangle with a municipal government seeking to avoid exactly such public deliberation.

### Block Parties and Working-Class Activism

The community mobilization kicked off, optimistically, with a party. Less than two weeks after the event at the St. James Centre, the newly formed community group hosted a Canongate block party, and despite the quick turnaround, the event drew a large and spirited attendance. Stimulated by rumors of the new development, residents gathered to eat, drink, make new acquaintances, and discuss possibilities for action. Sally and Janet had petitioned the council to host a second display, this time in the Canongate, and the council acquiesced, with the Canongate Kirk hosting a display of the Caltongate plans on November 2. At that display, community members were prepared with fliers announcing the inaugural meeting of the CCF, an affair that quickly became standing room only. Formulated to collect residents' views about the development, the CCF meeting produced a consensus to push forward with a campaign to engage the Caltongate process, which would become the SOOT campaign.

Deliberately claiming a historical tradition of women leadership in industrial working-class activism across Edinburgh and Glasgow (Crummy 1992; Goring 2018, 207–209; Rodger 1989, 31), the organization of the Canongate campaign (denoted externally as CCF or SOOT; the distinction devised to identify them as a community forum and campaign, respectively, was rarely perceived by outside observers) depended on the leadership of three women: Sally, Janet, and Catriona. Sally hailed originally from farming country in Angus, while Janet had been raised mostly in small-town central Scotland but maintained family ties to Edinburgh. Catriona had been raised in Edinburgh, where she regularly visited her great-aunt in the Canongate. Catriona now lived in her great-aunt's former flat, in a tenement roughly across Canongate Road from Sally and Janet. While the campaign relied on the input and labor of a core, though variable, group of rotating officers and an even wider group of volunteers, which included men in central and significant roles, these three women undertook organizational and communication roles for representing the group and engaging in political and public discourse. Their work, which in an average week during the campaign would command as many hours as full-time employment, has been well documented in local and national media, from the *Edinburgh Evening News* to the *Scotsman* newspapers, and various radio and publicity spots. Their voices, in person often raised to project across a full and bustling room, came to represent the Canongate community campaign. In my research among other community activist groups around Edinburgh during this period and beyond—from Porty Greenkeepers, to Save Glenogle Baths, to the Friends of Corstorphine Hill, many of which depended on the work of only a handful of dedicated campaigners—I found that these women gained through this campaign a reputation as determined and savvy activists. They were considered exemplars and resources for effective community campaign work, to the extent that leaders of such campaigns would seek them out for advice on activities like writing objection letters, sometimes attending CCF/SOOT meetings, in support of that cause and in cultivation of their own strategies.

The Canongate campaign, with its prominence of women in leadership roles, as well as its partnership with allies in the professional heritage sector, harked back to strategies and relationships that had been developed in response to problems of industrial urban life. This historical continuity speaks to both the long-term pattern of residence in the neighborhood itself, as well as continuity in the terms of conflict over development in Edinburgh. As noted in the first chapter, the residential patterns that have best supported the activism of working-class women have featured central residential locations, which facilitated women's involvement in public and political life. Interviews with women and men in the Canongate campaign, including both leaders and other participants, emphasized the desirability of the Canongate's central location, providing access to work, the shops, and activities in the city, distinguishing it positively from council housing options on the peripheral housing estates—aligning with housing arguments articulated by working-class residents in the nineteenth century (Johnson and Rosenburg 2010, 161). The exception to this pattern, the organization of the Craigmillar Festival Society by women in the peripheral Craigmillar housing estate, sought not engagement with the politics of development but rather the provision of arts activities for their housing estate. Nevertheless, this project merits a mention here, as both Old Town residents and conservationists identified in it an inspirational case of working-class mobilization and its positive social impacts.

As chapter 1 describes, the nineteenth-century industrial development plans in Edinburgh had, similar to Caltongate, pitted economic modernization against needs for residential housing and the conservation of the historic built environment, before conservative surgery was adopted as a compromise strategy. The Canongate-based campaign, as in the nineteenth century, united the interests of housing and conservation activists in an alliance that pursued the reform of development proposals for the Old Town and Canongate specifically. This campaign also looked to the past for the reformist development principles it would advocate: residents and conservationists deliberately and frequently invoked Patrick Geddes's ideas, most often in the terms of conservative surgery, in public statements, events, publications, and projects organized between 2005 and 2009.

In these ways, the features of the Canongate campaign reflected the residents' claims to represent a neighborhood characterized by continuity of long-term residence in Edinburgh's Old Town. Such claims were levied to strengthen the residents' influence in the development process, but as this chapter shows, the transformations of urban political economy that have produced the neoliberal program of development described in the previous chapter have reshaped the discourse and resources advocating modernization. According to neoliberal logics of development, priorities of conservation and housing provision become secondary goals, subordinated to the objectives of accumulation by property redevelopment. Through the discussion of the community campaign in the following pages, the impacts of this neoliberal development process unfold as obstacles, reframings, and denials of the Canongate residents' attempts to levy effective claims on the city council, as the local apparatus of the state.

The requirement of procedures for "consultation" by community organizations has become a key legitimator of urban development outcomes, but as chapter 2 shows, the processes of development decision-making have been largely removed from the sphere of politics and therefore meaningfully separated from the influence of community demands. This chapter argues that the appearance of public accessibility masked the depoliticization of urban development, even while discourses of aesthetic denigration served as an instrument of dispossession, supporting redevelopment projects like Caltongate and justifying the foreclosure of public debate. By elaborating these instruments of depoliticization, it is shown that the politics of urban space is replaced by a management of dissent strategy derived from the world of private corporate activity, by which difference and disagreement are acknowledged, but decision-making is surrendered from the sphere of politics to that of short-term economics. The desired product of such strategies is the transformation of urban space from political to the merely economic; that is, from public negotiation to private interest (Lefebvre 1996). The word *expertise* is deliberately avoided here, as in the case of Caltongate as well as other developments in Edinburgh; the advice prioritized could not be said to be more "expert" than that of its critics, who included some of Edinburgh's most prominent architects. Instead, it is more accurate to note that the sector prioritized was that of private commercial interests with a global purview. These conditions are not singular to Edinburgh, I suggest, but are broadly indicative of the experiences of working-class urban residents under neoliberal urbanization. As James Holston has shown in Brasilia, the ability of working classes to exercise a collective right to the city may serve to indicate their political efficacy in relation to the state (2009). I argue that the depoliticization of urban development processes thus presents a significant blockage faced by the urban working classes seeking access to the state, and this chapter shows the intensification of political activities stimulated in the Canongate through residents' navigation of these blockages while they sought mobilization as political agents.

The CCF/SOOT members participated in formal planning opportunities, pursued a public relations campaign through local media, organized a community project to link them enduringly to the Canongate history and built environment, and eventually took advantage of the opportunities provided by economic recession to take up a new, albeit circumscribed, role as community development agents in a neoliberal political economy. Through these political activities that focused on the material and social concerns of the Canongate, residents resisted their spatial-cum-political marginalization. The following chapter elaborates on their practice and discourse of dwelling that they came to assert as appropriate to this neighborhood. As chapter 5 argues, these assertions would find convenient and comfortable parallels in the rhetoric of the SNP, contributing to an affect of hope that would promise transformation and reform of the narrowed political avenues to influence, which campaigners had discovered to be discouragingly absent.

### Community Consultation as Dissent Management

As Andrea Muehlebach (2012) has shown, neoliberalism has adapted to specific formations of culture and history in which a given political economy is structured. Local frameworks of morality grant meaning, motivation, and sanction the sacrifice of individual well-being for the state's larger project. But as the rise of antiglobalist nationalisms in Europe suggests, moral frameworks such as secular liberalism or Catholic ethics may be tested by their own standards by those expected to bear the brunt of the sacrifice. When the state's realization of moral expectations is found wanting, however, those moral frameworks may cease to confer legitimacy on the state and offer the terms of its censure instead. In Edinburgh as in many European and North Atlantic cities, the idea of community has served to legitimate many decisions, processes, and sacrifices integral to the functioning of neoliberal urbanism. In the process of deliberation over the Caltongate development, this section shows that in the course of the campaign, Canongate residents moved from an embrace of community rhetoric to a suspicion of the term's invocation by the city council and private developers in the planning process. The promises that they initially understood to be secured by their identity as "the community" were rooted in the accountability structures of a managerial urbanism (Harvey 1989), itself secured within a Scottish/British welfare state.

The early meetings of the newly formed CCF, which invited discussion of the Caltongate master plan, drew standing room only crowds in the meeting hall at Old St. Paul's Scottish Episcopal Church. Those crowds consisted of Canongate residents, conservation professionals, architects, and other interested people from neighborhoods across Edinburgh; they brought tweed blazers and faded black hoodies elbow to elbow, heavy combat boots and sensible office footwear toe to toe, introducing themselves over cups of tea and biscuits. Discussion centered on sharing disgust with the Caltongate plans, and so disagreement over the proposal, let alone debate, did not typically characterize these conversations. Within the first few meetings, *calls* for action were turning into *plans* for action, and it is perhaps indicative of the scale of consensus regarding the Caltongate master plan that SOOT, originally formed to be the "action arm" of the CCF, eventually came to stand in for the community as the CCF meetings tapered off into nonexistence. Paralleling the activist strategies from other working-class Edinburgh neighborhoods, some of the earliest moves of the group were made possible by the city-funded computer lab at Edinburgh's only centrally located council housing estate, Dumbiedykes, adjacent to the southern border of the Canongate (Matthews 2015, 2016). Volunteers in the lab instructed the campaign leadership in the making of fliers and posters, even giving the campaign an internet domain name that one volunteer had been saving: eh8.org—a reference to the postcode of the Canongate.

Representing the community of the Canongate seemed initially to offer a pathway to influence through the formal planning process, but as the CCF/SOOT campaign would discover, such paths were confined to closed circuits. Canongate and Old Town residents, as well as Edinburgh's built heritage conservation organizations and urban planners not affiliated with the city council, recognized the CCF/SOOT as a collective representative of the local community. This recognition, however, was challenged by some supporters of the Caltongate proposal, including then-Council Leader Anderson, as well as an architect who contributed to the Caltongate master plan, whom I interviewed in 2010. Both insisted that the campaign represented only a minority perspective, citing a 2007 survey that was sent out to thirty thousand homes within a square mile of the Caltongate development (a designation that generated confusion), and of the seven hundred surveys that were returned, 53 percent favored the development, while 27 percent rejected it. Critics of the survey noted that it failed to mention potentially controversial aspects of the development, such as the demolitions of historic buildings, and presented the proposal entirely through the marketing material of the private developer, Mountgrange (who commissioned the survey). My fieldwork in the Canongate suggested no evidence of a hidden majority supporting the Caltongate master plan, but I did encounter a few individuals who expressed optimism about the new development, primarily local business owners who lived outside the neighborhood but hoped that the Caltongate development would bring increased foot traffic to their shops. From my research, the CCF/SOOT did convey the predominant feeling circulating through this area: dismay at the dramatic transformation planned for the Canongate and at the apparent disregard for the interests of current residents in that transformation. The reluctance of Caltongate supporters to acknowledge this representation, however, indicates the expectations of empowerment associated with the identification of a group as "the community" of the neighborhood in question. Such expectations can be attributed to the moralized affect of community as a concept (Creed 2006; Etzioni 1993; Williams 1976) and to the influence of urban planning as the professional discourse concerned with improving practices of development by amplifying community contributions.

The academic discipline of urban planning, the origins of which are often traced to Patrick Geddes, addresses, debates, and defines professional standards of good development processes and outcomes (Macdonald 2009). Since the 1960s, norms in city planning have increasingly advocated the involvement of local residents in planning processes (see Arnstein 1969). The discipline has since devoted much attention to questions of improving processes of community engagement in planning in particular from this period of its own professionalization and incorporation into municipal governance structures (Flyvbjerg 1998; Innes and Booher 2004). While planners attended to questions of minimizing the impacts of power relations on the planning process (Flyvbjerg and Richardson 2002), however, the city governments that employ planners were crippled by conditions of economic recession and austerity in the 1970s, an experience followed in the UK by a turn to an "entrepreneurial" mode of urban governance (Harvey 1989). The transition from what Harvey identifies as managerial to entrepreneurial governance modes accompanied a more profound shift from the British welfare state (in which the Scottish Office maintained some autonomy over national affairs) toward the neoliberalizing state regime of Thatcher. In my fieldwork, I found these transitions to be understood as largely merged: a general neoliberalization of state and city, characterized often as a turning from "the people" to "the economy," or as one of the campaigners' protest signs read, "Big Business." Despite their awareness of these general transitions, Canongate campaigners' expectations of their role in the planning process reflected both the moralized invocations of "community" and the managerial relationships of the bygone welfare state. The incongruities between these expectations and the neoliberal affect wielded by leaders like Anderson, who emphasized interurban competition as a global condition that conveyed urgency to the projects of urban development (Blackley 2007), would gradually emerge through the planning process. And so through their campaign, as Canongate residents came to recognize that the neoliberalizing of relations between state, city, and the spaces within complicated the outworking of the ideals of planners who are integrated into this governance system (cf. Goode 2006), the welfare state's managerial relationships seemed to withdraw even further out of reach.

In the CCF/SOOT response to the Caltongate master plan, residents' expectations of a moralized community voice, deserving of the right to influence the development of the neighborhood they inhabited (Baxstrom 2008), conditioned their program of engagement with the planning process. The planning process, however, was managed by city councilors and by the developers, and as two partners of the "growth coalition" (Logan and Molotch 1987) operating within the frame of neoliberal urbanism, these actors offered instruments for community consultation that were used to manage the impacts of the community group rather than to provide opportunities for communicating community inputs into the development. Through their interactions with these instruments, CCF/SOOT leadership eventually perceived their marginality to the process and came to treat the possibilities of community activism with increasing skepticism.

Such skepticism is justified by a robust literature on the uses of "community" as a key legitimator and instrument of a stripped-down state service delivery system. Research has found that communities are often tasked with the provision of services formerly distributed by the state (Creed 2006; DeFilippis, Fisher, and Shragge 2010; Kelly and Caputo 2011) and that the invocation of community tends to support the hierarchical processes of capitalism (Joseph 2002). Critiques of the impacts of governmental practices of community collaboration have questioned whether such collaboration actually empowers community members (Li 1996) or provides a cover for the actions of the state (Rose 1999) or parastate organizations (Goldman 2005). To complicate the translation of community input to actual city spaces, the logics of neoliberal governance value efficiency and the strategic maximization of profit (Gershon 2011; Ong 2007), priorities that directly conflict with the often-messy processes of gathering and incorporating community input.

At the outset, however, the campaigners had no such awareness, and they participated when and where they could. Initially, municipal leadership and the private developers offered three events to serve as community consultation instruments. The first two events were held in the spring of 2006: an invitation-only Planning Stakeholders Workshop in March, followed by an open-door Community Planning Day in April. An attendance of more than seventy at the open event indicates the hopeful attitude that prevailed in these first months of the campaign, but the lack of demonstrable outcomes from those events led the campaigners to present a letter to the city council in June arguing that, according to proper planning procedure, such events should have preceded the drafting of the master plan. In response to these critiques, the council recommended that the developer continue to offer ongoing opportunities for community engagement during this process. The developer thus organized the Caltongate Liaison Group, invited the newly appointed minister of the Canongate Kirk to lead it, and offered the group as a forum for residents to share their concerns.

Although skeptical of the possible impacts of this group, Catriona agreed to join one of the first meetings along with some other residents and a representative from the development firm. When she observed that the only discernible outcome of this group appeared to be a cataloging of residents' concerns, Catriona gave up the few hopes she had been harboring. At dinner afterward, she exclaimed, "The whole thing was traumatizing and unhelpful. It's a tragedy. The word 'community' should be stricken from its name." Although she mistakenly recalled the group's name, her reference to community indicates that she judged the group according to the planning ideals of community consultation. Discerning no evidence of the developer's intentions to respond to attendees' concerns, she concluded that the meetings were all for show and never returned to a meeting. The other campaigners took their cues from her. These events constituted the full program of community consultation regarding the Caltongate proposal, and a planning committee document I located later suggests that Catriona's observations about the developer's lack of intention to address the concerns of attendees did in fact reflect actual planning strategy.

In this 2006 document, the head of the planning committee advises the Scottish Executive to edit the wording on a new planning bill, suggesting that the "complexity" of community engagement be carefully considered and reminding Scottish Parliament members of the "Planning Bill's aims of using community engagement to develop trust and confidence in the planning system." He continues,

> To ensure that community confidence in the reformed system is not eroded by false expectations of delivery by planning authorities and developers, the Scottish Executive needs to use terminology with greater precision. In particular the PAN [Planning Advice Note] needs to strengthen explanations of how the *processes* of engagement can be used to *facilitate* greater involvement with a view to *obtaining a representative range* of views that will improve the *information available* to decision-makers within planning authorities. (City of Edinburgh Council 2006b [emphasis original])

The logic of community engagement expressed in this document focuses on mitigating potential conflicts (raised via "false expectations" of community members) to ensure efficiency in the delivery of the proposed development. By this logic, the community is represented as a local stakeholder—as reflected in the title of the council-arranged event—and a provider of "information," but the community is denied the special role as a moralized contributor. The goals of community consultation as perceived by the residents and by the city council planning committee are incommensurate with one another. By the standards of the city council, the community consultation events described here have fulfilled their obligation to "engage" and "involve" the Canongate residents, thus earning the accrual of moral legitimacy to this, and on principle to any, development proposal. The Canongate campaigners, however, judged the community consultation efforts according to their expectations that the community would retain a special moralized role. While the city council and developer sought to appropriate the moral framework of community for their own objectives in a manner familiar as the moral buttressing of neoliberal governance, the residents rejected this framing and wrested the moral association back to themselves. Supported by their alliances with architects, heritage conservationists, and urban planners who shared their understanding of the significance of the community's role in urban development, the Canongate residents resisted the instrumentalization of community terminology for the ends of neoliberal urban governance.

In their navigation of what was identified by some campaigners as an attempt at manipulation on the part of the city council, Canongate campaigners sharpened their sense of opposition against the council leadership. This oppositional stance only intensified when, in the same period, public narratives of neighborhood decline were leveraged to support the Caltongate master plan as a program for regeneration. While the community consultations were seen as attempts to deceive the residents as well as the observers, the aesthetic narratives, although often presented as inconsequential opinions even by those who espoused them, meaningfully threatened the Canongate residents with a loss of place-based identity. The subsequent aesthetic debates between Canongate residents and Caltongate supporters convey, in language that combines appearances with moral value, the very loss with which the Caltongate project threatened the Canongate campaigners. In their responses, the Canongate residents began to articulate the qualities, practices, and values of a political aesthetic that they would continue to elaborate in the years to come.

### Aesthetic Denigration: A Discourse of Dispossession

In analyses of urban development as in other academic discussions, the role of aesthetics is often undertheorized, replaced with matters regarded as more serious, in the vein of politics or ethics (Schellekens 2007, 28). A recent wave of attention to aesthetics has begun to speak into this theoretical gap, however, to noteworthy effect. Krisztina Fehérváry attends closely to Soviet "aesthetic regimes" in Hungary, which she defines as "politically charged assemblage[s] of material qualities that have provoked widely shared affective responses" (2013, 3). This designation applies to the opposed aesthetics of the Caltongate development and the Canongate neighborhood, as evidenced in the intensified associations of affect with the aesthetics debates discussed in this section. The concept of "aesthetic governmentality," discussed by D. Asher Ghertner, illuminates how aesthetic regulation serves the legitimation of social hierarchies and forms of exclusion entailed in their support (2015). Such regulation may take the form of laws concerned with the movements of the urban poor (2015), design stipulations and standards (Lawrence-Zúñiga 2015), or the mechanisms by which working-class neighborhoods are targeted for renewal. In this section, aesthetic debates over the materiality of development reveal both political concerns with working-class presence and ethical critiques of municipal leadership, and through aesthetic affirmations the Canongate residents ultimately assert their belonging in and to this neighborhood.

Suggesting that neoliberal urbanism adopts a recognizable pattern of aesthetic design falls into the analytic category of the blindingly obvious. Although it may be easily observed, this characteristic often fails to register in analyses of neoliberal development (see Pinson and Journel 2017). The proposed cityscape approved for the Caltongate development by Edinburgh's city council, I suggest, presents an aesthetic-economic taxonomy typical of neoliberal urbanism: the architectural icon, wedged into a backdrop of bland modernism. In the case of the Canongate neighborhood, the new parliament building serves as the icon, conveying the "faux-populist iconicity of postmodern design" (Foster 2013, 15), designed by an award-winning architect and carrying the considerable weight of expectations from the likes of then-First Minister of Scotland Donald Dewar, who wanted the building to become a national showpiece (cf. Yale 1992). The construction of the new city council building close on the heels of the new parliament building, however, was carried out in the style Ulrich Beck has called "banal cosmopolitanism" (1992). Not intended to convey singularity or locality, beyond the choice of locally resonant sandstone cladding, this building provided the modern backdrop for the parliament-as-icon, that modernity signified through coherence within a globally consistent system of modern design.

The construction of these two buildings, in quick succession and proximity, provided the immediate context by which the Canongate campaigners interpreted the Caltongate proposal, whose aesthetic paralleled that of the City Council Headquarters. When Canongate residents saw the aesthetic and economic consistency between the three projects, they interpreted the physical forms of the buildings—their scale and style—within the historical context of the anti–working-class political interventions of Margaret Thatcher, whom they, along with many working-class Scots, regarded as

Fig. 3.1 The Scottish Parliament at Holyrood, adjacent to the Canongate. Photo by author.

a primary villain (see Gilfillan 2011). The aesthetics of the Caltongate proposal thus enabled these residents to realize that their neighborhood was being redeveloped according to the logic of economic growth in an entrepreneurial arrangement with city councilors' support. Residents critical of such logic rejected the idea that the changes pursued ("upmarketing") were indeed "upgrades." One of the organizers of the campaign reflected ruefully on that logic's application to the "low-key" Canongate neighborhood.

> [Caltongate] is sort of like upgrading [the Canongate], upmarketing it. And it's like, do we have to upmarket every single bit of the town? People expect to see bits that are a bit more low-key—it's that kind of mixed balance that makes it interesting. You know? You can't have it all swishy-swishy, you know?

In this quote, the choice of the word *upmarketing* explicitly links aesthetics and economics, just as the designs themselves implicitly do. This individual, who had moved to the Canongate as a young mother and raised her children in one of its council flats, would not have been able to do so in a

Fig. 3.2 The council headquarters in the Canongate. Photo by author.

"swishy" neighborhood of the city center. Her wariness of the upmarketing of the Canongate should also be seen as an anticipation of the destabilizing effects that the development project would have on this largely working-class neighborhood. The aesthetic denigrations of the Canongate, discussed in the following pages, thus convey the power to destabilize a working-class neighborhood and in doing so to make the neighborhood itself unreadable in terms of personal and collective memory.

In his work on aesthetics and social order in Delhi, Ghertner has shown how a language of aesthetic impropriety, which he terms "nuisance talk," is used in Delhi to identify order and disorder in city spaces. This talk "moves quickly from being a medium for expressing taste or opinion into the bearer of force" (2015, 80), a movement he details in the progression from judgments cast on informal settlements to their eventual demolition. Although the Edinburgh neighborhood in question does not suffer from the total precarity of informal settlements like those Ghertner describes in Delhi, a similar practice of nuisance talk prevails in Edinburgh's public discourse around urban development, as a means of "determining the credibility of claims to public space based on how the speaker is positioned inside or outside the corresponding social order" (86).

The social order at stake in the Canongate concerns both the role of the working classes in a city being stripped of its working-class spaces and fundamentally the question of a working-class population's right to the city (Lefebvre 1996). That right becomes increasingly fragile as the neighborhood in question obtains a high imagined value for commercial extraction (Harvey 2005; Peck and Tickell 2002). In this context, such nuisance talk becomes a discourse of dispossession, reflecting David Harvey's (2004) identification of accumulation by dispossession as a primary spatial process of neoliberalizing cities. Such dispossession does not only occur through the privatizing of social housing stock or the sale of public land (although both practices have taken place in the Canongate neighborhood). The aesthetic discourse of dispossession works through public statements denigrating the appearance of a neighborhood, of which there were many examples following the proposal of the Caltongate master plan. Then-Council Leader Anderson characterized the neighborhood as "dingy" (2010 interview) while the leader of the chamber of commerce Ron Hewitt dubbed it "drab" (Edinburgh Evening News 2006d). In opinion letters that supported the Caltongate development, written to the *Edinburgh Evening News*, the Canongate was variously represented as "a blot on the Royal Mile" (*Edinburgh Evening News* 2006c), "crying out for being developed" (2006c), and "one of the less attractive parts of the Old Town" (*Edinburgh Evening News* 2006a), which contained "nothing interesting ... for tourists" (*Edinburgh Evening News* 2006b). While Anderson and Hewitt both dismissed any such aesthetic judgments as inconsequential—Hewitt writing an opinion letter to the *Evening News* in which he claimed, "Beauty won't boil the pot!" (*Edinburgh Evening News* 2006d)—research on such denigrations suggest the contrary, that these depictions serve to legitimate arguments for a neighborhood's redevelopment (see Chesluk 2008 on Times Square; Rutheiser 1999 on Atlanta).

Rejecting the social order that this "nuisance talk" supported, Canongate campaigners responded with outrage to these depictions of their neighborhood. They flipped the aesthetic discourse: not the Canongate but the Caltongate master plan was aesthetically inadequate. Countering Caltongate supporters' characterization of the Canongate as "dingy" or "drab," the Canongate campaigners reframed the Canongate aesthetic as "austere" and "stately" and named the proposed Caltongate development the "eyesore." While the discourse of the Caltongate supporters had linked aesthetic judgments with language fantasizing about the neighborhood's modernization and consumer promise, the Canongate campaigners connected the aesthetic question to issues of respect for the historic built environment. Although the aesthetic discourse of Canongate residents adopted the form of aesthetic talk, however, they lacked the power to transform their judgments into development decisions. The Canongate residents' talk reflects awareness of their disempowerment and concerns about the historic place being "forgotten."

In the pages of the *Evening News*, residents expressed fears about the Caltongate development and its like "erasing our past" (*Edinburgh Evening News* 2006f), such that they were "seeing Old Edinburgh vanish before our eyes" (*Edinburgh Evening News* 2006e). These comments often accompanied suggestions that the Caltongate proposal inadequately "respected" Edinburgh's history, such as in David's letter (*Edinburgh Evening News* 2007c): "The Caltongate [proposal] must respect and enhance the ancient buildings around it, not compete with or degrade them—and should be designed and built, like them, to last at least 200 years."

The idea of "enhancing" or "degrading" the built environment obviously refers to aesthetic concerns, and such aesthetic concerns are often embedded in narratives of the potential for damage and loss, such as in this anonymous letter (*Edinburgh Evening News* 2007a): "What will this frontage [on the Royal Mile] look like? Will it fit in with the traditional look of the rest of the Royal Mile, or will the facing be some kind of tacky plastic panel monstrosity beloved of Labour council-approved projects across the rest of the city?"

The loss threatened by "tacky" development materials and designs should not be regarded as merely a symbolic one, as if the aesthetics of development only *signaled* undesirable values, lack of architectural taste or even a threat of displacement for some residents of the Canongate neighborhood. In fact, the aesthetics of the Caltongate proposal did communicate these very things, as the Canongate campaigners made clear to me, in comments like those above. The aesthetic transformation promised by the

Fig. 3.3 Austere or eyesore? Canongate tenements under scrutiny. Photo by author.

Caltongate development could in itself effect a spatialized forgetting, enabled by the replacement of two buildings listed on the city's historic register and of the adjacent tenement building with a hotel, signature restaurant, and office building designed in the banal cosmopolitanism of Caltongate.

Campaigners asserted that the Canongate residents remember better and therefore understand the Canongate better than the Caltongate developer, who imports merely economic logic to the area. In a letter to the *Evening News* from May 2007, a prominent campaigner argued: "The Royal Mile's different architectural styles, responsive to the needs and aspirations of their time, tell the story of Edinburgh and Scotland's history. . . . [The Canongate has been] an area which, for generations, has been home to a mixed living and working community drawn from all classes. The [developers'] idea that the Canongate needs 'more extensive retails offers' and 'more night-time activities' to regenerate shows a basic failing in the developer's understanding of the character and importance of his historic area" (*Edinburgh Evening News* 2007b).

In quotes like this one, Canongate campaigners asserted their claims to be heard in development discussions based on their remembrance and recognition of the "character" of the Canongate neighborhood. Through all these quotes, the aesthetic discourse adopted by the Canongate residents affirmed and sought to uphold the historic identity of the place, represented both by an "austere" appearance and by the continuation of the working-class community inhabiting the neighborhood. These claims match well with the concerns of Edinburgh's built heritage sector, which challenged the necessity of demolishing the listed buildings and the MacRae tenement, while arguing that the Caltongate development's modern design clashed with its built surroundings. This aesthetic discourse of denigration thus provided a threat that encouraged working-class residents and conservationists to make common cause in the Old Town once more, even while the respective impacts of that threat were hardly equal. In the final section, the collaboration of the Canongate residents and heritage sector representatives on two resident-led projects indicates how closely these interests became allied, although the stakes of the Caltongate development promised to impact them in markedly different ways.

### Connecting Community Claims to Aesthetic Memory

Stephen Feld and Keith Basso note in their discussion of "senses of place" that displacement can form as powerful a place attachment as experiences of rootedness (1996, 11). The experiences of the Canongate campaigners suggest that such powerful attachments can also be mobilized by the *threat* of displacement. This displacement need not be a threat of physical eviction or loss of home, as indeed it was not for the Canongate campaign leadership, who resided in council flats rather than privately owned properties, none of which were in the buildings threatened by demolition. Instead, the imminent displacement affecting them promised "defamiliarization," a traumatic effect of destabilized mechanisms of place memory, described by Paul Connerton (2009, 32). Connerton argues that when people regularly outlive the forms of their physical environment, such as buildings, then the "accelerated metabolism of objects generates the attenuation of memory" (122). Therefore the "short lifespan of urban architecture" (4) is one of the primary causes, he suggests, for modernity's "particular problem with forgetting" (1). This defamiliarization and its concomitant forgetting is, I suggest, an important effect of the aesthetic transformation of the Canongate neighborhood and is an effect *intended* by the Caltongate development proposal, enabling both the rewriting of history and the reorientation of the neighborhood toward the objective of competition for capital in a global market of cities. As the quotes on previous pages indicate, Canongate residents perceived a threat to the working-class history displayed by the Canongate's built environment, and they responded by organizing projects to assert the value of that history, emphasizing the industrial and working-class history made invisible in the Caltongate master plan.

Returning to the February 2008 meeting of the city council's Development Management Subcommittee, the aftermath of the 17–1 vote to approve the master plan saw a surge of activism just when, so it seemed, all had been lost. In the minutes immediately following the vote, resident campaigners filed out of the meeting room. After a few tense hallway confrontations with councilors attempting to offer their light condolences, I walked with a group of seven or eight into the open courtyard outside the council chambers for a few minutes of warm but painful solidarity before each walking out into the bitterness of the winter's night. A young councilor wearing Converse trainers with his rumpled suit tentatively reached toward the loose knot of campaigners and called out, "Sorry!" as he passed by. This was received by the campaigners as an admission of guilt for wrongdoing, and they regrouped to heckle him angrily, with shouts of "Shame!" As the councilor slunk away to his car, Catriona commented in grim satisfaction, "He let us shout at him like that because he knew he'd done wrong." That sense of moral rightness was now compounded by convictions of wounded justice, and though they lacked formal planning avenues for intervention, for the moment, the fiery sense of having been wronged was far from cooling.

When I first wrote this chapter, the Edinburgh Old Town Development Trust (EOTDT) was still raising funds to refurbish the street-level space given to them. By the time of this book's publication, this space has come to indicate the scope of creative interventions generated by community residents. What was in 2017 an unassuming, unoccupied, and rather unloved space at the bottom of a tenement building has been transformed into a community center, which offers myriad activities throughout the week and makes them available to the public at no cost, encourages the renting of its rooms by community groups, collects and dispenses surplus food on a by-need basis, and runs the entire ambitious program thanks to the efforts of a small and dedicated staff. It will be the important work of a future project to document the long-term effects of this center on its surrounding built and social environment, alongside and in conversation with the adjacent new building projects still underway.

The first opportunities for creative community action soon presented themselves within weeks of the decision approving Caltongate. The campaigners learned that they had been granted funding for a "community research project" from the Scottish Community Action Research Fund (SCARF), a grant for which Catriona had applied months before. That funding allowed them to focus their energies (and newly freed time) on addressing the very concerns that the Caltongate proposal had raised: the forgetting threatened by the aesthetic transformation of the Canongate. The Canongate campaigners therefore determined to use this funding to support a multipart project of public remembrance, named "The Canongate Project" and carried out through walking tours, lectures, and films on the history of the Canongate. I was recruited to conduct and record reminiscence interviews with older current and former Canongate residents to capture for collective memory the assorted histories and scenes of the Canongate's recent industrial past. These memories of the Canongate, collected and shared among the campaigners and recorded in the final project report, reconstructed working-class histories and in doing so valorized the Canongate's built environment as a kind of working-class heritage. Laurajane Smith, Paul Shackel, and Gary Campbell have argued that heritage should be understood not as essentially elitist but as a "cultural process" that is potentially broadly accessible. For working-class communities, they suggest, heritage can be "one of the cultural tools used in the processes of individual and collective remembering and commemoration, while it is also a performance involved in a 'working out' and asserting identity and sense of place and the various cultural, social and political values that underpin these" (2011, 4). Canongate resident campaigners upheld the built environment and industrial history of the Canongate as a kind of heritage, and themselves as the bearers of that heritage.

Recognition of the Canongate campaigners as representatives of architectural and neighborhood heritage was affirmed by Edinburgh's major conservation organizations, which contributed speakers to the project's lecture program. Such depictions of heritage united architectural and social history in ways that affirmed the significance of the Canongate and identified the present-day campaigners with the long-term residential community characteristic of the neighborhood. In the final report produced by the Canongate campaigners, a resident was quoted as saying: "I just hope the planning that's going on with the Canongate is going to work. I just hope it doesn't take anything away from the Canongate and its looks and its history. That's a major thing that's upsetting so many people. Changing the historic Royal Mile like that."

The connection between the Canongate's "looks" and its "history" expressed by this resident suggests the union between the conservationists and Canongate campaigners that coalesced, in response to the Caltongate development proposal. The final report quoted here took the form of a fifty-nine-page document, submitted to Edinburgh's city council, that begins by describing the Canongate as a "vibrant community" and presents descriptions of the events organized for this project, summaries of data from neighborhood surveys, and excerpts from reminiscence sessions, and concludes with action steps to continue challenging the implementation of the Caltongate proposal. The working-class heritage highlighted through the Canongate Project thus included both histories of everyday life in the industrial Canongate via the reminiscences, as well as the built environment of the neighborhood, the significance of which was highlighted by lectures from members of Edinburgh's professional heritage organizations and local architects. Through this project, the SOOT activists positioned themselves as sources of knowledge about the Canongate neighborhood and as caretakers of the city's built heritage, and in these two tasks, they were assisted and affirmed by the participation of a number of citywide organizations and officials. While the Canongate Project did not directly engage the formal planning process, it did position the SOOT campaigners as public community representatives and asserted the aesthetic and social significance of the Canongate, which was framed as a neighborhood under threat. When opportunities for community engagement in the area's redevelopment did unexpectedly emerge through the impacts of the 2008 economic recession, their freshly affirmed status as the community of the Canongate and their reframing of the Canongate's built environment as important and historic opened an unforeseen window to impact the development process.

# LIKE THE VIEW?

Application Ref 07/01241/FUL

## SAY NO TO CALTONGATE
## OBJECT NOW
to the planning applications
Save Our Old Town
eh8.org.uk

Fig. 3.4 "Like the view?" A poster circulated by Save Our Old Town (SOOT), comparing an existing view in the Canongate neighborhood with a view of a building proposed for the site in the Caltongate master plan. Whether one likes the view suggests a host of factors—social, historic, and economic—bound up in their relation to this place. Image courtesy of Canongate Community Forum.

THROUGH RECESSION, OPPORTUNITIES FOR
COMMUNITY IMPACT IN DEVELOPMENT

Throughout this project, and indeed ever since the council meeting in which the Caltongate master plan was approved, I often heard a rueful, if cheeky, refrain along the lines of: "We can always hope the economy crashes!" or "Maybe we'll be saved by a recession!" "With Caltongate Developers

Mountgrange in financial distress, a window of opportunity for city planning and the council to reconsider their stand on how the New Street Site is to be developed" (Canongate Community Forum press release, February 19, 2009).

As these comments suggest, the campaigners regarded the supporters of the Caltongate development as having more to lose from such a recession than they would, and the idea of an economic recession appeared to promise an externally offered salvation from the threat of redevelopment and demolition that had been approved by the residents' own elected representatives. Much as the recession of the 1970s dried up the municipal leadership's enthusiasm for large-scale development projects, the recession that began to rumble up through the British banks in 2008 did succeed in freezing progress toward the Caltongate proposal. Neighborhood campaigners seized this opportunity to pursue their own projects of development, and as the next pages show, they achieved some notable success, helped along by both the recession and their previous work on the Canongate Project.

Throughout the eight weeks of the Canongate Project, the British banks continued to hold, albeit with increasingly evident precarity. Many campaigners saw this vulnerability as a window of opportunity, and some appealed to UNESCO heritage inspectors (succeeding in bringing them to Edinburgh for an assessment that summer), and one architectural historian submitted an appeal that queried the terms of the council's sale of bus depot land to the developer according to the legal frameworks of the European Union. Although these attempts stirred up some local media coverage, particularly when the UNESCO inspectors delivered a strongly worded rebuke on appropriate care of historical sites to Edinburgh's city leaders, they opened up no immediate opportunities for influence. This frustrating immobility began to show signs of change by the end of the summer of 2008, when the profits of Halifax Bank of Scotland (HBOS) had dropped by 72 percent, and within six months, in January 2009, HBOS was bought by Lloyds TSB. As HBOS had been financing the developer's proposal, this meant that the developer lost its funding and was forced to drop the council-approved Caltongate master plan.

In the absence of its developer, the Caltongate master plan remained merely a potential design, and this state of limbo facilitated one more burst of creative development energies from local residents. The original campaign leadership, hailing from the Canongate, joined with a handful of residents in other Old Town neighborhoods to form a development trust, a form of organization to which they had been introduced throughout the campaign. In 2009, the EOTDT emerged, with a website and a mission statement announcing its aim to pursue "community-led development" and "preserve the diverse culture and historic integrity of the Old Town" (Edinburgh Old Town Development Trust 2009). Multiple ideas for local development peppered the pages of the earliest versions of the website, evidencing the influence of Geddes's ideals for urban development both implicitly in the trust's interests and explicitly in the names of projects and publications.

Of these ideas, three obtained enough support to be pushed forward, and two have come to some fruition. The first idea suggested the repurposing of one of the two historic buildings intended for demolition in the Caltongate master plan, the Canongate Venture, into a local literacy center. That project initially garnered support from city councilors and one of the architects who had designed the Caltongate master plan—in fact, an architect who suggested to me that SOOT reflected the views of a local minority rather than the local community. The SOOT leadership regarded his support as fickle and bemusing; it made little sense to them, but in public, they withheld their skepticism in exchange for some newly plausible development hopes. Indeed, the project received several green lights and seemed to be moving forward toward council approval. Then in 2011, on a tide of rising stock prices, a new development firm put forth a bid to undertake the Caltongate development, and the literacy center project promptly lost its council backing. That firm's version of Caltongate would be modified, however, in response to both a humbled economic climate and the public influence of the residents' campaign.

Those modifications are discussed in the following paragraphs, but it is worth noting that the success of the second and third ideas of the EOTDT, in contrast to the literacy center, derive from their lack of encroachment on the neoliberal logic of real estate–based profit accumulation. These ideas have taken material and social form through groups organized around the activities of gardening and writing/publishing. They also explicitly invoke the legacy of Geddes: the Patrick Geddes Gardening Club organized to transform the neglected gardens of the

Old Town into local sources of fruits and vegetables, as well as spaces of community interaction. Its members have addressed multiple such sites, starting with the overgrown grounds of a historic house in the Canongate, which had for decades been used as a midden. These site-based transformations contribute to an aesthetic makeover of the area that is quite amenable to the interests of real estate development. The third idea, conceived in relation to the literacy center but carried on despite the loss of a key location, has resulted in the publication to this date of four volumes of poetry and prose by authors in the Old Town, titled *The Evergreen: A New Season in the North*. Its title gestures to the enduring impression left by Geddes on Old Town residents, having been taken from a periodical publication of multidisciplinary and perspectival interest by Patrick Geddes, last published in 1896. The EOTDT thus participates in a well-established tradition of appropriating Geddes as a voice of resistance to large-scale development in the Old Town, on behalf of a mixed-class collective of residents and conservationists. Without empowerment through the development process, however, such resistance fails to threaten the neoliberal development plans in a meaningful way, and one such development project may take advantage of an active community sector, appropriating its labors as an indicator of ongoing area regeneration or vitality.

The new developer has taken such steps, providing a circumscribed space for the community group within the development area and involving representatives in meetings to discuss the modifications of the plans at an earlier stage in the process. While the provisions of the plan have been largely modified due to economic necessity, the chastening of scale of the development—including the preservation of facades of two historic buildings that the Caltongate proposal had designated for destruction—and the provision of a small space for the community were counted as undeniable benefits of this new, modified development by the former Canongate campaigners. Combined with the fatigue of near-constant mobilization over the previous three years, these nods to community demands ameliorated the intensity of their previous engagement. The new development firm sought peace with, if not direction from, the community campaigners. This firm distanced itself from the confrontational legacy of Caltongate and renamed the modified development, disassociating it from the public controversies around Caltongate, but at the same time taking a move from the Caltongate developer's playbook: the new name for the development, New Waverley, sought identity outside the Canongate, allying itself with nearby geographic and cultural features, the adjacent Waverley Valley, and the well-known Waverley novels of Sir Walter Scott.

When I wrote this chapter, the EOTDT was still raising funds to refurbish the street-level storefront space given to them, so that it might serve as a space for community gathering. One of the historic facades has been transformed into the entrance to the Adagio Aparthotel, while the other is under redevelopment for use as a restaurant. The Canongate campaigners remain informally associated with the EOTDT, but the SOOT leadership have scattered to other locations, for reasons discussed in the following chapter. Under the auspices of the new developer, the area is still under construction, being intended for the largest concentration of offices for Scottish civil servants in the country. *The Evergreen* has just published its fourth edition, and the Patrick Geddes Gardening Club has moved on to gardens in the Grassmarket area of the Old Town. Old Town residents continue to pursue the adaptation of incoming development plans to their own community uses, but for those closest to the SOOT campaign, the plausibility of large-scale impact seems low.

One former SOOT campaigner—an officer in the organization from its earliest days—had remained in the area and continued to involve himself in the ongoing community representation work. In 2017, I asked him about a particular proposal that had been submitted to community consultation through a local representative organization in which he served. With an eye roll, he flung up his hands in disgust. "I just went, 'Right. Just do what you want. You're going to do it in the end anyway!'" From idealistic campaigner to a committed but cynical advocate, this Canongate resident exemplified the lesson in disempowerment that the SOOT campaigners gained from the experiences described in this chapter. And yet, he and the rest of SOOT's former leadership had by this time already thrown their support behind the SNP. As the following chapters show, the ineffectiveness of their resistance to neoliberal urbanism in the Canongate directly influenced the former campaigners' support for the idealistic rhetoric of liberal democracy they had come to hear from the SNP, whose political aesthetic closely resembled the presence and practices that they had attempted to protect in the Canongate.

Fig. 3.5 Ground-floor flat with the red door: the community space allotted to the Edinburgh Old Town Development Trust by the New Waverley developer. In 2018, when this photo was taken, funds were still being raised by residents for the refurbishment of this space. By 2021 the space was being used for community purposes. Photo by author.

### Looking Back, Thinking Ahead

In reflection on the development trajectory of the Canongate, the New Waverley development succeeded in managing the community demands precisely by minimally empowering them in a strategy of community management identified elsewhere as a hallmark of neoliberal governance. The cynicism about community consultation evidenced in the actions of the Caltongate developers, and even by members of the city council, in combination with the discourse of public denigration of the area's historic built environment provoked outrage among both Canongate residents and other conservationists. Their joint mobilization, in particular through the Canongate Project, though insufficient to sway the council committee vote,

Fig. 3.6 The public square behind the hotel on Canongate Road (with a view to the still-boarded-up Canongate Venture on the left and the council headquarters on the right) provides as much space for cars as for pedestrians. Photo by author.

did influence popular and municipal perceptions of the Canongate area. In the unanticipated (but hoped-for) circumstances provided by the onset of economic recession, a second take on the development proposal resulted in the carving out of a small space in the new development designated for community use, managed by the EOTDT.

Former SOOT campaign leaders look back on the campaign with incredulity at the enormous effort spent on political mobilization and the paltry gains they achieved. They struggle to regard those efforts as impactful on the neighborhood: although some facades were preserved, the uses of the space now serve tourists and other passers-through. A large arched passageway was knocked through the lower half of the MacRae tenement, creating access from Canongate Road to a new public square—in which one former campaigner observed cars lined up for a wash on a summer day. The arches on Jeffrey Street that SOOT campaigners wanted for affordable space for artists now house a row of consumer goods for purchase: from

Fig. 3.7 The formerly Caltongate, now New Waverley, construction site was still under development in 2017. (View toward the backs of the Canongate tenements and new hotel, with council headquarters on the right.) Photo by author.

sportswear to a "donutterie," and at the far end, a property management company specializing in Airbnb rentals. The defamiliarization promised by redevelopment has occurred with minimal demolition.

The former campaigners observe that through their mobilization, they may have gained their own shared space in the neighborhood, but their ability to meaningfully shape that neighborhood beyond this allotted space is firmly circumscribed. That pursuit of a right to dwell in the city, via the Canongate, expressed their claim on the state, and their actual role in the development process is suggested by the allocated space itself: one narrow, delimited area, a physical metaphor for their role as one minor stakeholder in a neoliberal urban economy. Through this experience, the SOOT campaign leaders learned much about their opportunities for realizing their demands through political processes. From sharing oral histories of collective working-class activism, a storied legacy of political mobilization on which they based their campaign, to organizing as stakeholders in an entrepreneurial city, these Edinburgh residents experienced a reframing of the basis of their claims on the state, from a collective political right to an externally ascribed market value.

As I have watched, walked alongside, and listened to these residents share their long, painful, and ultimately frustrating experiences campaigning against the redevelopment of their neighborhood, I have observed the extraordinary toll that political mobilization ekes precisely from its most successful activists. As individuals exercising their democratic right to organize themselves, the leaders of the SOOT campaign initially committed themselves to a struggle for influence in the decision-making of city councilors, a struggle in which they were outresourced and underinformed. As they acquired more resources, however—a website, access to the internet and to a printer—and gained more support from allies who provided expertise and free public lectures, along with some inconsistent financial donations, the labor required to manage the campaign only compounded in scale. Encouraged and validated by their allies in the professions of conservation, architecture, and urban planning, the Canongate residents rose to meet the challenge that only continued to grow as the planning process steamed ahead. Had the campaigners run a less organized and compelling campaign, they would have been spared the strain of its management by the council's implementation of a quicker and smoother planning process, but instead, the campaign succeeded well enough to stretch out the process and wring them out completely, without achieving their ultimate hopes. In reflection, I note that the mechanisms of neoliberal urban governance that offer merely the appearance of access do not only confer legitimacy on their decisions with the lightest touch of community involvement; they also eviscerate the community itself in this almost-politics of urban development. I cannot help but wonder at the scale of collective mobilization required to effect community-oriented change on the development of the city within such a model.

The losses from that campaign have both scarred and compelled the former Canongate campaigners to seek the realization of their social and political vision elsewhere. As the next chapter describes, following the approval of the Caltongate master plan, most of them left the Canongate for other working-class neighborhoods, but they continue to carry the political aesthetic of the Canongate with them. The former SOOT leadership by 2020 have largely abandoned causes of urban development, leaving the running of the EOTDT to allies in other Old Town neighborhoods, particularly Grassmarket. From the SOOT campaign through the present day, their experiences navigating the neoliberal state and its entrepreneurial city have propelled them out of the Canongate neighborhood to state activism in a collective politics of solidarity that seeks the repoliticization of their urban lives and a concomitant revitalization of working-class politics. While campaigners' attention understandably focused on the possibly vanishing aesthetics of the Canongate during the campaign detailed in this chapter, their imagination of a responsive state accountable to the city's working-class residents traced an idealized memory of the British welfare state, contrasted to the manipulations of the neoliberal state experienced in Edinburgh. This political ideal is explored in relation to Scottish independence in chapter 5, while chapter 4 elaborates the aesthetic that translates from the Canongate to the Scottish nation, suggesting that the former Canongate campaigners have politicized the home itself as an affirmation of working-class life that entails a rejection of entrepreneurial development logics. This conceptualization has added color and form to campaigners' imagination of the nation, as evident in their subsequent discussions of Scottish politics and independence and as practiced in the political mobilizations that have followed.

INTERLUDE 3

# DUMBIEDYKES

ADJACENT TO THE SOUTH BACKS of the Canongate lies Edinburgh's only centrally located council housing estate. The place name, Dumbiedykes, recalls the road that once skirted the walls of the park at Holyrood and ran past the first school for the deaf in the United Kingdom, its name immortalized in Sir Walter Scott's novel, *The Heart of Midlothian*. Since the mid-nineteenth century, this estate has referred to the housing development, initially of rather handsome, though ramshackle, stone construction sprawling along the eastern edge of Holyrood Park from the Canongate in the north to St. Leonard's in the south. Carved out of a wedge-shaped margin of land between the city to the west and the shaggy slopes of Arthur's Seat and the Salisbury Crags to the east, Dumbiedykes boasts the best views from council housing in Scotland, particularly from the west-facing balconies of its eleven-story tower blocks. As the nearest neighbor to the Canongate, Dumbiedykes has since the industrial nineteenth century maintained close ties with that historic burgh, sharing a working-class and poor community life replete with the range of problems associated with inadequate housing. The ties between these neighborhoods remained close throughout the Canongate community campaign, but though the working-class residents of the Canongate have largely dispersed since the approval of the area's redevelopment, the residents of Dumbiedykes continue to struggle with the city council and its simultaneous visions for and neglect of this part of the "east end" of the Old Town.

Compared with the Canongate, Dumbiedykes has housed larger numbers of more deprived populations, with less mixing of social classes, and in some respects resembles a blend of the peripheral housing estates with city-center working-class neighborhoods. While its low-rise tenements and two tower blocks do not visibly recall the blighted nightmare-scape of Knoxland, that fictitious peripheral Edinburgh estate described in near-apocalyptic terms by novelist Ian Rankin (2004), the paradoxical combination of centrality and neglect of Dumbiedykes has often made it a ready face for poverty in Edinburgh. In 2018, Edinburgh Council angered some Dumbiedykes residents by using it as the visual backdrop in its publicity for Challenge Poverty Week. One Twitter user summed up the sentiment: "We're more than a prop. How about Council sort dampness in homes? Make the high rise fire safe? Fix lifts? Tackle drug users & antisocial behaviour? Restore bus service? Anything?" (James Slaven tweet, October 3, 2018).

During the height of the Canongate campaign, a 2008 study from Sheffield University identified Edinburgh's Holyrood area, inclusive of both Dumbiedykes and the Canongate, as the "loneliest place in Britain," based on factors such as the number of people who are single, live alone, live in private rented accommodations, and have lived in their flat for less than a year (Dorling et al. 2008). Recognizing the dissonance between this study and the narratives of community campaigners, a reporter from the *Times* reached out to Save Our Old Town (SOOT) members for comment. The campaigners rejected the interpretations of the Sheffield study, and the *Times* reported, "A community action group had found a strong sense of belonging among residents, expressed in a long-running campaign against Caltongate" (Wade 2008). In fact, not only the Canongate campaign but also a Dumbiedykes-based campaign of working-class political activists (described in the following pages) had emerged from this area just three years before the Sheffield study. Despite the demonstrable deprivations, something about community life in both the Canongate and Dumbiedykes has evaded capture by the characteristics quantified in the Sheffield University study or by the popular media representations of these neighborhoods. An excursion to Dumbiedykes, with a brief sketch of its historical and contemporary ties to the Canongate, presents a more complex portrait of everyday life and political action in working-class neighborhoods at the heart of a capital city.

### Origins, Rebirth, and Repeat

The nineteenth-century origins of Dumbiedykes owe to the rural-to-urban migration of would-be workers in Edinburgh's industries, and their hasty construction reflects the urgency of the city's housing crisis rather than the deliberate consideration of a long-term investment in the built environment of the Old Town. From the late nineteenth century through the mid-twentieth, the tenements of the Dumbiedykes area obtained infamy for conditions of slum living as dire as any in Britain. Nevertheless, as narrated by former Canongate residents of the same era, deprivation and neglect became conditions in which a certain kind of community life not only survived but depended on the mutual support among families inhabiting these often crumbling and rat-infested tenements. Where there is community life but also tuberculosis, wood rot, and, as a young girl memorably recounted in a 1959 interview, mice running across her feet while she lay in bed at night, the need to address the plain and vicious inadequacies of housing tends to blot out the more everyday concerns of preserving relational ties between residents. As designing development that attends to the latter concerns generally has had the effect of making housing reforms seem prohibitively expensive from the perspective of councilors, this objective has seldom featured as one of the priorities in Edinburgh's processes of housing redevelopment.

The redevelopment of Dumbiedykes, accelerated by a campaign for public awareness initiated by local ward councilor Pat Rogan, constituted the last major slum clearance of Edinburgh. This project proceeded throughout the 1960s, demolishing more than 1,000 homes inhabited by more than 1,900 Edinburgh residents and replacing them with around 650 homes in the form of low-rise tenements and two high-rise tower blocks. Despite the relocation of many residents, a sizeable population of families remained in the new Dumbiedykes. The coinciding of this redevelopment with the onset of economic recession in the 1970s and the large-scale unemployment caused by disinvestment in industrial manufacture meant that Dumbiedykes' reputation for housing the very poorest and most disadvantaged in Edinburgh stuck stubbornly to it, despite the total redevelopment of its built environment. Owing to its central location, Dumbiedykes's neglect was punctuated by investment at fits and starts, as the facades of its council housing feature in many panoramic views of Arthur's Seat and the Crags, while its winding pavements deposit its residents on the same stretch of Holyrood Road where parliament officials and a growing population of university students step out for lunch or a coffee.

During the Canongate campaign in 2008, a campaigner and I arranged to meet with members of a community organization, the Dumbiedykes

Writers Group, in the Braidwood Centre, the nicely appointed Dumbiedykes community center that had been entirely refurbished in one of the fits of development from which the estate sporadically benefits. The Braidwood Centre owed its funding to the decision to situate the new parliament building in the Holyrood brewery land directly across the street from Dumbiedykes, and, since 2003, it has served the community by hosting events, classes, and meetings available to residents. The Dumbiedykes Writers Group, which predated this community center, had since that time scheduled its meetings there. While the group's essays ranged from the historic to the contemporary, redevelopment loomed large in the memories of the older members, and they handed me one of their publications, a 1999 booklet of essays and photos in which several entries reflected on life in the preredevelopment Dumbiedykes with a sense of loss, very similar to the nostalgia described to me by Canongate residents.

Resident writer John Bald (1999a, 19) reflected on Arthur Street, which had been demolished in the clearance of Dumbiedykes: "Arthur Street had the reputation of being rough and tough and was reputed to be the worst slum in Edinburgh. I spent the first twenty years of my life there. It was home. I never felt unsafe, never hungry or unwanted. When I meet my old neighbours we always remember Arthur Street with fond memories."

For Mr. Bald, acknowledgments of the bad reputation of his street accompanied the insistence that more was happening on that "rough and tough" street than was apparent to outsiders. Nostalgia for that neighborhood life colors his recollections, and the regret he expresses for its loss is shared by another resident, Jean Donaldson, who writes about the loss of Holyrood Square, "the most densely populated part" of Dumbiedykes, consisting in a group of 206 houses (1999b, 21). "The high-rise flats which took the place of Holyrood Square must have been regarded by the local residents as the lap of luxury after having only had the basic amenities and having had to rely on the local baths. A very strong community spirit existed then, but with the passage of time that has sadly disappeared."

These reflections that identify a moldering and cramped built environment with "community spirit" were common to reflections on both the midcentury Canongate and Dumbiedykes. As the collapse of one such Dumbiedykes tenement in 1952 indicates, the conditions in which this community life emerged were not to be regarded as satisfactory in themselves—Mr. Bald writes in another section on "the not so 'good old

Fig. Interlude 3 Arthur Street, of the "rough, tough" reputation, before its demolition in 1961.

days'" and the proliferation of boils and lice in these conditions, but suggests that this misery was leavened with the delights of the chip shop (1999b, 22–23). With these housing deprivations thus firmly in view, the commentary from both of these adjoining neighborhoods suggests a perspective on a resilient working-class life as embedded in these tenemented neighborhoods, performed through the everyday activities of women and children in particular. While the lives of the working classes are often understood to be attached to the fortunes of waged labor, the nostalgic reflections of Dumbiedykes and Canongate residents regard them as equally negotiated through the spaces of community life, beginning at home.

Indeed, home and the rights of the working classes to maintain a distinctively welfare state relationship with the city of Edinburgh council motivated a successful campaign from Dumbiedykes to reject the transfer of the city's council housing stock to a private housing association, against the will of the majority Labour Party. Having originated as a Conservative Party policy, housing stock transfer first took place in Britain in 1988, and since that time the strategy has been implemented widely and via an increasingly top-down process in England (Pawson 2004, 6). In Scotland, the policy was applied experimentally through parcels of stock transferred to associations and then embraced by the devolved government as a core housing initiative of New Labour (Daly et al. 2007). By the first decade of the twenty-first century, housing stock transfer had been used across Britain as a device for ensuring the quality of council housing, and it was touted as evidence of New Labour's commitment to individual choice. The legitimacy of both claims was challenged by its vocal critics, who decried stock transfer as an extension of Thatcher-era privatization of state-provided services, thus subject to similar critiques as the Right to Buy program (Pawson and Fancy 2003, 6). Labour guidance advised that stock transfer could redress local authorities' overdrawn and underresourced housing budgets via the transfer of some or all of their council housing to the ownership and management of private housing associations, and council money freed from their landlord responsibilities could then be committed to the construction of new housing. Several Scottish councils seized on this opportunity, and the proposal for complete council housing stock transfer was put to local ballot in Glasgow, Dumfries and Galloway, and the Scottish Borders in 2002; Edinburgh and Argyll and Bute in 2005; Na h-Eileanan Siar in 2006; and Inverclyde in 2007.

Considering the rich tradition of leftist political activism in Glasgow, it is perhaps surprising that the most effective resistance was mobilized not in Glasgow but in Edinburgh, that city regarded as Scotland's most "anglified" (Hearn 2003, 13), where a successful antistock transfer campaign defeated the council's stock transfer proposal. Edinburgh Against Stock Transfer (EAST) originated in Dumbiedykes among resident tenants ideologically opposed to the transfer that they regarded as the council's "plans to abandon their tenants and privatize their homes" (BBC News 2005). The leader of Edinburgh's city council, Labour councilor Donald Anderson, who had been a primary proponent of the stock transfer scheme, deemed the 53–47 percent defeat (at a 60 percent voter turnout rate) a "major setback," while the Scottish National Party and Scottish Socialist councilors rejoiced (BBC News 2005). The success of the EAST campaign marked a victory for working-class political mobilization, ironically in the face of their former allies, the Labour Party politicians. It also affirmed the potential in Dumbiedykes, a council housing estate in the center of Edinburgh, for shaping the city's political life despite the deprivations faced by its residents. A Canongate campaign leader identified this politically activist Dumbiedykes leadership as not only inspirational but also directly responsible for resourcing their own campaign. "Although it's always been quite poor and quite deprived in some respects, they've always had a strong sense of community and who they are, and, 'You're not going to take stuff away from us.' We would never have been able to set SOOT [Save Our Old Town] up if it hadn't been for the folk at Dumbiedykes. They were fundamental in helping us."

This assistance came in the form of tangible resources like assistance in the Dumbiedykes computer lab and the gift of an internet domain name for the SOOT campaign, as described in chapter 3, but as the Canongate campaigner's quote above makes clear, the activist residents in Dumbiedykes provided an affirmation-in-kind of the Canongate residents' cause. The working-class politics mobilized by the Dumbiedykes residents, however, which translated well to the direct democracy of a popular referendum, could not be applied as effectively to the centralized processes of council planning permissions. The Canongate campaigners, affirming values consistent with their fellow activists in Dumbiedykes, failed to obtain the support of their city councilors necessary in the planning process to realize their social and political vision. Thus, while the efficacy of the Dumbiedykes antistock transfer campaign may be celebrated as a political outcome empowering the working classes, the difference between that outcome and the outcome of the Canongate community campaign highlights the wide variability of working-class politics, according to the political processes and instruments that structure opportunities for influence.

### Two Dumbiedykes in 2021

The result of these two campaigns for the Holyrood area of Edinburgh has meant that while the Canongate tenements have experienced a hollowing out of family tenants, Dumbiedykes retains a substantial population of families, alongside its many single occupants. While council renting remains the norm, owner-occupiers have been increasing in the area over the thirty years of the Right to Buy program, and Dumbiedykes flats can regularly be found on property letting websites for long- and short-term rentals.

The ethnic composition of the Dumbiedykes population has shifted from the Irish and rural Highland origins of its earliest generation to include a range of Central Asian, Russian, and Eastern European immigrants. *Include* is used deliberately here; community groups like the Dumbiedykes Writers Group have gestured to the inclusivity of their community, printing their publication's title (though not its essays) in five languages. As I heard from a southern European resident, who sardonically identified himself as a "foreigner," and as I myself observed, Dumbiedykes can be experienced as two different places, one typified by community solidarity and inclusivity, and the other characterized by a rejection of (or perhaps by) the respectable community in exchange for temporary deliverance, via substances legal and illegal. The juxtaposition of these two Dumbiedykes creates a disturbing dissonance for many residents, but it is one they have gained little traction in addressing, despite their central location adjacent to the heart of the city's Old Town.

In 2017, I met with Paolo, a resident homeowner in Dumbiedykes for the past nineteen years. We talked inside his flat (with a glorious view), which he had double-purposed as a studio for his work as a sound engineer. He was a friend of a friend, connected by way of the Canongate, and we had been introduced because he was undertaking the documentation of police responsiveness to—or, more accurately, their disinterest in—residents' reports of vandalism, drug use and selling, and arson. A prominent theme of the conversation that followed highlighted the bifurcation of the neighborhood into two Dumbiedykes. The first Dumbiedykes, the one Paolo identified with, was the multicultural community of activists and families, including "a lot" of professionals and "two people with PhDs," although Paolo observed that this education "doesn't necessarily make you somebody who is proactive." While these highly educated residents would sign a petition when asked, they otherwise remained, lamentably, "quite out of action." This Dumbiedykes fit comfortably with the working-class cosmopolitanism I had observed in the Canongate, and it aptly described the ties between neighbors and activists in these two adjacent areas.

The second Dumbiedykes, however, had been consuming much of Paolo's time over the past two years. He showed me videos of youth burning building materials at a construction site on the estate, pointing incredulously in the same frame to uniformed police passing idly by. He regaled me with harrowing tales of his former neighbor, who had sold heroin and attracted a steady trail of clients who would often mistakenly beat on Paolo's door and shoot up, defecate, urinate, and pass out in their shared stairwell. Neighbors reported these events to the police, who directed them, as a rule, to call the Crimestoppers line whenever they witnessed something illegal. Following this advice over the course of a week, however, prompted a warning from Crimestoppers that, henceforth, any additional reports would be treated as nuisance calls. "We had been calling," Paolo shrugged, "twenty times a day." Despite having shared recordings of mothers screaming outside the windows of the flat, accusing Paolo's neighbor of having sold drugs to their children, and despite men pacing and moaning on the lawn below the flats about needing their fix, the police did not intervene to stop this activity, which one member of Parliament, whose assistant observed it firsthand, dubbed "light drug dealing." Rather, the residents were tragically delivered by the news of their neighbor's demise: the burning of Paolo's neighbor in his own flat under what Paolo, but not the police, regarded as suspicious circumstances.

Over two years of trying to direct the attention of police, city councilors, and members of Scottish Parliament to the neglect suffered by his neighbors and his neighborhood, Paolo marveled angrily at the consistency with which issues of governmental neglect were framed as personal matters. When a resident broke her leg in one of Dumbiedykes's many gaping potholes, the council pointed to her state of drunkenness, while Paolo pointed to the potholes. "So what? She could've been an alcoholic! If that hole wasn't right in the ground, with no barriers around it, she wouldn't have broken her leg!" After an hour of discussing a litany of similar cases, which Paolo identified as the council/police/parliament's refusal to act in Dumbiedykes, he concluded, "But really, there's nobody in charge. It's your problem if you live in this area. . . . People in this specific estate are punished, because [councilors and members of parliament] think, 'Oh what do you want? Right in the middle of town, you've got the views—what [more] do you want?' . . . Law and order!" Paolo laughed bitterly in reply.

As I left my meeting with Paolo and walked back toward Holyrood Road, I looked around at the meticulously cleaned lace curtains of twentieth-century working-class respectability adorning ground-floor windows in the low-rise tenements. I saw signs of children's play—a plastic toy accidentally left behind, a small shoe—on the lawn before them. But beyond these green squares, lines of low buildings wore water-stained pebbled exteriors, and stair doors testified in dents and other scars to violent episodes recently past. Dumbiedykes demonstrates that the potential benefits of social and political integration enabled by a central location cannot compensate for governmental neglect, from social housing to police services. The stymied activism of Paolo and his neighbors and the efficacy of the EAST campaign together show that working-class activism navigates proximity to social problems, bearing out the impacts of social and political history on the bodies of activists themselves. That these social problems have traditionally, under the auspices of the British welfare state, been designated the responsibility of local politics heightens the sense of betrayal and abandonment that drives residents' deeply felt desire for change. From the much-lauded views of Dumbiedykes, the image of a Scottish welfare state appears to provide a fresh, familiar, and hopeful horizon.

# CHAPTER 4

# THE POLITICS OF HOME

### The Right to "Be at Home"

Following the completion of the Canongate Project, I left Edinburgh for a new home in the US to take a position teaching anthropology. I kept in touch with the Save Our Old Town (SOOT) campaigners via email and social media, and I returned for research visits in 2010, 2017, and 2018. When I first left, Sally had planned to relocate from the Canongate to a neighborhood just north of the city center. This seemed in some ways a surprising dislocation: at the height of the SOOT campaign, Sally's seemingly tireless activities had inspired a newspaper reporter to dub her "an Erin Brockovich of town planning" (Allan 2008). But the campaign had taken an extraordinary toll on her physically and emotionally; she decided she just couldn't stay in her flat on Canongate Road while the neighborhood as she knew it disappeared. As she moved her family to the new home in a nineteenth-century block of purpose-built working-class housing, she desperately needed both distraction and joy. She decided this was the time to finally pursue a long-nurtured interest in art, and she enrolled in a painting course at a nearby art school.[1]

I first saw an emergent collection of her work on social media in an array of blues—bright teal, pale sky, and deep ocean—accented against warm whites and buttery yellows, soft leafy greens, and bold rosy pinks. When we reunited in 2017, painting was taking up most of Sally's daily labor, arranged around the lives of her now-teenage children and punctuated by episodes of political action. I was eager to see the work in person, and Sally obligingly led me on a tour of her paintings, hung throughout her house for a show. I peered at the brushstrokes and stepped back to admire the composition, while she explained the collection as a body of work. Sally mused, with a wry expression, that when she had first begun painting, she expected that she would create angry, exclamatory protest art, coming hot on the heels of the unjust Caltongate decision. But once she began to compose her canvases, she discovered to her great surprise that she was most drawn to domestic scenes, living rooms and stairs and shared gardens. The paintings we perused offered perspectives of and from her house, kitchen to living room, bedroom to front green. Reflecting on the unexpected turn her work had taken, Sally concluded thoughtfully that it expressed what had motivated her all along, in her campaign work, volunteer work, and now her art: a deep appreciation for home—and at the heart, a belief that everyone should have a home.

Sally's personal domestic scenes, so directly connected to that SOOT campaign, recalled evocatively the moments I had spent in campaigners' homes, sharing couches, eating meals, and meeting the neighbors. Those experiences of shared spaces, alongside the campaigners' discourses of home, highlighted for me a persistent thread of the campaign, one that is underrepresented in scholarly literature on urban planning or working-class political mobilization. The idea of home as an organizing basis for urban political engagement appears to contradict divisions of the social into private and public domains, and yet the history of working-class housing activism suggests that the home as an idea and an ideal represents a compelling instrument for collective mobilization.

This chapter shows how a modified politics of home has become important as a form of working-class activism responsive to the conditions of neoliberal urbanism in Edinburgh, which have produced shared experiences of the insecurity of housing and the relocation of formerly city-center working-class communities via city renewal projects. I suggest that the qualities attached to home and "being at home" in the critical discourse of resident campaigners informed a vocabulary of dissent from the trends of neoliberal development, one that asserted the inalienable relationship between the place as home and its residents as well as the indivisible nature of the place as their home, inclusive of both private and public spaces. In this way, the idea of home offered an idealized concept that allowed residents to politicize the Canongate aesthetic as an alternative to the commodification of place instrumentalized in the Caltongate proposal. The discourse of home discussed in this chapter thus expresses the residents' resistance to neoliberal urbanism and in its elaboration as a distinctly Canongate aesthetic connects this resistance to their involvement in national politics (in chapter 5). In the sections below, I discuss the material and social contexts of "home," consider the historical contexts in which home has become a site of resistance to neoliberal urbanism and engage the particular invocations of home as inalienable and indivisible by residents of the Canongate. Finally, I consider both opportunities and limitations for this politics of home to mobilize and challenge the dominant logics and practices of urban development.

As city-center development projects displace working-class residents, a shared sense of injustice has united them across neighborhoods of Edinburgh, as in the formation of the Edinburgh at Risk group. Campaign leaders perceived a similar plight in other cities and nations, naming Harlem, New York, and Barcelona, Spain, among those urban communities facing similar dislocations, when they made a case for the global scale of the development problems in their campaign meetings. But such citations, despite campaigners' claims to solidarity, did not generate interaction between campaigns outside of Britain, as far as I could tell; the internet provided information but not new relationships. The reasons for this did not, I observed, indicate lack of interest but lack of time; the Canongate campaigners already labored to extremes and exhaustion pursuing opportunities, action, and allies in Edinburgh and had little time, energy, and possibly imagination left for online networking. The potential for building a broad-based program of sustained action must be qualified therefore by recognition of the difficulties imposed by the local and temporal particularities of each redevelopment event. This pattern of redevelopment and relocation would perhaps generate more generalized objection if it were attempted all at once, with all the hubris (and budget) of a twenty-first-century Robert Moses. But unlike Moses's breathtaking plans to carve through Manhattan with a superhighway—and unlike an abortive 1960s proposal to pave an inner ring road around Edinburgh—the projects that dislocate the urban working classes of cities like Edinburgh today have tended to be smaller and more locally specific in their influence. Any given project might thus generate a handful of relocations and, therefore, a manageable amount of public critique; because each project is place- and time-specific, the solidarity generated between one neighborhood and another, some two or five years later and five blocks or one mile apart, is limited. As the Canongate case makes clear, the sheer scale of effort required to contest these proposals, which falls heaviest on those most committed to the cause, also constrains the scope of activist innovations, focusing engagement on the formal processes of planning. While it may be the case that Scottish working-class activism around housing issues has historically generated a core project of working-class politics, in the neoliberal era, collective mobilization around housing issues requires the difficult conceptualization and practice of solidarity across time, space, and bodies.

> She walks the fog to get the colours home
> The pigments then assembled rub against each other.
> Each swiftly landing on this canvas turns
> What was into what's meant to be.
>
> From "Woman Painting,"
> Deborah Warner (2014, 49)

## At Home in the Canongate

Undoubtedly home, like community, is a "warmly persuasive idea" (Williams 1976) that connotes many different qualities to many different people. In popular use in Scotland as elsewhere, a house is invoked as a structural approximation of home, although the structures of the house vary from flats to semidetached row houses, detached bungalows to cottages. For the Canongate campaigners, the universally shared housing structure was the flat in a tenement building, consisting abstractly in a "volume of space off the ground" (Robinson 2005, 103). In their program of activism, however, the idea of home invoked exceeded the spaces and activities of the individual flat and its residents. The conceptualization of home invoked by these campaigners incorporated both these personalized places of belonging and shared spaces of collective interaction; a nested materiality that residents navigated in processes that manifested as "being at home." It was this right to *be at home* that the Canongate campaigners claimed through their program of activism, I suggest, rather than merely a right to *have* a home in this neighborhood. This distinction is not merely semantic; it suggests the broader scope of the campaigners' concerns and demands, and it helps to explain why Sally would leave the Canongate following the approval of the Caltongate proposal and from her new house launch a painting project focused on home.

The ideal of "being at home" has been discussed as a matter of individual movement, habits, and discourse (Rapport and Dawson 1998). Through such a lens, home becomes not a site of resistance but accommodation to the lack of stability faced by groups like migrants, tourists, and commuters. But the Canongate campaigners, claimants to a Scottish tradition of political activism for working-class housing rights and built environment conservation, challenged the conditions of enforced mobility. In the Canongate Community Forum (CCF)/SOOT campaign described in the previous chapter, the ideal of being at home suggested the aesthetic intertwining of material and social identity, forging a physical site of resistance to the spatial liquidity of neoliberal urbanism. In the sense that the campaigners invoked this idea, being at home implied the satisfaction of basic material conditions—there must be a physical structure of the home—the smallest unit of which, in the Canongate, was the tenement flat. Although the campaigners did refer to their flats as homes, and, as a subsequent section shows, this depiction could itself be leveraged as a form of resistance, the flat-as-home depended on its surrounding built and social environment, such that in the campaigners' politicized usage, the Canongate itself became home, iterating a collective sense of belonging identified with its material environs as place, a "knowing" that enmeshes people and place (Degnen 2013). Being at home thus combined a pragmatic knowing with a practice of dwelling, in the sense elaborated on by Heidegger: knowing as a mode of "dealings in" the world, through everyday appropriation and use (2008, 95), and dwelling as the event of being that unfolds in place (Heidegger 1954; Malpas 2021). Confronted with a competing, even threatening, world of practice, campaigners knowingly levied their practices of dwelling as an alternative model, an affirmation of a better way (cf. Rasza 2015).

This material and social conceptualization of home suggests the conjoining of the built environment and collective memory that Connerton observed in his treatise on forgetting; a materially enduring built environment is essential, he argued, for collective memory (2009). Memory is considered as an instrument for achieving continuity in identity, both individual and collective (Halbwachs 1992), and a positive relationship between memory and the capacity to "be at home" is supported by research among dementia patients (Dekkers 2011). The ties between space, memory, and identity described here indicate the scope of campaigners' interests in the stability of the Canongate's built environment. From the event initiated by the proposal of the Caltongate master plan, that stability could no longer be presumed but rather had to be pursued (Huyssen 2003, 17). I suggest that the idea of being at home, or knowing and dwelling in the Canongate, invoked the act of remembering as a claim of right to continuity in individual and collective identity. The dependence of this continuity on the built forms themselves and the memories and identities hung on their structures of stone and harl entailed their claims on the state. The continuity of home constituted a primary concern of the Canongate campaigners articulated in their aesthetic discourse and through the projects they undertook as the Canongate community, discussed in chapter 3. While closely related to historical housing activism, the demands of this campaign could not be confined to that tradition. Examining the practices and claims of home in the Canongate illuminates the significance of this social and material concern around which the Canongate campaigners mobilized as a project of resistance to neoliberal urbanism and an affirmation of their own alternative practices as having built and indwelling a better world (Heidegger 1954).

Elaborating on the campaigners' discourse and practices of being at home suggests the kind of "holistic focus" that Carsten and Hugh-Jones call for, one that embeds the house in the larger spatial, social, and historical context through which its meanings are negotiated (1995, 36). That larger context of Edinburgh, described in chapter 1, had by the time of my research produced the Canongate as a largely but not exclusively working-class residential neighborhood of Edinburgh's Old Town, its built environment part of a UNESCO World Heritage site, a significant portion of it put to use since the early twentieth century for social housing. The idea of "home" in working-class neighborhoods has been identified with a "we-being" of collective sociality, practiced in the individual house (Allen 2008). Such we-being in the Canongate, shaped by the collective practices of dwelling, could better be represented as unfolding in a network of neighborhood places, held together by the primary artery of Canongate Road and the tributary closes that acted as street addresses ("I stay in Dunbar's Close," and so on). Canongate Road supported social interactions that interpret in a local register the "street life" of James Holston's Brasilia (1989) or the "sidewalk ballet" of Jane Jacobs's New York (1961). As the experiences of Agnes and other mothers illustrate, the small spaces of the council houses encouraged a public social life, oriented around and along Canongate Road. In my own passages, alone or with residents, the streets, closes, and shared green spaces functioned as places of encounter and recognition.

During my fieldwork, I worked on that road at a women's clothing store (which has since become a tourist-oriented whisky and tobacco shop) and learned its rhythms through the tasks of my labor, from the early-morning lifting away of metal grates, walking them into the adjacent close and leaning them against its walls with a nod to the employee doing the same at the shop next door, to the late-afternoon binning of garbage and retrieving, replacing, and relocking of the grates. I looked forward to visits from residents popping in to chat and was occasionally surprised at the public intimacy evidenced in the many ways residents used the street: alternately as a dog run or a sidewalk, a place for starting conversations, extending invitations, and determining plans. Whereas the idea of the sidewalk ballet suggests a public material stage for social interaction, separated from the private home, what I observed in the Canongate softened the border between public and private spaces. One essential component of the street I discovered in the gaze of women whom I accompanied on walks along the tenement-lined road. This gendered gaze sought knowledge of the interior life of neighbors but did not intrude on domestic scenes like a voyeur peeping through the curtains. Instead, the women I walked with considered the material condition of the windows themselves as indications of the moral and social conditions of their caretakers.

Inverting Walter Benjamin's casually strolling and observing male flaneur, walking with residents in the Canongate was a decidedly feminine, rather hurried affair. Rather than an idle, disinterested activity of leisure, walking served as a transportation mode—to work, to shop, to school—with a gaze on the go. As we passed between row after row of tenement windows, the women who accompanied me would glance sidelong at the panes in our wake. With an angle of the chin and a sudden diversion of our conversation, I might be directed to notice an offending set of dusty, streaky windows. Most often the assumed explanation was that a council housing property formerly inhabited by a family had been bought by a private landlord and let out to transient residents, such as students or tourists, who felt no sense of responsibility for the place or for their neighbors, who would be forced to view the offensive panes. This process of turnover was evident in the Canongate, as throughout the Old Town, and although it has been slowed somewhat by Scottish Parliament's ending of the private Right to Buy council housing provisions in 2016, the entry of Airbnb and similar internet-based property businesses into the area has made short-term subletting an even more profitable venture.

I walked the Canongate with Catriona in 2017, catching up on personal lives and politics. As we crossed an intersection, we were hailed by another former campaigner, who made plans to meet with me later. Walking with him, a young man new to me but known to Catriona tried to press his cause on her, to her politely concealed impatience, but as we walked on, she exclaimed about how exhausting it is to be constantly recruited for causes because, as a well-known activist, she was assumed to be ever available for political action. As I started to sympathize, she cut me off and gestured across me, slowing abruptly. "That was Sally's house. Don't tell her about the state of her windows!" Shaking her head in disgust, she picked up the pace again, and I reflected on chance encounters, activist intrusions, and dirty windows. The unsightly windows that Catriona and others had drawn to my attention pointed to the moral failings of the neoliberal state and the moral and social uprightness of the residents themselves, who remembered their responsibilities to neighbors and the role of their own dwelling in building a world in the Canongate. The interpenetration of public and private and the expectation of the private world's display to a passing public situate the social judgments of home in the Canongate, a criterion of moral behavior. The window judgments suggest the "surplus" of meanings only partially expressed by the anticipated vocabulary of ethics and morality: this material lens unites social and economic obligations in an everyday, and decidedly aesthetic, ethical practice (Zigon 2014).

While visitors like myself may not be as likely to notice the windows, the signs of residential departure have grown increasingly apparent throughout the Canongate. In 2017 and 2018, at many stair doors, residents flagged for me the telltale indicators of the repurposing of the area's housing for a rental market: anywhere from one to half a dozen key boxes clustered like barnacles along a single ground-floor door frame. The Canongate's significance as home to such families and neighbors not only compelled residents but also attracted would-be allies from other parts of the city. This progressive depopulation, from the vantage point of 2005, seemed like it could be halted, at least to the most optimistic of the campaigners. One such campaigner, the most actively involved ally from outside the neighborhood, was an architect who had recently given up trying to live in the Old Town.

Explaining why she came to commit so much time and energy outside her private architectural practice to the Canongate campaign, she identified the residential nature of the Canongate as the primary factor that attracted her to join the campaign: "I just thought, this should be supported. These people are living here, they're bringing up families here; they're the kind of people the Old Town needs. It's going to be nothing without the residential population, and I could see the trends that were happening in the area round about where I was living, so I just decided I'm going to see what I can do to help."

This middle-class ally's desire to support the Canongate's residential population derived from its delayed participation in the "trends" she observed in the rest of the Old Town, trends related to political-economic priorities of entrepreneurial city development (Hall and Hubbard 1998; Harvey 1989). Such commitments were also expressed by members of Edinburgh-based conservation organizations the Cockburn Association and the Architectural Heritage Society, but as chapters 2 and 3 show, distaste for the specific physical features of the Canongate, combined with the city's investment in turning the neighborhood toward visitors and tourists prompted most city councilors to reject such a framing of the Canongate as the home to an existing population (Spirou 2011). As a Conservative Edinburgh city councilor during the campaign period complained, "There is nothing to *do* there!" Similarly, in a conversation with a Labour city councilor about the Canongate, he indicated that he would not feel "comfortable wandering about at night" in the area. According to the entrepreneurial logic of urban spaces appropriated by these Caltongate supporters, the Canongate as a built and social environment should invite external access and consumption, whereas, according to the residents' practices and judgments of home, the Canongate should support their efforts to make a home in and of the neighborhood.

Resistance to the Caltongate development principles was practiced in everyday life, long before the threat of development. Out of that everyday practice, the working-class residents claimed their rights to maintain the Canongate as home, to be at home in the Canongate. The support they gained from architects, built heritage conservationists, academic urbanists, and planners achieved a kind of political solidarity around the idea of home as an appropriate driver for development. That idea of home, as this section has described, entailed the interpenetration of public and private spaces—street, sidewalk, back gardens, and interior rooms—particular to the social and ethical life of the Canongate. Through the Canongate campaign, the residents' rights and practices of home were politicized by residents and their middle-class allies as a moral site of resistance to ascendant development practices in Edinburgh. Despite its centrality to this campaign, and the history of ideals relating to home mobilizing political activists in Edinburgh, home as a social and political idea has often been overlooked in place-based analyses of capitalism, cities, and social class.

## AT HOME IN WORKING-CLASS POLITICS

The Canongate residents' campaign described in the previous chapter could be tacked on to a rich narrative of housing activism in Scotland. Throughout urban Scotland, political mobilization around housing demands has provided a basis for working-class politics since the early decades of the twentieth century. Working-class women and men organized to demand fair rents and "adequate housing [as a] basic social right," and indeed the organization of rent strikes in Glasgow facilitated the consolidation of Labour's position in Scotland as the political party of the working classes (Melling 1989, 78). In that century of housing activism, the enemy of working people was most often the exploitative private landlord raising rents without necessary upkeep of the property. Popular belief in the right to obtain housing that was not overcrowded, unsanitary, dilapidated, and overpriced motivated a slate of Scottish policies, which produced a large-scale commitment to public sector housing in Scotland (Rodger 1989). As described in chapter 1, while housing activism in Edinburgh's early twentieth century involved a coalition of middle and working classes, by the latter decades of the century, the construction of council housing on the city's peripheries, the introduction of the right to buy for council housing tenants, and the drifting divergence of conservation and housing interests contributed to a diminishing sense of solidarity between these groups. For the Canongate residents in the early twenty-first century, the increasing scarcity of city-center council housing meant that fewer working-class allies shared their predicament, in which the conservation of the historic built environment appeared as a corollary of housing concerns. While the Canongate campaign might thus appear to continue the tradition of Scottish housing activism in residents' advocacy for the retention and even for the expansion of council housing in their neighborhood, as the previous chapter indicates, their campaign activities additionally sought conservation ends only sporadically addressed in twentieth-century working-class housing activism.

Recognizing home as a site of resistance is both old hat and new news. Ideas of home have been represented as sites for moral and material agency, significant to individual acts of resistance (Buch 2015), psychological well-being (Radin 1982), and the construction of both individual and larger social identities (Carsten and Hugh-Jones 1995). As ideas, *home* and *house* are often used interchangeably in everyday talk, but they have represented objects of interest for rather distinct streams of academic study. The material house has been the object of greater interest to analyses of architecture and material culture (Miller 1987, Waterson 2014), social class (Zhang 2010), inequality (Klaufus and Ouweneel 2015; Taylor 2013), and state power (Fehérváry 2013). Studies of home have been embedded within research on memory (Bahloul 1996), social change, and loss and migration (Sa'di and Abu-Lughod 2007). A few works have bridged the streams, seeking to understand the roles of houses as home in events and processes of everyday life (Carsten and Hugh-Jones 1995; Miller 1988, 2010; Waterson 2014).

Studies of life in urban capitalism have foregrounded the material properties and economic costs of housing as central concerns, illuminating a spatialized pattern of inequality that both indicates and determines differentiated access to public resources (Desmond 2016; Taylor 2013). Analyses of urban development have shown how concerns with housing stock drive private and state-sponsored gentrification, and residents' concerns with neighborhood transformation at least implicitly indicate that the home is perceived as encompassing more than the structure of a privately owned or publicly rented residence (McDonogh 1999; Sawalha 2010). Ethnographic studies in particular provide the social and cultural contexts that suggest what having a house means to individuals and families, but few of these have sought to understand the imagination and invocation of home as a means of engaging these political-economic processes. The Canongate campaigners invoked the idea of home, and particularly their right to be at home in the neighborhood, as a localized logic for resistance to neoliberalizing urban development, especially refusing the concomitant representation of houses as "commodities" or "property," in the words of the campaigners, as the following section explains.

That the idea of home should provide motivation to resist the imposition of capitalist market logic might surprise us. It might at the least have surprised Marx, who in his correspondence dismissed the ideals of home as "petty-bourgeois sentimentality" (1978 [1846], 142) unsuited to a modern socialist society. Instead, Marx focused on the shared experience of waged labor as the basis for uniting workers to overturn the capitalist order, and property as the means to politically recognized power in the capitalist state (Barclay and Carr 2013; Folbre 2009). While Engels, in his travels to English manufacturing cities, detailed the deplorable conditions within and around many houses of the poor (Engels 2009 [1844], 66), his and Marx's critical interests remained focused on the socioeconomic manifestations of capitalism: wealth and divisions of waged labor, from the individual household to the state. Their interests in place primarily derived from the necessary link they perceived between territory, property, and the state (Engels 2010 [1884], 211). As subsequent ethnographies have shown, the political and economic ideals of Marx and Engels, in translation by Communist states, produced specific household arrangements (Fehérváry 2013), but Marxist critiques of capitalism and political-economic ideals have placed little stock in the ideals of home as sources of revolutionary fervor.

As one of the most influential Marxist scholars writing on cities, Lefebvre's concept of the "right to the city" skirts the idea of the politicized home in his identification of "habitation" rather than citizenship as constituting the basis of urbanites' political claims (1996, 158; see Purcell 2002, 102). But the significance of habitation for Lefebvre lies not in the material basis for dwelling but in its constitution by the practices of everyday life; it has been the critical interpreters of Lefebvre's intellectual legacy like James Holston who has expanded his framework to highlight the impacts of, for instance, Brazilian peripheral housing practices on urban and national politics (Holston 2009). Many Marxist interpretations of working-class activism in late twentieth-century welfare states emphasized the role of the workplace and the experience of labor in fostering solidarity for political mobilization (Challinor 1977; Coates 1981; Hinton and Hyman 1975), an interpretation maintained even by their critics (McKibbin 1984; McLean 1983). As contributors to Rodger's volume on nineteenth-century Scottish housing have pointed out, however, housing concerns mobilized working classes more effectively in early twentieth-century Britain, from Glasgow's rent strikes (Melling 1989) and across urban Scotland, including Edinburgh, through northern England's industrial towns and London (McCrone and Elliot 1989, 225). These two gendered streams of political mobilization fed one another; the organizing of labor through unionization was often assisted by neighborhood-based activism in which women played a prominent role, in both the United States and Britain. This working-class organization presented a credible threat to capitalist dominance, with both states ultimately avoiding more comprehensive revolution by enacting a series of legislative reforms in the practices and guarantees of laboring life, as well as provisions for working-class housing.

The popular account of working-class political mobilization has, despite the contributions of women and housing campaigns, come to be represented as a masculinized triumph of labor union organization. Though the mythologized events of "Red Clydeside" in Glasgow depended on rent strikes organized by women like Mary Barbour, Helen Crawfurd, and Agnes Dollan, the heroes of that historical movement have typically been men. Socialist leader John Maclean was lauded as a "pioneer" on a commemorative memorial in 1973 (and, more recently, as a "hero" [Bell 2018]), long before Mary Barbour got a statue in 2018. The contributions of working-class women to the causes of political mobilization and influence, despite being excluded from trade unions, have often been acknowledged but overshadowed by the masculine politics of labor (Gordon 1991). A growing body of literature has taken up the rewriting of this historical narrative, foregrounding the contributions of women (Breitenbach 1993; Gordon 1991; Goring 2018; Hughes 2010), and Edinburgh-based researchers have been writing the previously invisible histories of women reformers working in the Canongate (Darling 2015). Since labor politics has long represented the manifest political agency of the working classes, the task of reframing working-class politics remains as urgent as ever (Barclay and Carr 2013).

The urban geography in which women had engaged in political activism would shift over the twentieth century, however, distancing them from the public spaces of organization at the same time that strategic political developments dealt blows to the labor activism and influence of working-class men. The transitions in housing development following World War II, which saw Scottish cities like Edinburgh investing in the large-scale construction of peripheral council housing estates, had the effect of isolating women in households distant from the city centers. While labor-based activism continued to speak for working-class causes in Scotland for decades as these estates continued to be constructed, the onset of economic recession in the 1970s ushered in a political era in which Margaret Thatcher in Britain and Ronald Reagan in the United States were elected on agendas that sought to break this instrument of collective working-class influence. While the impacts of these events on labor politics have been well documented, I suggest that the estate-led retreat of women from the public political sphere contributed significant yet underappreciated blows to working-class political influence. In Britain, not only did Thatcher's government close mines that had formed the laboring backbone of working-class communities from the English Midlands to the Scottish Lowlands; the provision of working-class housing suffered when state funds to cities were dramatically cut, ultimately reducing the total housing stock available to low-income families and ensuring that the majority of their housing options in cities like Edinburgh would be situated on peripheral estates.

As discussed in chapter 2, the imposition of Thatcher's neoliberal policies has reframed city responsibilities and in doing so demoted working-class residents from a central concern to an indirect one. The welfare of urban working classes became an outcome derivative of the city's short-term economic gains, thereby situating urban working classes in a depoliticized public sphere in which decisions about their benefit were directed to economic experts, which they awaited in neighborhoods with the greatest differential between actual and potential revenues (Harvey 1989, 2005). In other words, working-class homes became the most likely targets for urban renewal projects, creating housing precarity reminiscent of the industrial era and yet at a moment when the working classes' instruments for political influence, via development consultation, were rhetorically valued but pragmatically neutralized.

In the Canongate, the labor basis for political action had been removed with the closure of the breweries in the 1980s. Unlike the experience on many peripheral estates, the centrality of this Old Town location facilitated the political involvement of women, as reflected in the leadership of the CCF/SOOT campaign, but this activist program could not rely on support from proximate workplace associations. Experientially and geographically distant from labor bases of organization, the campaign mobilized its supporters around the idea of home and supported that cause by invoking the lack of available opportunities for both labor and consumption. To me, it seemed that the class character of the neighborhood and its residents were distinguished not by the labor they participated in but by the council houses themselves; working-class residents almost by definition rented their homes from the council. Parallel to twentieth-century working-class politics that levied demands addressing laboring conditions based on shared laboring experiences in a capitalist workforce, this twenty-first-century working-class campaign organized around home has made claims that speak from residents' experiences of precarity due to neoliberal urbanization. Assertions of the right to home, a knowing and dwelling practice essential to the coherence of a Canongate aesthetic, afforded a distinctively political challenge to the neoliberal order, one appropriate to the material and social threats to their neighborhood posed by the Caltongate master plan.

The precarity of the Canongate residents' material and social world, which became apparent to them in light of the Caltongate proposal, suggests a potential breakdown in the processes of "reification" and "world-building" described by Hannah Arendt. Arendt draws Marxist analysis into a more enduring material domain productive of everyday life, thereby providing a framework for recognizing the Canongate residents' attachment to home as a form of political-economic critique. As Arendt has argued, ultimately the most consequential human effort is that of "world-building." Dissatisfied with Marx's characterization of humans as the *animal laborans*, Arendt points out that Marx failed to fully parse the associated processes and products of productive activity, and she provides a corrective distinction between labor and work, associated respectively with spheres of short-term and long-term productivity (cf. Bloch and Parry 1989). She describes labor as a never-ending process, due to the almost immediately sequenced activities of production and destruction, which occur in the form of consumption, the results of which fill our wastebaskets and landfills. Work, by contrast, produces enduring things that may be used rather than consumed, and she argues that work and its products should be recognized for their contribution to "stabilizing human life" (Arendt 1958, 137). The "worldly" character of life is achieved through work, she explains. "Human life, in so far as it is world-building, is engaged in a constant process of reification, and the degree of worldliness of produced things, which all together form the human artifice, depends upon their greater or lesser permanence in the world itself" (95–96). The increasing ease of material productivity, observed presciently from 1958, suggests the possibility of a mismatch between the things of the world and their consumption: of properly permanent things being consumed as if they had been intended for the sphere of labor rather than work. Consumption, in Arendt's use, is restrained to a more narrow definition than is common in contemporary anthropological discourse, indicating the "using-up" of a given thing rather than any activity outside the sphere of economic production (see Graeber 2011). "In our need for more and more rapid replacement of the worldly things around us, we can no longer afford to use them, to respect and preserve their inherent durability; we must consume, devour, as it were, our houses and furniture and cars as though they were the 'good things' of nature which spoil uselessly if they are not drawn swiftly into the never-ending cycle of man's metabolism with nature" (Arendt 1958, 125–26). I suggest that this inappropriate transfer, from the sphere of work to that of labor, from use to consumption, and by implication destruction, describes well the move that Canongate residents identified in the proposal of the Caltongate redevelopment plan. The proposed demolition of historic buildings, entailing the replacement of a properly durable cityscape, as well as services for an enduring population with amenities for a transient one, entailed a loss of the "worldliness" of the Canongate.

Arendt's observations, from conditions of an economy still thriving on industrial manufacture, nevertheless provide insight into a later stage of capitalist development and the still-accelerated processes of demolition and replacement characteristic of neoliberal urbanism. The enduring quality of Arendt's observations lends credence to the continuity of economic logics from mid- to late-capitalist formations of political economy. The neoliberal political shifts that loosened the governmental fetters that had once constrained the application of such logics have drawn urban built environments into a metabolic cycle of strategic destruction in service of urban capital accumulation. With this corruption of the processes of work in view, Arendt's conceptualization of world-building anticipates the political mobilizations around the crumbling of the world, even though she herself conceived of political action as a sphere separate from economic activity.

Inconveniently accompanying the attenuation of labor politics as an instrument of working-class mobilization, urban working-class communities that inhabit neighborhoods of perceived economic advantage have become the most vulnerable. The Canongate campaigners' emphasis on home as a right of the working classes suggests not a retreat from the political but a politicizing insistence on their collective right to be at home as a means of contesting what Deleuze and Guattari have termed "deterritorialization," the reorganizing of places and their replacement by novel configurations of persons, names, and functions in service of the capitalist generation of wealth (1987). Efficacy in the politics of home as in the politics of labor, as well as the host of social and political movements leveraged against such deterritorializations (Rasza 2015; Graeber 2009), depends on collective solidarity, advocated by anthropologists of labor like Paul Durrenberger, that requires the "joint action of all in the support of any individual"—or, as the case may be, in support of any neighborhood. Such action is made more difficult by the popularization of a neoliberal economic consciousness that focuses on "individual rather than collective interests" (2009, 16), or the triumph of Edinburgh councilor Donald Anderson's logic of "bettering oneself" over the Canongate campaigners' logic of accountability to the communal group. The transition from industrial to neoliberal capitalism, with its accelerated turnover of the built environment and weakening of collective labor-based mobilization, has motivated the politicization of home as a new, or perhaps renewed, form of oppositional and affirmative working-class politics.

### The Politics of Home: Singular and Inalienable

Sally, throwing her arms wide to gesture toward the Old Town around her, exclaimed, "These are the dying embers of the residential city center!"

I first heard these words as I stood with Sally, hands stuffed deep in my jacket pockets to shrug off a spitting July rain, on the pavement in front of the Jeffrey Street Arches, a street level below the tenements of the Canongate on the edge of Waverley Valley. In 2008, the arches had been a sloping street of rather grim, boarded-up spaces that the campaigners had hoped to get redeveloped into affordable art spaces, but in 2017, we stood before a bright row of new shops, selling goods to higher-end visitors. At the time, I was focused on what Sally was saying about the larger spatial pattern of the city center, particularly the exchange of functions represented in the built environment: commerce replacing residence. When we walked through the Canongate neighborhood in 2017, it was Sally's first return to the area since its redevelopment had commenced. We had discussed the possibility of this visit the previous morning over mugs of tea as we sat on the front steps of her house, when she confided the reason for her avoidance,

> After I moved here, I had an aversion to the [Canongate]. I couldn't go. It was almost like this invisible electric fence repelling me.... [The Old Town] is not a living space any more... Edinburgh is just this event that's

happening three hundred and sixty-five days a year. And when you're still trying to have normal life and your three hundred and sixty-five days is being here with your family and school or work, you just feel more and more like that [the Old Town] is corralled off. . . . Well, I've got a couple of friends still alive in there, but what would I want with tartan bagpipe music being piped out?

After we had talked more about the changes in the neighborhood, about which Sally was well informed despite her self-imposed distance, she decided, despite my offer to forgo a potentially unpleasant walk, that she could "work up to" the visit. The next day, we met in front of the Scottish Parliament building under a low ceiling of rain clouds, and for the next hour, Sally evaluated out loud the changes in her former home, shop by shop, block by block. I had a notebook with me, so she suggested we take inventory of the shops along Canongate Road. She warmed rapidly to the role of tour guide, guiding us along a newly unfamiliar path. Sally called out the shop names, along with impromptu histories, as I scribbled hurriedly, naming the owners she still knew and speculating as to the whereabouts and occupations of those who had left, like Mike who used to run the bacon roll shop that had been knocked out by the New Waverley development's arched pend. We counted twenty-two gift or tourist shops selling a spectrum of "tartan tat," ten cafés and three restaurants, three pubs and two hotels, and fifteen shops or other spaces, like the Museum of Edinburgh in the historic Huntly House, which Sally identified as "local."

Sally's intimate knowledge of these shops, the tenements rising above them, and the former occupants of both, reminded me, step by step, that residence was never and is never general but always particular: not *a* home but *someone's* home. The Canongate had been Sally's home, and she claimed it through her knowledge of the people and places that had made it singular, the knowledge that gave her both pleasure and pain to recite to me, in the aftermath of its dissolution. In guiding me through her home, Sally allowed me to understand that her home, and in fact each place called a home by someone, is a representation of spatial and social character that is identifiable by its singularity, a trait of objects and persons that are "uncommon, incomparable, unique . . . and therefore not exchangeable for anything else" (Kopytoff 1986, 69). This trait of singularity therefore suggests the home's resistance to the kind of generalization necessary for establishing market value; to conceptualize a place as home removes it from the marketplace of commodity exchange. As Igor Kopytoff and others have shown, however, such identities are not permanent but processual; material objects may move through various stages, becoming more or less singular and therefore less or more available to market exchange (Appadurai 1986). A given structure may be fondly regarded as the family home one week and then, due to a change in circumstances—happy or unfortunate—the next week may be transferred to commodity status, as "real estate" for sale.

Neoliberal urban development practices incline toward the ever-increasing commoditization of the built environment, representing places as "goods," identifiable "ultimately as figures in the ledger" (Tuan 1996, 156). The particularities or "genius" of a given place are assessed with respect to the "economic advantage" they convey, but according to the depersonalized expectations of commodity exchange, beyond the determinations of payment for real estate purchase, there are few requirements for accountability to the people who, by their own reckoning, belong to that place. This extraction of place from localized contexts of its production and significance for exchange in the generalizable form of real estate suggests the "alienation" process that Anna Tsing has identified as "that form of disentanglement that allows the making of capitalist assets [in which] capitalist commodities are removed from their lifeworlds to serve as counters in the making of further investments" (2015, 133). While Tsing's analysis addressed this process in global commodity chains, the application to urban development practices helps to explain the contests over the appropriate relationship between people and place that so typically characterize public debates. When the Caltongate proposal was under consideration, for instance, I heard multiple proponents of the development, from city councilors to an architect working on the proposal, express their indignation that the residents of the area believed they had a special right to accommodation of their expectations. According to these commodity exchange assumptions, the residents' demands were inappropriately personal and therefore selfish, easily dismissed as characteristically shortsighted NIMBY (Not in My Backyard) protests.

But for Sally and the community campaigners—and, more to the point, likely for most people when their home is under consideration (see, for instance, Eric Avila's 2014 research on the American freeway revolts)—assertions of a place as home serve as political claims. Identifying a place as home asserts its appropriate removal from the sphere of market transaction as a singular and fundamentally unexchangeable material good. Neoliberal urban development, in the form of the Caltongate proposal, threatened to subsume the Canongate in an ever-expanding commoditization of Edinburgh's built environment, and so the residents sought to reclaim the Canongate by marking it as home and therefore inappropriate for this transaction. Against the generalizability of the Canongate as real estate, residents asserted a political and moral claim to its particularity as *their* home and their right as residents to continue to *be at home* there. They rejected outright the alienation necessary for conversion to the real estate commodity, and through the commodity's sale, for accumulation by state and private actors.

This claim is political in the sense articulated by Appadurai (1986), concerned with contesting the terms of exchange and value set by the neoliberal logic of property-based capital accumulation (Gordon 1999; Harvey 1985; Smith 2002). Such a claim also levies a moralized challenge to the processes and effects of this regime of transaction. When the Canongate residents represent the Canongate as home, this claim situates the place as belonging properly to that restricted economic sphere identified by Maurice Bloch and Jonathan Parry, in their comparative analysis of exchange and morality, as the sphere of long-term social reproduction, as against an alternate construction of Canongate as real estate that is dedicated to exchange in the pursuit of short-term profits (1989). In these ways, the politics of home, as the strategy that emerged in response to the Caltongate proposal, represents a locally specific counterclaim against the processes of neoliberal urbanism. It is a politics that emphasizes particularity in the face of generalization, and by this means it elevates the role of the local community over a centralized, and distant, decision-making process. The idea of home as invoked in the Canongate campaign politicized a Canongate aesthetic as an ethical alternative to the commodifying plans for the Caltongate proposal. As discussed in the next chapter, the ethical framing of home has emerged again, in significantly related ways, in the arguments for Scottish independence made by these individuals.

The invocations of home in the residents' campaign sometimes explicitly identified an individual family house and at other times connected that house to the larger neighborhood, thus including both private and public spaces. The following paragraphs explore several invocations of home, representative of a larger pattern of discourse and practice, which indicate its part in a place-based vocabulary of resistance. The examples described below emphasize home as an ideal communicating embeddedness—in spatial and social context—and thus indivisibility, regardless of the value of the place on a real estate market and regardless of ownership structure, state or private. The essentially social and relational nature of the home additionally enabled residents to invoke this idea to assert the singularity of their individual houses and to add a relational stipulation to the eventual market transaction when this transaction was seen as inevitable. Such claims to home represent individual acts of resistance to the despecifying deterritorialization of the Canongate, asserting their personal relationships to this place over Caltongate's market-based reorganizations of the same place.

### *"Common Good" Property*

Residents often contested the generalizing alienation of the Canongate by asserting a fundamental difference between home and property. This contrast depicted the Canongate as home, embedded in a network of social relations, as against the Canongate as property, which was identified with private ownership by the socially disembedded individual. As one campaigner put it, frustration with the Caltongate plan for the Canongate's redevelopment was "not just . . . personal" but reflected the plan's impacts on "my home and my community!" Such residents argued from collective rights to home rather than individual rights to property, a pattern that reflects the fact that many of the campaigners were not property owners but municipal authority renters. No representation of the residents as the "community" of the Canongate, or of the Canongate as the place identified with this community, could therefore rely on most residents' rights to private property appropriation and its "social entitlements" (Hann 1998, 7). The identification of the Canongate as socially embedded home, however, did produce one remarkable attempt to resist the disembedding of the Canongate represented by the sale of the land to the private developer by reforming the legal property terms themselves. The goal of this attempt was to enable residents to attain property rights to their home, but as members of a collective trustee organization rather than as individual owners. For a brief period during the campaign, residents fashioned their claim to the Canongate in the form of collective property rights by invoking the common good designation of the land in question.

In 2006, the Canongate campaign leaders discovered that the land being sold by the city council to the developer was designated in council documents as held in the common good. Sally collaborated with a future

Green Party Member of the Scottish Parliament to research common good law to attempt to leverage a collective property claim or at least collective resistance to the sale. Ultimately, the claim was unsuccessful, as common good land has effectively become land transferred to ownership by the local authorities in Scotland, a designation that has provided the councils with a sizable source of potential revenues but has produced little political accountability as to its use. Residents thus found that they lacked the support of contemporary property law, with no comparable securities afforded to renters from the state, as individuals or as a community. Their resistance could not marshal state law for ideological or legal support of their claims as the insurgent citizens of Brazil have been able to invoke their constitutional right to a home (Holston 2009).[2] While discussions about common good land continued throughout the campaign, after the first flurry of research and some public commentary, the campaigners decided to pursue other avenues for influence. This claim always fascinated me, however, as an attempt to leverage property law in support of their own collective belonging. Marilyn Strathern argues that the ability to claim ownership over some thing as property has the social impact of "effecting an identity" (1996, 30). In the invoking of a collective or "common" property claim, I suggest that the Canongate campaigners, in keeping with their claims to represent the community of the Canongate, claimed an identity with the Canongate that was expressed in the assertion of inalienable relationships between people and place as foundational to the terms of property rights. This attempt to leverage property law, even a disappointingly defunct one, resonates with a global array of varied expansions of property claims that have proliferated as adaptations to neoliberal contexts seeking to "disrupt" traditional divisions between persons and things (see Hirsch 2010 for a review of these examples). For the campaigners, this common good property claim offered just one example of political claims made in the name of home, by which they contested the alienation necessitated by the real estate transaction-as-accumulation strategy of neoliberal development.

### *"Not a Commodity"*

This strategy of claims to home as a rhetorical removal from the world of market transactions has continued to be invoked by Canongate residents long after the campaign has ended, indicating that this framing was not only a campaign strategy. In this case, claims to the inalienable quality of home were also leveraged significantly by one of the few property-owning campaigners, indicating the prevalence of this moral framing of home independent of the experience of council renting. Framing a tenement flat as a home has served to critique the possibility of a home's premature transfer to the general category of real estate, when it properly resides in the sphere of the personal and particular. When I visited the Canongate in 2017, I met for tea with one of the few former campaigners who has remained in the Canongate, primarily because he owns his flat. This man Tom, a retiree who has continued to be involved in the work of the Edinburgh Old Town Development Trust, relayed to me his aggravating "harassment" by a neighbor who repeatedly contacted him about buying his flat. The flat, owned by Tom for more than a decade, occupied a desirable position on an upper floor of a well-kept tenement, and his neighbor across the hall continued to hint at his interest in purchasing the flat, to Tom's growing annoyance. After his initial refusals were not respected, Tom looked his neighbor in the eye and stated flatly, "Look, my house is a home. It's not a commodity. Think on that." Tom reenacted the scene for me with the same injury and indignation. As with the other campaigners, Tom's identification of his flat as a home rather than a commodity enabled him to remove it conceptually from market circulation as a relational object. In this case, the neighbor's proffer of immediate or even deferred transaction for the flat provided the backdrop against which the singularity of the house as his home was constructed as support for its proper circulation in a world of personal relationships. Tom affirmed the decisively relational quality of his flat when he confided to me that, whenever he did eventually sell his flat, he would use whatever power was available to him as seller to prevent his neighbor from being the one to buy it.

This stipulation indicated that the inevitable, eventual market transfer of ownership for this flat would require a positive *personal* relationship: the flat would therefore move through a market that is not impersonal but relational, not as a generalized commodity but as a singular good. In this case, then, Tom imagined that he could transform the conditions of the market itself to accommodate his singular home. Asserting the social conditions of this sale thus constituted an act of resistance against the encroaching marketization of the world of goods and services, reclaiming Tom's flat from this properly (in principle if not always in practice) impersonal market. The tenuous nature of this resistance, as an act counter to standard real estate practice, caused Tom some anxiety, and he wondered what legal safeguards he would need to employ to protect his repersonalization of the sale of his flat. In his refusal to commodify, this Canongate resident was carrying on as a property owner the resistance in which he had participated as a campaigner: resisting the abstraction of place for economic gain, even though as owner of his property, he bore the legal privilege to do so. Tom's resistance was echoed by the Canongate residents who had reported to me that they had refused their right to buy their council-rented properties on the principle that the council should provide homes for people; in both cases, the impersonal market circulation of property was rejected precisely for the weakness of its relationships—between individuals or between individuals and the state—and therefore the lack of accountability for its transactions.

### *"A Private Green"*

While Tom's refusal of his neighbor's offer exemplified a resistance among Canongate campaigners to the marketization of place in the Canongate, this resistance had never been unanimous, as indeed the offending neighbor suggests. Although the campaigners believed strongly in the rightness of their framing and practice, their spatial practice caused them to come into conflict with a property owner in the Canongate on at least one other occasion. In 2008, during an afternoon of strategizing and reconnoitering in a Canongate storefront, one of the campaigners, a usually free-spirited woman in her fifties named Jess, drew up a chair and recounted a bewildering encounter. On this rare (and therefore much prized) sunny spring afternoon, she had taken a blanket and a book to one of the beloved "back greens" of a tenement near her flat. Then, as she lay on the blanket reading her book, another woman approached her with a stern and unusual injunction, "This is a private green, and you cannot use it." The campaigner protested, "But I live just 'round the corner in Gullan's Close!" The back greens were generally presumed to be accessible to all Canongate residents, and policing of private access was virtually unheard of. "I'm sorry, but no. You'll have to leave." The campaigner gathered her blanket, muttering her astonishment, and returned home to deposit blanket and book before marching straight to the Canongate Project's community space to tell her story. The tale was greeted with outraged head-shaking and adamant exclamations: "It shouldn't *be* like that!" The woman's framing of private property as space generally treated as common land, whatever its official status, highlighted both the practice that had been normalized among campaigners and its vulnerability to legal exception. The indignant responses that this exception generated from the resident campaigners confirmed the uncommonness of the interaction while indicating the precarity of norms that counter property law, even in the Canongate before its redevelopment.

The actions of Sally, Tom, and Jess convey closely related framings of the Canongate as a common asset to its residents, its private spaces mediated by their relationships, and its public spaces open to use by all. Their insistence on the primacy of these socially embedded meanings of a resolutely particular built environment resisted the disembedding transformations and reorganizations of these built forms as "figures in the ledger." This form of resistance expresses well a political aesthetic advocated by these residents, which described a moral relationship in the order between material, individual, and community life (Rancière 2004). These emic distinctions between home and property or home and commodity attempt to resocialize the practices of urban development and, in doing so, to reject the deterritorializing logic of neoliberal capitalism. The discourse of home in the Canongate—as inalienable, singular, and consisting in the entanglement of public and private—affirmed the practices of everyday life and elevated them to an idealized aesthetic, opposed to the neoliberal aesthetic of the Caltongate proposal in virtually every possible way.

### Forging Solidarity through a Politics of Home: World-Building and Everyday Life

The claims to home made by Canongate campaigners were not levied by individuals or groups who had produced the built environment; they had rather inherited and inhabited its forms and spaces. Arendt's emphasis on the "enduring" quality and "permanence" of the world so built, however, suggests that a compelling link may be fostered between generations through the material world, even as Agnes's recollections of parenting in the Canongate convey her socialization into practices of inhabiting it. While Canongate residents did not produce the stone and mortar forms of their tenement buildings, they did accomplish the considerable work, in Arendt's sense of the word, of transforming standard council house provisions into personalized and relational spaces (Miller 1988), which were invested in the social reproduction of their community. Sometimes this work involved biological reproduction, as at least one of the campaigners had given birth in her flat, a practice that appeared in the reminiscences of former residents as well.

The worldliness of the Canongate thus combined the internal spaces of the tenements with their austere, often water-stained faces, both of which increased their significance due to proximity to buildings on the national historic buildings register and their participation in a UNESCO World Heritage site. These historic buildings would provide a material key to the solidarity that formed between residents and conservationists, both of whom, for related but distinct reasons, identified the Canongate's built environment as an inalienable resource (Starecheski 2019). The degree to which the histories of these structures were considered significant by the residents, before the proposal of the Caltongate development, is suggested by narratives like Agnes's, which were common among Canongate residents. My experiences strolling through museums with residents, as well as listening to many stories of neighborhood history and personalities like the one conarrated by Agnes and Margaret, lend credence to the ordinariness of such practices, but my position as an American and an outsider to the Canongate who arrived during the campaign, necessarily limits my perspective on what constituted "ordinary" practice before that campaign. In the aftermath of this proposal and the subsequent founding of the CCF and SOOT community organizations, remembering, particularly within a UNESCO World Heritage site, offered resources to empower the campaigners in their resistance (see Cole 1998; Sawalha 2010). Whereas according to resident reminiscences, sharing stories of the Canongate helped to socialize residents into their relationships and responsibilities in the era before the development proposal, the names, dates, architects, and functions of the buildings threatened with demolition suddenly became essential information once the Caltongate development was proposed. The everyday practices of social memory took a decidedly architectural turn, inflected with the urgency of justifying the permanence of the Canongate's built environment, and both knowledge and affect reinforced their shared cause with the city's conservationists.

The CCF/SOOT campaigners brought a succession of speakers, activists, architects, and building conservationists to speak during the Canongate Project and to give presentations at campaign meetings on the necessity of permanence of both the built environment and its occupants. The resident campaigners' emphasis on the historic character of the Canongate appealed to the academics and professionals with an interest in built heritage conservation, and the residents' goals of continued habitation of the area promised to conserve the patterns of everyday life characteristic of the historic Canongate. Thus the home discourse of the campaigners resonated with the aesthetic discourse of their allies in built heritage conservation, and the politics of home, though originally marshaled to mobilize Canongate residents, facilitated the expression of solidarity between these allies. In interviews with members of the Cockburn Association, discussions of "good" versus "bad" development advocated ideas like "sympathetic design" and a "heterogeneous mix" of buildings that convey a "sense of identity," ideas that fit easily with the Canongate residents' discourse of the characteristics of their home. Shared perceptions of the inalienability of the Canongate as a historic neighborhood persuaded heritage advocates and residential campaigners to make common ground with—and to achieve coherence between—each other's interests in challenging the threatened deterritorialization of the Canongate.

Additionally, the lone city councilor who voted against the Caltongate plan, a Green Party member with whom I met following the vote, articulated a rationale in keeping with the aesthetic-moral critique of the campaigners. On viewing the plans, he observed that they "didn't look striking in any way," and concluded that they failed to fit with the local area architecturally. But more problematic, he emphasized, was the plan's lack of consideration for the needs and interests of local residents, and he argued that "there are quite a lot of people still living in the Old Town, whereas a five-star hotel and conference center doesn't fit with that." The perceived injustice of the lack of consideration for residential concerns also prompted the involvement of other local political activists, who supported the campaign by giving free lectures, hosting guided tours of the area and showing documentary films on topics like "Activist Edinburgh." The solidarity that formed around this mix of interests, from building conservation to environmental sustainability and political justice, temporarily mobilized local residents, practicing architects and urban planners, and local political activists in the politics of home.

Despite its grounding in neighborhood-specific practices and discourse—what I have called a Canongate aesthetic—the politics of home as presented here sought to build alliances and solidarities external to the neighborhood itself. The openness of the Canongate campaign suggests an important quality of the neighborhood itself. As a central, densely traveled area, which grants its residents access to the city and the city access to its own streets, the connectivity and visibility of the Canongate have been echoed by the political networking of the campaigners themselves. As the following chapter shows, campaign leaders perceived a sympathy between the sense of life defended in this Canongate campaign and the boldly aesthetic political vision cultivated by the Scottish National Party.

CONCLUSION

Muriel Spark's Edinburgh, introduced as an central character in her 1961 novel *The Prime of Miss Jean Brodie*, recognized the multiplicity contained in a city that was constantly being built and interpreted by, even as it sustained, its inhabitants. "And many times throughout her life Sandy knew with a shock, when speaking to people whose childhood had been in Edinburgh, that there were other people's Edinburghs quite different from hers, and with which she held only the names of districts and streets and monuments in common" (Spark 1961, 33).

Such multiplicity may very well strain at the solidarities cultivated within a city like Edinburgh, but this chapter has shown how from the neighborhood of the Canongate, a distinctive sense of place gathered in such a way as to extend and incorporate persons and projects beyond the geographical and experiential boundaries of that location.

Arendt's emphasis on the role of the objective world in sustaining human life and meaning making suggests some distinctions between a politics of labor and a politics of home, and the gendered history of each begs comparative study. Both require solidarity expressed through collective action, and as the Canongate case indicates, the politics of home does not necessitate closure or exclusion. Both residents and conservationists forged solidarity based on the singularity and inalienability of place. As anthropologist of labor Paul Durrenberger has shown, possibilities for collective action among working classes and their allies must constantly contend with the powerfully mobilized collective organization on behalf of private corporations (2009, 16; see also Doukas 2003; Fones-Wolf 1994). Both the politics of labor and the politics of home are vulnerable to the geographies of dispersal that are characteristic, even instrumental, in neoliberal urban processes. As these processes have generalized and transacted places for the processes of capitalist accumulation, however, locally specific aesthetics offer alternatives for evaluating and conceptualizing places. While it is a rare neighborhood that can claim the conservation interests focused on Edinburgh's Old Town, the cultivation of solidarities around a particular, shared aesthetic may be pursued from many locations (see Interlude 4).

At the time of writing, Sally resides in a nearby neighborhood, Tom has moved to a small town in East Lothian, and Catriona lives in a council-rented flat in the historically working-class, but rapidly gentrifying, area of Leith. One might expect that the Canongate aesthetic, having served as a place-bound instrument for mobilization, would have lost its significance, or at least its plausibility, when they departed that neighborhood. But instead, in my ongoing relationships with these individuals, I have observed that this political aesthetic has been adapted to a new geography linking place and persons in inalienable relationships. This new geography, however, is hardly new at all: it is Scotland, or rather an idea of Scotland as a nation whose moral order bears more than a passing resemblance to the ideals of home once pursued in the Canongate.

While the campaigners have mostly moved out in anticipation of the neighborhood's redevelopment, the Canongate of course remains. When I visited in 2018, I rented a room in the hotel that now inhabits the stripped-out shell of the MacRae tenement building. I insisted on a room overlooking Canongate Road to the south rather than the newly created "plaza" and the construction site cum council headquarters on the north side of the building. After booking my room, I wondered what perspectives the room would reveal—and what it would feel like as an anthropologist and friend of the former residents to suddenly obtain access to what had been a council flat and a home, via my market transaction, without permission of anyone personally invested in the flat. As the key card mechanism clicked and I swung the door open, I stood for a moment on the threshold, deeply ambivalent but admittedly professionally and personally curious.

The unobstructed view told me that I need not have bothered with the ceremony. "If IKEA made a hotel," I muttered, dragging my suitcase across the wood-printed laminate floor and pressing the light panel out of habit. The whole place could have been navigated by rote; as a habituated traveler

Fig. 4.1 View of Canongate Road through a dirty window in the hotel formerly known as the MacRae tenement. Photo by author.

of conferences and lectures, I knew the smooth surfaces and artful angles, the laminate, plastic, and aluminum accents designed according to a minimalist Nordic aesthetic. This place was designed for me, I realized, or for the visitor I was supposed to be, the tastes I was supposed to prefer—and despite my disappointment, I have never been one to dismiss the charms of IKEA. My eyes failed to register this room as a place; however, it instead read glaringly as an arrangement of imported consumer postures and desires. I walked straight through it to the window, the opening that I knew would provide details for my eyes to examine, views to study. As I approached, I could see hewn stone through the sheer curtain and the vague shapes of dark windows on the tenement across the road, so I eagerly drew the curtain back—and abruptly stopped, my eyes distracted by the streaky, dust-patterned pane of the window instead. I heard Catriona's disapproving voice in my head, "Look at the state of these windows."

## Notes

1. In a surprising coincidence, an Edinburgh councilor—who had been one of Caltongate's chief proponents and was voted out of office in 2007 following a scandal in which he made a rude gesture to the Canongate campaigners on his way into a reception hosted by Caltongate's would-be developer—took up a painting course at the same time. While Sally finds her own place making art in Edinburgh, she is often faced with the art of her erstwhile political opponent.

2. See Hohmann 2013 on the challenges of enforcing any such right, due to limitations of resources.

## INTERLUDE 4

# DOOCOTS AND COMMUNITY LAND USE IN GLASGOW

IN 2018, I FOUND MYSELF stepping up to a sturdy wooden ladder to climb some eight feet into a dark, close space lined with wire-caged rows of rustling pigeons. They cocked their curious, glassy stares at me, and I marveled at the unexpected turn in my fieldwork that had brought me inside this sheet metal–clad doocot on a former industrial estate in Glasgow. After a few photos, I clambered back down into a comfortable, tiny living room while the doos above continued to coo pleasantly. Next to an armchair and a radio, a small space heater created a rather startling cocoon of warmth—in fact, a saturating heat that I had not expected from the raw-seamed, green-painted metal exterior. Squatting on its prime location along a paved path between the estate and the canal walkway, this boxy metal tower offered little charm to passersby. When my companions and I struck up a conversation with the owner, who had stepped outside to soak up some treasured rays of sun, we had been invited into a carefully cultivated space of masculine leisure. These doocots were a far cry from the tenement living rooms in which I had joined Canongate activists to strategize against their exclusion from Edinburgh's city center. Nevertheless, the spatial claims signified by these doocots on this and similar estates across Glasgow resonate with working-class experiences of long-term neglect, followed by unwelcomed land revaluation, which were painfully familiar to Canongate activists. That these parallels exist despite great variation between the geographic, social, and historical conditions of these two largely working-class populations offers an opportunity for commentary on those conditions that produce distinctly working-class experiences of agency and frustration in urban Scotland.

Doocots and doos, the Scots rendering paralleling the English terms "dovecotes" and "doves," hark back to a history of structures created to house pigeons, once intended for conspicuous consumption by aristocrats in medieval France and England, and more contemporarily for the competitive leisure activity of fleeing doos (in English: flying doves or pigeons). In this account, I break with the transcription practice that I explained in the introduction of using English over Scots throughout the rest of this book precisely because in this conversation, in both Glasgow and Edinburgh, only the Scots term for "doocot" was ever employed, and the dialectical distinction between "doocot" and "dovecote" thus respectively renders Scottish and English cultural domains, in both written and oral accounts. Both "doo" and "pigeon" were used to indicate the birds themselves. Though I note that parallels exist between the Scottish and English versions of these practices, this discussion of doocots is limited to Scottish—and primarily Glaswegian—urban contexts and the discourse in which they make sense.

Despite the felicity of my introduction to the "doo men" and their doocots, I have wrestled with reluctance in conveying this view of Glaswegian working-class life, which seems to reproduce widely "known" tropes. In the stereotypes of urban working-class Scots, the hobby of fleeing doos evokes images of a gruff, lager-drinking, football-watching masculinity, which is tempered by tender care for a man's doos. Such a stereotype is not limited to the Scottish working classes; the long-running English drama *Coronation Street* featured until 2010 a character named Jack, whose difficulty maintaining a job and navigating a rocky relationship with his wife and son were made more forgivable by his gentle faithfulness toward his pigeons. Whether or not the doo men all maintain such sweet relationships with their pigeons is not a question posed in the narrative that follows. Indeed, when I asked two such men about their pigeons, the answers I received focused entirely on competition and the canny strategies they employed to trap each other's birds. The birds were discussed as a means to personal victory, a triumph over a rival doo man, rather than as a source of pleasure in themselves. From such casual conversations as we had, however, I cannot pretend to comment on the quality of the relationships between these men and their pigeons. Instead, I was struck by the doocots themselves and the claims to land that were levied by the act of their construction, which rested not on ownership of that land but on the council's willing neglect of it.

FROM CANONGATE, EDINBURGH, TO POSSILPARK, GLASGOW

The experiences of the Canongate campaigners, which I have observed for more than ten years, have been shaped by the competition of interests for space in a city center. While the leaders of the residential campaign identified themselves as working class and their negotiations with the Caltongate redevelopment as a class-based struggle, their city-center location provided them with access to transportation, public spaces, and amenities of social and political life that I knew from other writings on British working classes to be more typically scarce in such communities (Edwards, Evans, and Smith 2012). Narratives of more extreme working-class deprivation also circulated among the Canongate residents, associated almost exclusively with the council housing estates that have ringed the city centers since the buildup of council housing in the 1960s and 1970s (Glendenning 2005). Primarily, the stories of these estates that I heard from Canongate residents narrated brushes with estate housing in the first decade of their construction: an offer by the council to take a new house there or a brief period living in one of these houses before moving on. Sally, one of the campaign leaders, had lived initially on an estate when she moved to Edinburgh, and a council house swap had allowed her to trade her flat for the Canongate one that she inhabited for seventeen years. Beyond a handful of these experiences, however, the working-class Canongate residents maintained few if any ties to the estates. In fact, I found a notable feature of working-class community life in the Canongate to be its separation from working-class life on those estates.

Seeking to better understand the distinctiveness of these geographically and socially distant working-class worlds, I began in 2017 to search for any social ties to the estates that I could trace. The answers to my initial inquiries were discouraging. A long-term resident of Dumbiedykes, the council housing estate adjacent to the Canongate neighborhood, assured me that the peripheral estates were a "totally different world," from that city-central estate, even as he went on to confide the many ways that the central estate suffered its share of neglect (see Interlude 3). As I spoke to a variety of individuals with diverse and ongoing ties to Old Town activism, social distance from the estates persisted as the norm, and I began to guess that I would need to start fresh with some introductions to people and organizations based in those locations. Just before the end of that 2017 research trip, however, an unexpected connection emerged from the rather unlikely personage of the director of a prominent built heritage organization in Edinburgh.

At the time, that organization was being led by a man I will call George, a town planning professor and practitioner, and we initially arranged a meeting to discuss development trends in Edinburgh and the role of the organization in a raft of ongoing projects throughout the city. When I asked—near what I expected to be the end of that meeting—about any connections or ties to council housing estates, our conversation took an unforeseen turn that eventually led me to a former industrial estate in Glasgow. George explained that he had taken early planning work in housing estates facing extensive demolitions in Glasgow in the late 1960s, and after moving to Edinburgh for his work at a university there, he had become actively involved with the Craigmillar Festival Society throughout the 1970s and 1980s. The significance of this connection requires some explanation. Craigmillar, a peripheral housing estate in the south of Edinburgh, was already suffering the deprivations of neglect by the turn of the 1960s. A group of its women residents, among them Helen Crummy, sought musical education for their children and so organized to found the Craigmillar Festival Society, which blossomed into a community arts movement and along the way gained recognition throughout Britain, as well as funding from the European Commission (Crummy 1992; Rodger 2017). At its peak in the late 1970s, the Craigmillar Festival drew crowds of more than seventeen thousand people and included the likes of comedian Billy Connolly and artist Richard Demarco, the latter eventually joining the Canongate activists' work and contributing to the Canongate Project. The Craigmillar Festival Society, though dissolved in 2002, not only overlapped with some participants of the Canongate campaign; in the imagination of working-class activists like the Canongate residents, it continues to stand as a record of the enormous potential for creative organization and influence of the urban working classes. George, having witnessed the rise and decline of activism in Craigmillar, noted that issues currently faced there, like vacancies and subsequent large clearances, their rebuild stymied by the economic recession in 2009, were just beginning to threaten another community to which he had some rather fragile connections but a keen interest. Next week, he planned to visit a colleague working in this community, which was located in Possilpark, a former industrial estate in Glasgow that had been identified in 2012 as the second-ranking area of multiple deprivations in Scotland. He offered me the chance to tag along.

At the other end of the hour-long bus ride that connects Edinburgh and Glasgow, this visit introduced me to a neighborhood of striking disparities. Located near the northern edge of Glasgow, Possilpark had been planned in the late nineteenth century to serve an iron foundry, whose success and national renown sustained a working-class community there through the end of World War II. The history of the neighborhood since midcentury followed familiar themes, with a locally specific twist: having been designed as an industrial suburb complete with main street shopping and tenement housing, the closure of the foundry in 1965 had effectively set the community adrift, cut from its economic moorings and pathways to social respectability. Lacking reliable transportation links to the city center, and with the only remaining retail jobs dependent on increasingly scarce local wages, the neighborhood that had served the global interests of the British Empire became a desperate island turned unto itself. This untenable condition prompted some entrepreneurial Possil families to organize their own far-reaching trade, not in iron but in heroin, a trade that throughout the Western world has exploited the miseries of deindustrialization in urban working-class communities. By the early 1980s, the main street of Possil had become the hub of Glasgow's, if not Scotland's, heroin trade, and in 1995, sociologist Alex Meikle dubbed it "the heroin shooting gallery of the world" (Ibrahim 1996).

The legacy of heroin in the intervening generations of Possilpark has brought community development workers, sociologists and social workers, drug treatment programs, periodic injections of city investment in the form of a sports center opened and eventually closed, bus routes scheduled and then dramatically trimmed back, schools shuttered, and children bused to a handful of nearby locations. Most efforts have focused on bandaging the individual and communal wounds left by heroin's ravaging, and a walk along Saracen Street, Possil's high street that marches along under the handsome red sandstone tenements once meant for industrial managers, presents a stage for quiet battles fought here daily. The vacancy of many storefronts, their names printed in fading color above metal shutters, suggests a potential for commercial density, but the most represented commercial trade here is pharmaceutical, with chemist shops providing two separate counters: one for methadone and one for all other prescriptions. Bookies such as Ladbrokes attracted the people identified by social workers with Possil's defiantly resilient drug trade, but they also acted as social hubs, particularly since one of the two primary pubs had recently closed due to violence. At midday, the pavements were not crowded, but we walked past young women pushing toddlers in strollers, two older men standing on the corner engaged in voluble discussion, and a few single men ambling slowly. Our destination—and George's contact—waited inside one of those Saracen Street storefronts, a community center run by a church that had been planted in Possil some ten years ago. Leaders of this church, which I will refer to as Cornerstone, had worked with local residents in those years to designate local brownfield land, now overgrown with trees and grasses, as a nature reserve named the Claypits in reference to its foundry origins. It was this collaborative planning work that had led to George's informal involvement and ultimately to my own presence in Possil as well.

We were welcomed by Gerry, the outgoing minister of Cornerstone, an enthusiastic young man who was transitioning the church into the care of a new pastoral team in the following week, as he was moving his family to another part of Scotland where he had enrolled in a degree program in city planning. Following a warming cup of tea, he led us on a wander along a wet but passable path into the Claypits reserve. This former brownfield site had long outgrown its industrial origins, with its tall grasses and thickets of mature trees bordered by a few incongruously tall and lichen-flaked iron gates marking the former edges of the foundry property. Gerry brought the hike to its scenic conclusion on the brink of the hill's far slope, gesturing expansively to the panorama of Glasgow's towers and rooftops stretching out before us—as neat as a postcard and just as distant from most residents' everyday experience. He gestured to the paved walk winding toward the city below, lamenting, "this is the least travelled path in Glasgow." Much of his work, Gerry explained, focused on trying to persuade youth in his community programs to recognize that they are part not just of Possilpark but of the greater city of Glasgow, and he encouraged them to see the city and its amenities as belonging to them as well. As we walked the short distance back to Saracen Street, I ruminated on the isolation indicated by Gerry's comment and on the wealth of land at the doorstep of the working-class residents of Possilpark.

Had not the abandoned bus depot at the Canongate's edge attracted the attention of Edinburgh city councilors, eager to identify sites for major redevelopment, regardless of current residential use of the neighborhood roundabout in that location? Could the distance between Possilpark and the Glasgow city center protect this neighborhood from the profiteering agendas of such externally focused development? Would the residents of Possil mobilize to consider and to subsequently represent their own interests in such a negotiation, given the personal and communal toll of drug trade and addiction still pressing on this community? Despite the different historical trajectories and characteristics of the respective working-class communities in the Canongate and in Possilpark, these questions relating to urban land use, representation and agency in development, and in particular the viability of development for the benefit of the everyday lives of the working classes suggested powerful continuities between the experiences of these communities.

Those questions had to be temporarily shelved, as the academic year and therefore my classes were beginning, but one year later, I returned to Possilpark to follow up on the process of negotiations for urban space in this postindustrial estate. Beyond the heroic origin story of this nature reserve, I soon learned, the issues had become almost instantly more complicated—a tangle of different use interests, class habits, and aesthetic expectations. Doo men, dog walkers, and day trippers, not to mention Scottish Canals, had differing expectations for the Claypits Nature Reserve, and negotiations were already well underway.

### Space Takers and Place Makers: Rising Challenges of Representation

In 2018, I was walking again through the Claypits, this time with Graeme, a Cornerstone church member who serves on the Claypits Nature Reserve Committee, and we were discussing recent meetings between the community members and Scottish Canals. The new path we trod, now wide and flat enough for two parties to pass, had been dubbed the "yellow brick road" by Possil residents for the pale hue of the gravel covering it, seasoned with a knowing dab of irony. A faint buzzing from somewhere behind us had been intensifying while we conversed, and as the noise suddenly burst into a crazed pitch, we stepped quickly off to the side of the path and turned around. A four-by-four recreational vehicle careened into view some thirty yards back, heading along the path toward us. I expected to remain in the grass and watch it pass, but Graeme stepped back onto the path and faced the oncoming vehicle with arms held out to his sides, so that the driver was forced to slow to a stop in front of him.

"These paths aren't made for four-by-fours," he called out to the driver, whose broad face looked bemused. The man shrugged and shot back, "I grew up here, and me and my pals have always been riding four-by-fours and bikes here!" Graeme explained that things are different now, with the new path, and "we have to follow the rules if we want to use it." The four-by-four driver, remaining astride his vehicle, attributed those rules to the police and therefore resisted, countering, "I don't trust 'em. It's one law for one person, and another law for the other person. And anyway, they leave the boys alone here; they're scared of us," he boasted. Appealing then to Graeme directly, he went on, "I paid eight-hundred pound for this, and the police won't let me ride on the road. If they catch me on the road, they'll take it away! See," he turned and pointed back along the path behind him, sketching out his route in the air. "We come down here, we jump that hill, then we go all the way down there." The only other possible place to take the four-by-fours was too far away, he concluded, and it was too hilly for real fun.

Graeme hesitated only a moment in the face of this appeal, which he obviously regarded sympathetically. "Well, I can represent your concerns to the Claypits Nature Reserve Committee, if you'd like. They're taking views of what the community want to use this space for." The driver responded with an enthusiastic "Aye, that'd be great." He gave Graeme his first and last names, with instructions to tell them to the committee along with his views. Graeme thanked him, and with an amicable parting, he stepped aside and the driver revved his engine again, driving off with pebbles flying and dust ballooning in his wake. As Graeme and I walked on, he mused wearily, "I should probably just get off the committee. How are you supposed to represent the views of 'the community,' when some of them contradict each other? Old ladies walking their dogs on this path could get run over by a four-by-four!" But he acknowledged a resigned sort of sympathy for the plight of the four-by-four driver as well. "I just don't know how these things will get resolved."

The weariness Graeme expressed is known intimately by community development workers, who are responsible for impossible tasks like the "representation" of complex communities. Notwithstanding the irreconcilability of the requests of four-by-four drivers, old ladies, and doo men, this work of representation is no less an important one. The issue of doocots, for instance, had already been raised on the Claypits committee, requesting feedback from Scottish Canals as to whether they would continue to support the informal claims to space that these doocots represented: could the doocots stay, in Scottish Canals's vision of the Claypits Nature Reserve? The doo men had no legal claim to the space in which they had erected their sheet metal structures, but the competition between them on this land had preceded the nature reserve by many years and had become by this time a de facto part of the community's life. The leadership of Scottish Canals acknowledged some informal claims by the residents' doo fleeing *practices* to this land, but they have thus far expressed ambivalence about the structures themselves. In an initial committee discussion of the doocots, a workaround suggestion was floated that as an alternative to the individual metal towers, perhaps a communal doocot could be constructed, which the doo fleeing men could share. This suggestion produced guffaws of disbelief and dismay among the community representatives, who knew what the Scottish Canals professional apparently did not: the entire enterprise of doo fleeing revolves around schemes to entice a rival's pigeon to one's own doocot, then trapping it there. The joy in fleeing doos is not merely an interest in raising and keeping a pet but in the fierce competitive pride granted by pulling the trap cord and snatching another man's doo. A communal doocot would not, with all apologies, do.

Only four months after my visit to Possilpark, the accessibility of doocots as well as that of the yellow brick road through the Claypits Nature Reserve suffered a blow of the sort that the Canongate residents know all too well: a development project required the entire area to be cordoned off, initially for a six-month project intended to improve accessibility to the area. As of September 2020, that project has taken two years and counting. One of the doocots in the reserve was forced to close as well, as part of this project, but another one, at the top of the hill nearest the Possilpark houses, has been allowed to remain open. Having met with that particular doo man, I expect that he has been disappointed without the competition of his chief rival—although one to whom he considered himself demonstrably superior; by his own reckoning he did, after all, take doos off the man all the time. Without the urgency of sorting out use issues relating to the gravel path, or determining the claims of aggressively aging metal towers on Scottish Canal property, the Claypits Nature Reserve Committee has not been meeting lately. So the issues of space use and claims to this postindustrial reserve wait to be taken up again.

### Follow the Doocots

In the meantime, Scottish Canals navigates other aesthetic hurdles in its redevelopment of formerly industrial land. In August 2020, a permit was granted to the Glasgow Magnet Fishing group to hunt for watery treasure in the form of interesting relics like old swords and coins in the canal at the foot of the Claypits. Instead of the usual finds, the group turned up a hoard of more modern weaponry: machetes, axes, knives of various sorts, a meat cleaver, and a handgun (Sabljak 2020. Reactions to the group's social media post that day speculated about the cache of "murder weapons," and this ode to Possilpark's recent epoch of violent postindustrial history brought a swift and indefinite suspension of the fishing permit by Scottish Canals (Sabljak 2020). As a resident observed to me in the recent aftermath of the incident, the community's actual history did not appear so welcome in the emerging narrative of accessible urban nature space being written over the Claypits.[1] Whether doocots as a working-class claim to space will survive this narrative shift depends on the generosity of the aesthetic of public space supported by this collaboration between Scottish Canals and local residents.

The question of aesthetics, as with the Canongate campaigners, expresses claims to both place and history, and the working out of these issues in the Claypits will determine whether its public space can be marketed to the city at large while it retains visibly working-class elements—elements that can be both large and noisy. If it is determined that public nature spaces like the Claypits must contrive to present a middle-class aesthetic, then the implications for working-class residents not only of Possilpark but of neighborhoods throughout other Scottish cities point to a shrinking realm of public space and a correspondingly diminished political voice. Where the working classes exercise political agency, they must also visibly take up space, and thus we may look to the doocots as signals of the course ahead.

### Note

1. The magnet fishing group eventually regained their permission from Scottish Canals to fish in the canal in April 2021, thanks in part to public pressure applied by the growth of interest in magnet fishing during the Covid-19 pandemic (Sabljak 2021).

CHAPTER 5

# SCOTTISH COSMOPOLITANISM
# From Neighborhood to Nation

SCOTTISH POLITICAL COMMENTATOR AND WRITER Gerry Hassan observed in 2018 that Scotland seemed in recent years to be undergoing a tremendous shift, from an idealized vision of civil society dependent largely on elite influence to a "new political culture" characterized by "self-organized people power, social media platforms and new forms of campaigning" (2018, 42). To showcase this new approach to politics, he outlined the events that led to the exposure of corruption in the Glasgow Rangers Football Club in 2012 by "social media commentators and campaigners," and he suggested that this campaign could be read as a "harbinger" of the "unprecedented political engagement" that would come to characterize the 2014 popular referendum for Scottish independence (Hassan 2018, 42). My research among Scottish community campaigners suggests that Hassan could have looked even further back, to the mobilization of neighborhood organizations that were proliferating in the first decade of the millennium. And yet, the resonance that Canongate campaigners perceived between the Scottish National Party's (SNP) rhetoric and their political hopes shows that elites continue to matter in this new political culture. The most intriguing task for political analysis may be the identification and elaboration of resonances between elite discourses and "self-organized people power," a project to which this book contributes (Hassan 2018, 42).

Concurrent with the Canongate Community Forum (CCF)/Save Our Old Town (SOOT) campaign, multiple similar, albeit smaller, campaigns organized across Edinburgh to challenge municipal development decisions for their neighborhoods, campaigns with names like Porty Greenkeepers, Save Glenogle Baths, Friends of Corstorphine Hill, and Save Meadowbank, to challenge, respectively, construction in a public park, the demolition

Fig. 5.1 Individually, the successes of the community organizations that mobilized in Edinburgh in 2005–2007 varied, and so they united as Edinburgh at Risk, which identified itself as a "non-political umbrella organisation open to all who value the city's culture, history and future.... It is concerned at the many present and planned sales of public land and facilities and wishes full recognition of Edinburgh's Common Good." The politics denied here signifies a lack of party affiliation rather than a lack of interest in public advocacy. Image courtesy Canongate Community Forum.

of public Victorian baths, the loss of a public nature area for the expansion of the adjacent zoo, and the demolition of a public recreation facility.[1] Like Hassan, I see in these political mobilizations not a scattering of isolated events but rather a constellation of connected concerns represented through political engagement that has sought the collective appearance of a public whose voice would not be heard in the usual processes of governance (Rancière 2004). Pursuing the amplification of their voice through collective appearance, the leaders of these organizations joined with the CCF/SOOT to form an "umbrella organization" called Edinburgh at Risk (EAR) to facilitate sharing of information and political strategies and to raise a collective voice in negotiation with city leadership. Through their joined-up political mobilization, these Edinburgh residents from a range of social class backgrounds have contributed to a more "disputatious environment" in which a multiplicity of actors and organizations engage in the public questioning of relations of power and the terms of their accountability (Hassan 2018, 43).

As I have observed in the years since the CCF/SOOT campaign was mooted by the 2008 council approval of the Caltongate master plan, the aesthetic politics of residents stimulated by that proposal has articulated with elite discourses of Scottish independence. Paralleling the alliances of working and middle classes in the independence campaign of 2014, I have observed that the Canongate residents' working-class cosmopolitanism resonated with the politics of their middle-class allies in conservation, architecture, and planning. Both neighborhood and national political mobilizations of these Canongate campaigners suggest the "politics of forging new identities" proposed by David Featherstone (2005, 268), by which "place-located identities" become invested in opposition to neoliberal policies and practices (2005, 267). In the Canongate, the campaigners forged their place-located politics not as an elaboration on a felt opposition between local and global, or familiar and foreign, but rather as the grounds for articulating two competing aesthetics of social and political life. On the one hand, the Canongate aesthetic reflected the enduring legacy of welfare state political arrangements manifest in tenements of council housing and integrated into a central, historic built environment. On the other, the neoliberal aesthetic—associated with a potential rather than already-existing place—for its realization would require property-development engines to shunt the working classes to housing in peripheral locations, from which they would be encouraged to take service jobs in the centrally located consumer spaces of new developments. The Canongate campaigners upheld the Canongate aesthetic as a moralized arrangement of the built environment and social and political life, the terms of which are discussed at length in chapter 4, against which any competing aesthetics would be judged.

The primary terms of the opposition, therefore, between the place-based political aesthetic advocated by the Canongate residents and the aesthetic of neoliberalizing urbanism promoted by the Caltongate development's supporters concerned the value of the area's built heritage and provision of amenities for working-class life. Unlike the place-based political movements discussed by Featherstone, the invocation of the Canongate as place does not challenge neoliberal globalism by asserting a place-delimited identity marker over and against a sense of cosmopolitan belonging but rather challenges the dispossessive mechanisms of neoliberal urbanism by explicitly affirming the presence of working-class residents and implicitly idealizing the welfare state's attentiveness to their livelihoods. As this chapter shows, in their subsequent mobilization to national politics, the Canongate campaigners deliberately claimed multiculturalism, an idea increasingly prominent in SNP rhetoric, for their own moralized aesthetic rather than surrendering it to their opponents in the neoliberalizing processes of urban development. Through the Canongate residents' strategic politics of resistance to neoliberal urbanism and their desires to revision a Scottish welfare state, the values of twentieth-century European liberal democracies such as multiculturalism gain fresh relevance to both ends. Though part of the system of political elites, the SNP appeared to suggest a means to achieve a "fairer Scotland," invoking the historic legacy of Scottish liberal democracy and thus offering terms by which the Canongate residents could maneuver toward a more responsive state that, they hope, will be motivated to make space for the working classes.

The Canongate campaigners thus opposed the elite cosmopolitanism materialized in the Caltongate development proposal, with its accommodations to globally mobile professionals, from their own working-class cosmopolitanism. While during the campaign the Canongate residents' aesthetic discourse focused on more immediately consequential politics of the proposed redevelopment, they quickly appropriated the public rhetoric of multicultural Scotland in Europe from the SNP in the years following the campaign. Indeed, this socially democratic working-class cosmopolitanism had facilitated the forging of alliances between the campaigners and a variety of actors and organizations from across Edinburgh and Glasgow, many from the left-leaning middle classes. Thus a cosmopolitan posture among the leaders of the resident organization, even before the discursive emphasis on these elements in the rhetoric of the SNP, has made more comfortable the "intersections and alliances" that have organized around place-based identities, which continue to shape the practices of the new public sphere ascendant in urban Scotland (Featherstone 2005, 267).

Before engaging Scotland's well-established literature on national identity and its associated cultural and political movements, the following section situates Scotland within Europe and the politics of the Canongate campaigners within the anthropological study of nationalism. The characteristics of nationalist politics and identity articulated in this research suggest processes, principles, and stakes of such political projects within the larger field of Europe and the still-unfolding history of empire. Finally, the mutuality of influence between residents' mobilizations to both urban and national politics is presented through a comparison of their actions with a Dutch case that reflects dynamics both familiar and strange.

### Nationalism and Urban Politics

In the years following the campaign, resemblances formed between the CCF/SOOT campaign concerns and the public discourses of Scottish nationalism and independent Scotland. Scottish nationalist imagery and promises of Scottish independence, two overlapping but distinct discursive projects (Bechhofer and McCrone 2015), have both influenced the campaigners' affective responses to the SNP's visioning of national and political futures. Embracing the images of a Scottish social democracy rooted in both projects has enabled campaign leaders to contest the political aesthetic of neoliberal urbanism and reject its affective urgency. Though they differ in some important respects from one another, the individual campaigners' political imaginaries, discussed in the following pages, chart a deliberate course between a neoliberal version of globalism represented by the Labour council leadership (with their instrumentalizations of working-class neighborhoods and lives) on the one hand, and exclusionary racialized versions of nationalism (with their fixations on creating, and divesting the nation of, Others) on the other. Although Scotland differs in important respects from patterns of nationalist politics across Europe, European nationalisms nonetheless provide the field and the historical context in which the nation has come to make sense as a political and social unit, and so a consideration of these patterns and Scotland's relationship to them follows.

The construction of identities individual and collective requires attentive labor, and as a collective identity of both large size and political consequence, nations necessitate the imagination of cohesion and legitimation of its instruments (Anderson 1991). In Europe, the imaginations of nations have marshaled language (Bourdieu 1991), religion (Fekete 2016), and secularism (Silverstein 2018), essentialized conceptualizations of culture (Grillo 1998), race (Gullestad 2002; Silverstein 2018), and kinship (Gullestad 2006) as the bases of their unity. Such principles have been applied to define the contours of Europe's internal others: colonial migrants such as temporary laborers (Partridge 2012), refugees and clandestine migrants (Andersson 2014), Muslims and Jews (Bunzl 2005; Silverstein 2018), and Roma (Halmai 2011) for a decidedly noncomprehensive list. Scotland's own whitewashed history of nation-building has often occluded the dark colonial infrastructure that has made international migration feasible, and the manufacturing strength of Scotland, as elsewhere in Britain, has depended on colonial resources and markets (Devine 2003). Within Scotland, bitter sectarian clashes clove its lowland cities in the twentieth century, while nonwhite residents experienced discrimination and racial violence in the same areas. Scottish national discourses have yet to foreground these experiences and therefore risk glossing over the complicated realities of race, class, and nation in Scotland in service to a self-congratulatory narrative that bolsters the rationale for independence (Davidson et al. 2018). This book opposes any narratives of national innocence and seeks to illuminate the conditions under which a particular vision of Scotland—as multicultural, cosmopolitan, and decidedly democratic—has come to appeal to the mostly white working-class individuals discussed here. Although this image of the nation is appreciably "different" from exclusivist constructions of the nations mentioned above, difference cannot be mistaken for innocence. Indeed, rhetorical difference must be held accountable to the experiences of people of color in Scotland if it is to mean anything at all. This book seeks to contribute to the larger project of grounding such political rhetoric in the lives of a full spectrum of Scottish residents, contributing to that project this consideration of the relationships between national political rhetoric and the political activities of mostly white, working-class residents in Edinburgh.

This chapter shows that these forms of national discourse matter in the interpretation of everyday experience in Scotland, consequentially shaping the terms of both political imagination and action for the former Canongate campaigners. For these residents, the discourse of the nation, represented in particular in the rhetoric of the SNP, is also judged according to the political aesthetic that they cultivated in their Canongate activism, such that the two scales of political action interpenetrate one another in the residents' aesthetic project of imagining both city and nation. Particularly compelling for the Canongate campaigners has been the affective transformation of public political discourse, accomplished by the rapid ascent of the SNP.

As the following section shows, the SNP's rise to power in Scotland, long regarded as unlikely, has wrought a dramatic transformation on Scotland's landscape of political affect, as evidenced in discussions with the former Canongate campaigners. The unprecedented electoral popularity of the SNP, bringing with it the apparent plausibility of independence, exemplifies well the processes of what Rancière has termed "aesthetic activism." Rancière defines this activism as action in the world where, supposedly, such action is impossible, and he argues that in the taking of that action, the conditions of the world are changed, from incapacity to capacity. To act in this way, he explains, is to produce the world you want by acting as if you already live in it (Rancière and Gage 2019, 22). While Rancière focused on the worldly effects of this presumption of equality, I want to draw attention to the affective component of these acts. The kind of action that produces formerly inconceivable political outcomes, such as the absolute majority of Scottish Parliament seats won by the SNP in 2011, wields considerable and even transformative affective power. In Scotland, the SNP has appropriated the affective impact of its electoral successes in its own implausible rise, making both independence and political change appear suddenly plausible.

That the SNP has marshaled such affect to its cause is undisputed, and as one exasperated political commentator complained, the SNP has "monopolized the terrain of public hope" in Scottish politics (Scothorne 2020). While some critics may regard this hope as illusory and even diversionary from "serious issues," the significant role of affect, as aesthetics, in politics is perhaps not adequately appreciated. As this book has shown, conditions in Edinburgh grew ripe for such a change under Labour leadership that had operationalized an affect of urgency, with the effect of shrinking the space for public voice via processes that an Old Town community leader judged to be "totally undemocratic." In retrospect, these actions may be seen as a kind of affective mismanagement, and as chapters 3 and 4 have shown, such mismanagement has taken a heavy toll on the city's working-class activists. The cumulative wear of affective mismanagement provides an important piece of the narrative of campaigners' gravitations toward the SNP, presented in the following pages. The appeal of the SNP rhetoric to the Canongate campaigners reflects therefore a congruence between moralized visions for Scotland and the party's affective transformation of the political sphere, from a critical urgency that foreclosed public debate under

Labour leadership in Edinburgh, to an opening of public discourse that foregrounds an affect of hope and anticipation of change.

The mutuality of national and urban political discourses in constructing the sense of possible futures and a plausible present is illuminated by comparison with a study of urban residents with a very different interpretation of their precarity. In his research on Amsterdam residents navigating the redevelopment of their superdiverse neighborhood, Paul Mepschen argues that "the way people negotiate self-understanding and alterity in everyday life is intimately entwined with political and public discourse, which imposes meaning upon everyday life" (2017, 75). Mepschen found that public discourse effecting the "culturalization of citizenship" in the Netherlands influenced the sense that residents made of their failed attempts to influence their neighborhood's redevelopment (2017). When refracted through the lens of cultural citizenship, residents produced a "discourse of displacement" that highlighted their autochthonous identities, entitlements as "natives," and racist characterizations of threats to their community (Mepschen 2017). The contrast between residents' narratives about development in Mepschen's Amsterdam neighborhood and those circulating in the Canongate in Edinburgh highlights the role of political and, in particular, national discourse as a key to the interpretation of urban experiences. But the example of the Canongate campaigners also indicates that urban politics shape the terms by which city residents imagine and engage the nation. As previous chapters have shown, Canongate residents not only appropriate national discourse; they also judge the national political project in terms of the concerns developed in their neighborhood campaign. Urban and national politics thus shape, interpret, and critique one another in the life of a given activist.

Unlike the Netherlands, in its public national discourse, Scotland has not undergone a "culturalization of citizenship," which associates true belonging with an autochthonous majority under threat from immigration and racialized others. Scottish nationalist political discourse, the most prominent mouthpiece of which has become the SNP, frames the nation's dilemma as one of democratic sovereignty manifest in an underrealized governmental structure. The objectives of independence are thus cast as the structural rather than cultural realization of Scottishness. As the following sections show, however, even such arguments for independence maintain a footing on culturalist foundations in the depictions of Scottish culture and history that are emphasized in national political discourse. This chapter shows that historic discourses of the Scottish nation and the appropriation of its familiar narratives by the SNP have shaped the Canongate residents' national political aesthetic, consistent with their pursuits of a more democratic and welfare-oriented state relationship in urban politics.

The following section situates the nationalist discourse, as currently expressed within the SNP, in a long history of Scottish nationalism and sketches the rise of the SNP to replace Labour as the premier Scottish political influence. I argue that the interpretations of the SNP by campaigners, which were refracted through their negotiations with a dismissive and unresponsive state, helped render an everyday working-class cosmopolitanism compatible with the place attachments expressed by Canongate residents. These residents rejected the affective, moral aesthetic of neoliberal urbanism in favor of resurrected but adapted images of the Scottish welfare state, the edges of which they have sharpened against the darkening backdrop of an increasingly exclusivist strand of popular English nationalism.

### Scottish Nationalisms: Personal, Cultural, and Partisan

The literature on Scottish nationalism is rich, interdisciplinary, and historic, and a comprehensive summary lies far beyond the scope of this chapter. From Enlightenment-era authors to the recent (2015–2019) slates of elections that have brought record numbers of SNP members into parliamentary positions in Westminster and (since 1999) the Scottish Parliament, nationalism in Scotland has always consisted in a complex assemblage of symbols and attachments, including for some but not for all a call for political independence from the United Kingdom. As illustrated by this book's narrative of the campaigners' cultivation of coherence between everyday life and politics from the Canongate to the nation, expressions of Scottish nationalism should not presume acquiescence to a preexisting or normative construction of the Scottish nation. Instead, following Anthony Cohen's (1996) conceptualization of personal nationalism, I explore the formation of Canongate campaigners' political imaginaries through the experience of their community activism and argue that the identification of these campaigners with the Scottish nation should be seen as an agentive process invested in the aesthetic construction of that nation (see also Hearn 2017). That is to say, if Scotland is not to be relegated to "a mere figment of the nationalist imagination" (Cohen 1996, 805), it must be imaginatively appropriated to resonate with the everyday lives, material realities, and experiences of individuals. At a time when nationalism as a political subjectivity is reasserting itself across the world (if it ever actually ceased to be compelling; see Keating 2009), asking, "Whose nation? What nationalism?" seems ever more necessary. What does nationalism have to do with "actually existing politics," political engagements inextricable from the lived experiences of individuals and communities (Spencer 1997)?

Scottish nationalism is rooted in a configuration of people and place in the windy reaches of a northern isle, which has been engaged since the earliest-known histories in migrations, trade, and political interests with the European continent and elsewhere on the isle of Britain. Scotland's historic connections with Europe have long been highlighted, from Muriel Spark's eponymous antiheroine Jean Brodie, to architectural critics (McKean 2001; McKee 2018), as well as the conservation professionals I interviewed, as a means of decentering England in the history and identity formation of Scotland. England, as Scotland's closest neighbor and erstwhile rival kingdom, has long exercised profound political, economic, and cultural influence in Scotland, and since the signing on January 16, 1707, of the Acts of Union, this influence has been formalized in a shared parliamentary structure, uniting the formerly distinct English and Scottish Parliaments in the single body convening at Westminster. These Acts of Union have long been regarded as an anomaly in the history of European nations; Scottish leaders voted to dissolve the Scottish Parliament and adopt a role as second partner in Great Britain during a period when other European peoples were agitating for national sovereignty (Nairn 1977). The Acts of Union, therefore, mark the opening of an enduring cleavage in Scotland—a conflict internal to the stateless nation over what Cohen (1996) calls cultural versus political nationalism; that is, respective framings of the nation as constituting a culture or "Geist" (see McCrone 1992, 204, cited in Cohen 1996, 809) on the one hand, or a state on the other. The question of great interest to Scotland's national pundits centers on political self-determination: can Scotland achieve maturity as a nation without a corresponding state identity?

This issue raises the fundamental constitutional question of Scotland's independence, put to public referendum by the SNP-controlled Scottish government in 2014 and defeated with 55.3 percent against independence and 44.7 percent in favor. As Hearn notes, the 2014 referendum did not "arise out of the blue, but was instead yet another episode in the gradualist path to greater autonomy within the UK (and more recently within the EU) that has characterized modern Scottish history" (2014, 506). This gradualist path suggests a bent toward state sovereignty, and that bend has twice steepened since 2014, owing firstly to the 2016 Brexit referendum that set into motion the uncertain and complicated process of removing the UK from the European Union—against Scotland's 55 percent vote to remain—and secondly to the onset of the COVID-19 pandemic in 2020. The cautious and deliberate handling of national lockdown procedures by Scottish first minister Nicola Sturgeon compared favorably in the press to that of British prime minister Boris Johnson, which was widely perceived as mismanaged. Despite Scotland's high-ranking total of COVID-19 deaths, this comparison has been maneuvered adroitly to build public confidence in both Sturgeon's SNP government and the case for independence (Dickie and Burn-Murdoch 2020). From March 2020, surveys found that popular support for independence was initially strengthened by the effect of the pandemic, and despite some back and forth during the following two years, polls have not yet found a margin of even ten percentage points between "yes" and "no" responses to the independence question. As of December 2022, support appears to be rising again, following a Supreme Court ruling upholding Westminster's right to administer judgment over a Scottish referendum vote for independence. When considering such votes or surveys, Hearn's admonition to respect the complexity of desires and perceptions concealed within these numbers is instructive: a referendum vote should not be seen as a vote either for or against the Scottish nation but rather as a vote about the political vision and structure of that nation (2014, 508). In this sense, Hearn argues, nationalism is "normal" in Scotland—that is, nationalism constitutes a field for an "ongoing debate about identity and values" (2014, 511) appropriate to the nation.

In the partisan debates over Scotland's identity and values, the SNP has taken a leading role since 2007, and despite some electoral losses in 2017 to the Scottish Conservatives following the turmoil of two popular referenda, in 2019, the SNP won the most seats in each of Scotland's four largest city councils: Edinburgh, Glasgow, Aberdeen, and Dundee. The SNP's climb to power has surprised political commentators, not least because before 2015, it was believed that no single party could win an absolute majority in Scottish Parliament. I suggest that the unexpected dominance of the SNP, in

Rancière's terms, changed the conditions of possibility. The electoral successes of the SNP, however, should not be overinterpreted as an indicator of the widespread sharing of convictions regarding independence. Instead, the popularity of the SNP and its messages of independence are widely understood as an index of prevailing feelings of disempowerment in and dissatisfaction with the present political structure (Scothorne 2020), and as this book illustrates, such dissatisfaction derives from experience across multiple scales of the state. The SNP's precipitous rise would suggest therefore the concomitant fall of a political party associated with the dissatisfaction of Scottish voters: Scottish Labour.

The party that since the postwar period has represented unionist nationalism and the Scottish working classes, with a seemingly iron hold on the Glasgow urban region, Labour has imploded in the postdevolution twenty-first century. From 1999 to 2007, Labour stood as the incumbent party of Scottish leadership in Parliament, riding high on Tony Blair's promise and delivery of devolution. Once delivered, however, devolution rather rapidly hemmed Labour into an untenable space between the Scottish electorate and increasing political and economic sovereignty. For voters like the Canongate campaigners, Labour has come to represent the establishment version of Scotland, a culturally expressive but politically hobbled Scottishness in Britain, which has become associated with the evisceration of the state and the prioritization of economic growth over welfare. In trying to coax the fledgling Scottish national polity back into the confines of the British nest, Labour political imaginaries have managed to appear regressive, repressive, and reactionary.

Surveys of dissatisfaction with Labour have highlighted a loss of public trust in the party and the growing convictions that they have failed in their managerial responsibilities (Henderson et al. 2020). Having sent fifty-six Labour MPs to Westminster in 1997, in the 2019 elections Scotland sent only one, while in Scottish Parliament, Labour has declined from fifty-six Members of the Scottish Parliament (MSPs) in 1999 to twenty-three MSPs in 2020. In the face of this electoral chill, Labour retains its strongest hold among the postwar generation socialized into unionist nationalism (Gilfillan 2011), a fact I observed in the political party activities of the Canongate campaigners. Only one campaigner, a woman in her seventies, continued throughout the campaign to support the Labour Party, and she did so not only with her votes but also as a volunteer in her local Labour office; hers was the only voice I encountered in the Canongate stridently opposed to Scottish independence. "I'm Scottish *and* British," she insisted. "That's just the way it should be."

In the 2007 Edinburgh council elections, in which the Labour leadership that had promoted Caltongate was replaced by a coalition government led by the Liberal Democrats, most Canongate campaigners perceived Labour as the party agent of neoliberal urbanism—a more present and credible threat to their lives than the less numerous and thus less powerful (though no less reviled) Conservative agents of neoliberalism. As the Caltongate proposal was still live in the planning process at the time, the stakes of local political power had been ratcheted up, and Canongate campaign leader Catriona ran for office as a councilor for that central district, as a representative of the Scottish Socialist Party (SSP). She did not succeed in her bid for a seat, but at the time, as a lifelong, third-generation socialist, this party—which in the previous elections had placed six MSPs in Scottish Parliament—seemed to offer Catriona and thus the campaign a viable opportunity to contest the power of Labour in the city council chambers to push Caltongate and developments like it forward. Had the development process waited a few years, however, Catriona may have looked to the SNP to provide such an opportunity; by then, the SSP had lost its parliamentary seats, the SNP had gained an absolute majority, and the SSP had endorsed the SNP's plan for Scottish independence. The rapid arrival of the SNP, in short, changed the field of political plausibility. In the face of the narrowed space for political negotiation experienced by the Canongate campaigners, an affect of hope would offer restoration of the political agency that, in 2007, they were already beginning to perceive to be lost.

While the neoliberal urbanism that had foreclosed debate over the built environment was rightly associated by the campaigners with both Labour and the Conservatives, the addition of an SNP councilor to the Development Management subcommittee in 2007 did not serve the Canongate residents' cause at the fateful February 2008 meeting, which passed the proposal. That SNP councilor voted along with his Labour and Conservative colleagues for the Caltongate development, a vote that one campaigner commented on when we went for drinks afterward. Over a tiny, sticky table in a too-loud bar down the street from the council chambers, we leaned in and tiredly shouted our recollections of the day's meeting. A self-employed photographer who lived in a flat along Canongate Road, Carys had sat next to me at a crowded campaign meeting a few weeks before. Having gotten involved early in the campaign, Carys had been drawn into its excitement and urgency. She had attended meetings and joined protests and events as often as her irregular professional schedule would allow. We had observed from the council gallery for hours without many breaks for discussion, and so at the end of this long, wearying day, we recounted the meeting and its many moments of agitation together. Between sips from our lukewarm glasses, Carys speculated on the motive for the councilors' votes, whether personal profit, party requirement, or conformity, noting with approval the Green Party member's lone vote of refusal. The Green Party member had acted honorably, she decided, but then she mused over the behavior of an SNP member at the meeting. "My friend Elaine emailed—I'm not sure if it was all the MSPs or some of the MSPs and the councilors—it was more than twenty of them, and she got about four replies. The first reply was from Kenny McCaskill, who is the SNP guy at the Parliament, and his reply was quite supportive, and he said that it was his understanding that the SNP members were to be voting against [Caltongate]. Well, that's quite interesting, because they didn't, actually!"

She then switched to talking about an "unpleasant" Conservative councilor's comments in the meeting, and we did not return to discussing the SNP councilor's vote. The Canongate's own SNP councilor had built trust with the Canongate residents by speaking on behalf of their development concerns to the planning committee, and the SNP was generally held to be more responsive to residents than Labour or Conservative representatives, while nobody mentioned much about the Liberal Democrats. The regard that the SNP was beginning to build among the Canongate resident campaigners, when accompanied by frustrated recollections of their voting records like Carys's, gestures to the ambivalence of the SNP record, particularly on austerity provisions, promotions of home ownership over renting, and other issues that square poorly with a regard for the lives of working-class Scots. To understand the popularity of the SNP among such groups, however, I suggest that the party's record should be subordinated to—or at least qualified by—its affective transformation of Scottish politics.

The Canongate residents had recently emerged from a dispiriting planning process that had bracketed out dissenting voices like theirs, justified by competitive necessity and an affect of urgency. By contrast, the SNP's affective strategy has emphasized concern and attentiveness, offering an apparent opening-up of political debate to voices demanding fairness and equality. The affective climate as experienced by the Canongate residents has thus changed dramatically, lending plausibility to the expanded accountability of the state in particular. Affective anxieties, fears, and anger have animated exclusionary national identity discourse in recent years, and as Silverstein has shown, the surveillance of affect has served to control nonwhite populations in France and elsewhere (Silverstein 2018, 150). As the antidote to such toxic affective politics, Silverstein commends to the reader action pursued out of love, as "an act of solidarity and mutual recognition, the condition of possibility for a future together" (2018, 156). I suggest that in the translation of love as a desire for action to love as action, the key affective component is hope; specifically, hope for change. The affective transformation around Scottish national independence has injected public discourse, and working-class politics in particular, with an affect of hope, and this shift has profoundly impacted the participation of working-class Scots in the public sphere (Rancière and Gage 2019, 5). The sudden plausibility of political change, combined with the resonance of SNP political rhetoric with the welfare orientation of the Canongate residents has enabled them to imagine the Scottish nation in the aesthetic register of the Canongate.

Affect and aesthetic, as Alanna Cant has observed, represent "two sides of the same coin" (2019, 33). The aesthetics of the independent nation that the SNP continues to offer to the Scottish public; that is, a moralized sense of life associated with the affective experience of places, people, social life, and political life must also resonate with the experiences and desires of would-be supporters. This need for resonance brings the cultural and historical components of the Scottish nation to bear in the project of political vision casting. As the following section shows, the SNP aesthetics lay claim to a familiar construction of the Scottish nation rooted in cultural narrative, practice, and "normal" politics (Hearn 2014).

### "Normal" Nationalism and Egalitarian Scots

Nationalism as "normal"; that is, as consisting in a popular, ongoing, and widespread debate over political claims rather than as an ethnicized construct of belonging and exclusion (Hearn 2014), bears strikingly little resemblance to narratives of nationalism ascendant elsewhere in Europe in the early twenty-first century. In Scotland, the politics of nationalism has long been associated not with the closing of political processes to certain factions and populations but with the opening of these processes to more democratic participation and increased accountability, characteristic of the cosmopolitanism discussed in this book's introduction (see Hearn 2000; Stolz 2020). Representing this perspective, sociologist Lindsay Paterson has advocated for attention to the Scottish model of "pragmatic nationalism" as a means of pursuing democratic reforms to the welfare state, arguing that in Scotland, for the past century, "social democracy and nationalism remain intimately linked to each other" (1997, 70). These intimate links characterize Scotland's celebrated civic rather than ethnic nationalism, but in telling the history of Scottish nationalism, its flirtations with fascist and ethnic formulations of the nation should not be swept under the civic rug. During the 1920s and 1930s, Scottish nationalist groups in both Edinburgh and Glasgow organized demonstrations, and Edinburgh's Canongate in the mid-1930s briefly became one such battleground for control by a group calling itself the "Kaledonian Klan" (Bowd 2013). That the impact of such groups created comparatively smaller ripples on discourses of Scottish identity than they did in English nationalist circles indicates the minority voice of these groups in the movement, but such histories complicate any narrative of Scotland's exceptional civic nationalism (Davidson et al. 2018). Because this chapter focuses on the relationship between public discourse of Scotland and the political aesthetic cultivated by Canongate residents, a history of this discourse and its supportive mythology follows. The elaboration of campaigners' discourse highlights the idealized portrait of Scotland that they navigate, not uncritically, in the following section.

Appreciating the "persuasive nationalist rhetoric" of civic Scotland (Cohen 1996, 810) requires one to delve into the earthy domains of cultural myths. Such myths reflect not falsehoods but a language replete with meaning (Lévi-Strauss 1955), the public narratives and rhetorical traditions through which Scots have come to know themselves.[2] One of the most deeply held myths of Scottish distinctiveness centers on the Scots' egalitarian character (Hearn 2000). This character works at both the individual and societal level, such that Scottish society is itself held to be a more fair society, and the comparison most regularly made cites England as inferior in this respect: a more hierarchical society (McCrone 2017, 79). While the causes of this egalitarian nature are often identified with Scottish institutions of education and democracy, and even with the presbyterian structure of the Church of Scotland, as McCrone notes, it can also mimic a "primordial" or even racial characteristic of Scots (2017, 239). This primordial framing of egalitarianism rubs uneasily against Scottish nationalist claims to a civic or liberal democratic nationalism, over and against an ethnic or racial idea of the nation. As Jonathan Hearn (2000) has shown, while this egalitarian myth has in tangible ways impacted the development of nationalist discourse in Scotland, it does not reflect an accomplishment but remains an influential aspiration. This aspiration itself constitutes one of the resources people use to make sense of their experiences and levy their claims on the state, but as Liinpää has argued, concluding that Scottish egalitarianism reflects a fully accomplished reality actually mitigates against the push toward its realization (2018). Egalitarianism thus represents a complicated component of the Scottish imaginary.

As a myth of egalitarianism in a society of unequal means, benefiting from a global empire and slave trade, this narrative of the nation has always been ambivalent at best, exploitative at worst, but its roots in Scottish history delve deep. Allan MacLaren has argued that this myth predates industrialization and was shaped by the mutual obligations of "rural paternalism" (MacLaren 1976, 9, cited in McCrone 2017, 240). Indeed, the symbolic figure of the egalitarian myth is the "lad o'pairts," a country boy whose potential has been recognized by a prominent sponsor (such as a landowner or church minister) who enables the country boy to attend university, where his aspirations and innate capabilities are brought to fruition. Lingering influences of the gendered relations of rural paternalism thus inflect this character's journey, while his success is ultimately attributed to an inherently democratic and meritocratic education system. The philosophies buttressing this education system are generally attributed to the Scottish Enlightenment, itself heralded as a native cultural-intellectual expression, which has contributed many Scottish institutions adapted to serving the social good as part of a distinctively Scottish civil society (Hearn 2016).

As an example of this Scottish civil society, Richard Rodger has shown how in Edinburgh throughout the nineteenth century the city dispensed a Common Good fund "in equal measure to the inhabitants of the capital," the ideological base of which was that "the citizenry acknowledged the legitimate claims of all members of the public, individually and collectively, on a basis equivalent to their own" (2004, 176). These Common Good disbursements, according to Rodger, typified the interest of Scottish elites in "contributing to the social welfare of the disadvantaged," and he argues that the nurturing of a distinctively Scottish civil society "was the very essence of the Scottish Enlightenment" (2004, 177). The egalitarian myth is thus closely tied to the Scottish Enlightenment's effects within Scotland and the social and political will of its elites, but as a mode of contemporary identification, it has not been restricted to intellectuals and upper economic classes; research among Scottish working classes has found it embraced among these Scots as well (Gawlewicz 2020).

Having predated industrialization, the egalitarian myth cannot be said to have originally involved concern for the plight of working classes or a critique of social inequalities formed by capitalism itself. Nevertheless, Scottish people's belief in this egalitarian ideal shaped philanthropic and reformist concerns when such inequalities emerged through the economies of industrial labor, as capitalist class relations came to typify Scotland's urban centers (Darling 2015; Morris 2013; Smyth 2019). This concern for the social inequalities produced by industrial capitalism may also be seen in the influence of leftist politics, particularly socialist and labor movements in Scotland's urban areas, most prominent in Glasgow, from the working-class labor organizing and rent striking of Red Clydeside, to the Socialist Sunday School movement from the 1890s through the 1930s, and throughout the postwar dominance of the Labour Party anchored in that region. Having been formulated in the context of rural paternalism, the egalitarian self-beliefs of Scots adapted to the contexts of industrial urbanism, in which class relations shaped the terms in discourses of equality. As Hearn (2014), Davidson et al. (2018), and others have shown, this myth has never reflected an actual society without inequality, and indeed much of the support for the growth of Scottish civil society derived from imperial economies. This self-belief, however, has materially impacted the shape of politics in Scotland across classes and party affiliations. As a following section shows, this egalitarian vision of Scotland has offered imaginative resources for working-class political agency and alliances in both democratic and socialist formations.

While the welfare state was the political framework that presided over working-class political representation through the postwar twentieth century, at the turn of that century, socialist mobilization—which presented an alternative vision for an egalitarian society—suggested a possible path to political efficacy for the urban working classes. The recognized (and feared) plausibility of this path motivated municipal governance to accommodate its concerns in both Edinburgh and Glasgow (McCrone and Elliot 1989). The shape of the welfare state, which has become a moralized political imaginary in urban Scotland thus reflects the influence that socialist political mobilization played (and, equally as effective in Edinburgh, threatened to play) in producing municipal attentiveness to working-class housing demands in particular. Socialist mobilization therefore indirectly contributed to working-class political efficacy, while the movements in Glasgow's Clydeside area would become a motivational story in Scottish radical history. As signified by the experience of Canongate campaign leader Catriona, discussed in a following section, twenty-first-century socialists have found inviting parallels in the egalitarian rhetoric of Scottish nationalist politics. Although most of the campaigners did not pursue radical politics, the campaign still invoked the activism of industrial-era working-class socialists as an exemplar of effective working-class mobilizations; for instance, showing a documentary of "Radical Scotland" as part of the Canongate Project. Although socialist mobilization did stimulate a panicked reflex toward fascism among a small group of Scotland's elite in the 1920s and 1930s, that impulse has proven much less durable than the appeal to egalitarian social and political rhetoric by Scottish nationalists (Bowd 2013). Indeed, as the example of the Canongate campaigners suggests, socialist ideals have long found small but persistent purchase in Scottish political spheres. Rory Scothorne has depicted the vigorous activism of the left in Scottish universities from 1968 (2018), and Scottish electoral politics has featured socialist parties in some form since devolution, at its peak in 2003 sending six SSP representatives to Holyrood. Although no socialist party members currently serve in Scottish Parliament, since 2013, the SSP has officially supported Scottish independence, characterizing the Scottish government's vision for independence as a "very significant advance for the people of Scotland" (Fox 2013).

This deradicalization of socialist politics in exchange for measurable gains took place in the Canongate campaign as well. Rather than pitting democratic and socialist political visions against one another in the manner that typifies much popular political discourse, the Canongate campaign accommodated Catriona's socialist values into its dominant practices of liberal democratic politics (cf. Graeber 2009), not only through public events celebrating socialist mobilization but also in everyday discussions and interactions. Exploration of the degree to which the movement for national independence in Scotland has rehabilitated the social and economic ideals not only from its socialist heritage but of other social and political movements as well highlights the contingency of political identity formation and its dependence on the conditions of a social and political field.

The egalitarian mythology of the Scottish nation has provided supportive rhetoric and imagery for affirmations of working-class presence integral to the political activism of the Canongate residents. The egalitarian myth affirms the basis of solidarities required for collective action, whether between Canongate residents and conservation professionals against a particular urban development or between university lecturers and council housing residents against state austerity measures like benefits and social program cuts. As a historic and live component of public discourse about the Scottish nation, this myth has served to affirm equality—an affirmation that constitutes the very definition of political action, according to Rancière. Following Rancière's characterization of politics as dissensual and polemical, a "political culture" of engagement as Hassan observed at the start of the chapter might be expected to take shape in a society with a public discourse of egalitarianism. Indeed, a political culture in which all voices, especially the marginalized and otherized, claim their equality in public and political space, would make significant strides toward the realization of an egalitarian society in a manner that closely approximates the aesthetic politics described by Rancière. As other countries with claims to egalitarian social structure and values have expressed, if this mythology is appropriated by a culturalist discourse of the nation, such myths can be leveraged to devastating effect against racial and ethnic others. That the egalitarian mythology has not been culturalized to the same extent in Scotland indicates that other dynamics are at play in the appropriation of egalitarian ideals and rhetoric of both the SNP and the Canongate campaigners.

### Negotiating with Nationalism: Cosmopolitanism, Socialism, and Englishness

Closely related to the mythology of egalitarian Scotland is the rhetoric of cosmopolitan Scotland, a Scotland "in Europe" that affirms multiculturalism against ethnic or racial exclusivism. This political rhetoric of inclusivity distinguishes the SNP's platforms from most other nationalist parties in the twenty-first century, as evidenced in this statement on the SNP website,

"Immigration strengthens our economy, helps our public services thrive and enriches our society" (SNP). But the research on immigrant experiences in Scotland paints a more ambivalent scene: Hunter and Meer find a disconnect between the "elite visions of Scotland and popular opinions on [race and migration]" (2018, 383; cf. Leith and Soule 2011; Liinpää 2018), while McCollum, Nowok, and Tindal find "the public in Scotland being less hostile to migration than elsewhere in Britain" (2014, 82), and a Manchester University analysis of the 2011 census results concludes that "Scottish national identity is currently more ethnically inclusive than English [identity] is in England (Simpson and Smith 2014, 2). The realities of the immigrant experience in Scotland have been characterized as a "mixed bag," but as David McCollum has noted, the narrative of Scottish exceptionalism on migration may well exert a positive effect on those realities (2020, 428). For the SOOT campaigners, the prevalence of public proimmigration discourse made such positions easier to take up, both in their neighborhoods and in their alliances with left-leaning conservation professionals, planners, and architects. The path of greatest social and political resistance in these circles would have been any open discrimination or hostility. That the discourse of immigration more easily drifted toward affirmation does not address the experiences of black and brown Scots, however, which often diverge significantly from formal or official rhetoric. As with the egalitarian ideal of Scottishness discussed in the previous section, this ideal must be regarded as a noteworthy ambition rather than a fait accompli.

Nevertheless, as an ambition and an imaginary, multicultural Scotland and its constituent cosmopolitan Scots present a nationalist discourse that does distinguish this civic or liberal form of nationalism from the more ethnic or cultural forms that have gained traction throughout England, and most especially in the heartlands of postindustrial English towns (Hearn 2000; Leith and Soule 2011; McCrone 2017). This contrast between respective nationalist rhetorics and images becomes all the sharper when the concerns of the English nationalist voters are considered. With her lens focused on England, Gillian Evans writes about the rising popularity of "far-right cultural nationalism" among "left-wing white working-class voters," attributing these votes to their protest "against New Labour, which was now perceived to be mainly preoccupied with courting big business, and the middle classes, whilst supporting multiculturalism, and the drive to individual self-sufficiency" (2017, 90). Evans explains that the nationalist rhetoric of the British National Party (BNP) in England assisted in the breaking up of solidarities between working-class Brits of varied racial and ethnic backgrounds, and in so doing "reconfigure[d] working-class politics" (Evans 2017, 90).

The concerns that Evans articulated with New Labour's orientation toward business, the consumer classes, and a lifestyle-driven design probably made an appearance, very possibly in rhyme, on a banner outside Edinburgh's city council chambers at any given protest during the CCF/SOOT campaign. But in their rejection of the logics and values of neoliberal urbanism, the Canongate residents never targeted multicultural Scotland. As suggested in previous pages, the multicultural interactions and cosmopolitan attitudes of the campaigners indicate their lack of interest in such a scapegoat. Of the three campaigners discussed in the following pages, Sally has promoted and marched with ethnic groups in Edinburgh; Catriona advocated developing campaign links to neighborhoods facing similar development threats in Harlem, New York, and in Prague, Czech Republic; and Tom's social media posts regularly display artwork celebrating varied cultural and ethnic backgrounds.

But elaboration of racial or ethnic components to their social vision—either restrictive or inclusive—did not feature in their campaign for two reasons. Firstly, residents identified their opposition as their own council leaders who promoted a neoliberal urban development aesthetic rather than any proposed demographic group. Secondly, the discourse of multicultural Scotland or a virtuous cosmopolitanism had not yet gained prominence in the SNP's public political discourse at the time of the campaign. Such discussions circulated through SNP messaging in 2009–2015, which presented a "social justice frame" that moralized such images of Scotland (Breeze et al. 2015, 427). As the SNP's case for an independent, multicultural Scotland gained an ever-growing audience, multiculturalism as a feature of Scotland and cosmopolitanism as an orientation to the global gained significance, morally distinguishing the Scottish nation. Canongate campaigners, almost all of whom were white or could pass as such, participated in a limited neighborhood multiculturalism: mostly Scottish, Irish, or English, or migrants from elsewhere in Europe. As the social justice framings of the SNP circulated more widely, residents could and did appropriate cosmopolitan language to describe the Scottish nation. Their use of this language and its construction of a de facto multicultural and ideologically cosmopolitan

Scotland required only a minor adaptation of the political aesthetic that campaigners had cultivated in the SOOT campaign. The SNP's articulation of a familiar moral platform, rooted in Scottish cultural myths, could be appropriated by the former campaigners to expand the Canongate aesthetic into the sphere of national politics. Such appropriation did not invent political interests out of whole cloth but called up their experiences of intercultural engagement and the pursuit of international connections through their activism. The SNP's public rhetoric thus both resonated with their experiences and served to shape their participation in Scottish politics.

The SNP's vision of Scotland has affirmed the political aesthetic of the campaigners' Canongate, amplified certain aspects of their experience, and conferred an affect of hope to the campaign's ideals of an egalitarian, socially democratic politics in which working classes may expect to lay effective claims on the state. But as the following personal narratives of Scottish politics show, the SNP's agenda of national independence carries questionable entailments of nationalist political sentiments, even in this liberal invocation. Three engagements with Scottish national politics by three campaigners—Sally, Catriona, and Tom—are presented below. While all three former campaigners affirm the SNP's pursuit of a social vision more broadly and view the party as oriented toward greater democratic accountability, uncertainty remains regarding how this socially democratic vision relates to nationalism. Interpreting Scottish nationalism through their own social positions and experiences, each campaigner articulates their view on national politics, nationalism, and the possibilities attendant to political independence.

### Sally

Of all the former CCF/SOOT campaigners, Sally has become the most ardent advocate for Scottish independence. She is the one most likely to slip into the language of "banal" nationalism (Billig 1995), combining her own agency with Scotland through the word "we." As I visited with Sally one morning in 2018, we sat on the concrete steps outside her home, which is on the upper row of a colony development that was built in the late nineteenth century for working-class laborers and their families. She left the door ajar for the cat to come and go, and we took our tea in the late summer sunshine, discussing Scottish politics. As our conversation ranged widely, Sally mused about immigration in Scotland, with the implied contradistinction of England in the background, "*We* don't want to be the small backward exclusive country. The way a country grows and thrives is to have many people coming in and out" [emphasis mine]. "We" was not used to demarcate a Scottish "other," although as Tom's narrative below suggests, an external "they" was implied: the English nationalists voting to remove the UK from the EU, covered constantly in the British news. To list some benefits of immigration that she had come to appreciate, Sally enthused about the educational experiences her child was having in her Edinburgh school: "There are Australians, Spanish, French, Polish, Romanians, and Muslims. It's a fantastic school." Pausing, she reflected,

> You know, these people and their children are growing up knowing it's completely normal for people to come from all over, and you don't have to be born and stay somewhere your whole life. But on the other side, there are some people who have [stayed somewhere their whole life]. I've encountered them; they were born and bred in Edinburgh, and even if you're Scottish and you come from somewhere else, you are seen as an in-comer [when you move to Edinburgh]. [laughs] So I think it's easier for people to not see others as "the other" when you've experienced being "the other."

Those personal moral claims to cosmopolitanism bore a clear aesthetic resemblance to the life that Sally has cultivated since coming to Edinburgh: as an artist, her influences and interests range widely, and in the city, so does she. The food she cooks (and is praised for among friends) is as influenced by Greece and North Africa as by Scotland, and she enjoys sampling new flavors and combinations. Although she no longer resides in the Canongate, Sally notes that her city-center location is key to the life she has cultivated. Her cosmopolitanism is practiced within an urban geography with robust transportation networks and is characterized by a connectivity that differs from both her early years and many of her working-class peers.

Sally was born and raised in rural Scotland, and in coming to Edinburgh, she was initially placed on a council housing estate on the city's peripheries. Disliking the marginal location intensely, Sally made contact with another woman living in a council flat in the Canongate, who was interested in Sally's comparatively larger house in which to raise her children. The two families swapped council houses, a not-uncommon practice, and Sally became a city-center Old Town resident. When I asked her during that conversation on the front steps whom she knew in the peripheral estates today, she raised her eyebrows expressively and admitted she did not know anyone. That theme carried throughout my interviews across the Old Town: from the Grassmarket to the Canongate to Dumbiedykes. City-center working-class residents maintained largely clustered social networks with few, if any, connections to the outer estates. The apparent spatial and social distinction between working-class social networks, quite apart from shared social class positions, highlights the specificity of working-class experiences and the importance of those factors in social and political life. Much of the social science research on the working classes in Britain has been conducted in fairly isolated locations, such as council housing estates (Koch 2015), formerly industrial villages (Gilfillan 2011; Tyler 2004), and suburbs (Mollona 2009; Smith 2017). These accounts represent the residents' institutional and communal engagements in everyday life and often directly address the negative stereotypes and demonizations of these populations (Tyler 2013). But research in isolated locations, and on council estates in particular, cannot be made to stand in for research on "the working classes"; rather it describes particular cocktails of class precarity and spatial isolation, just as in the Canongate, the working-class experiences reflect residents' social and spatial integration within the city center.

For Canongate residents like Sally, being working class without the deprivations of geographic distance meant that "if you've not got much money—You know I can walk to the park, I can walk to Waverley [train] station, I can walk to shops, I don't feel cut off like I would on a peripheral estate—because they are not suburbia, they're still peripheral estates, and they've got issues because you've gotten so many people who have got different social problems, all compact." Sally suggested that her city-center location offered a bundle of material, social, and affective qualities, which have shaped her sense of the possible. Her cosmopolitan affirmations of cultural sharing and her high degree of mobility in Edinburgh, complemented by her travels with her family, have enabled her to sample the delights of grilled halloumi, continental painting, and South Asian textiles. Although these practices predated the SNP's ascendance, the connections between these practices, as part of the sense of life that she has cultivated by dwelling in the city center, and a morally freighted aesthetic of multicultural Scotland have been brought to her attention by the social justice frame of the SNP political rhetoric.

Sally's practices have not merely been folded up into a national discourse that interpreted them for her, however; as an agent invested in the aesthetic construction of the nation, she has judged the SNP vision of the nation by the Canongate aesthetic, with its commitment to the right of the working classes to shape material and political processes. As easily as Sally's practices have accommodated the SNP platform, they have clashed with the neoliberal, elite cosmopolitanism materialized in the Caltongate proposal. Whereas Sally's working-class cosmopolitanism emphasized and defended the particularity of the Canongate neighborhood, the Caltongate proposal refused any sense of locality, its cosmopolitanism defined instead by a fluidity of place and its lack of "a specific local commitment towards belonging," on which Sally's habits of interaction, engagement, and exploration, in her own description, depended (Ramadan 2014, 57).

Whether the SNP social justice frame would continue to resonate with experiences from a flat on a council housing estate cannot be answered definitively, even by Sally. Certainly, these estates have produced social movements concerned with social integration and cultural exchange and more recently participated in national politics. The Craigmillar Festival Society in Edinburgh brought together international rosters of visual and performing artists in the 1960s and 1970s, and the 2014 referendum on independence succeeded in mobilizing youth on postindustrial housing estates in both Edinburgh and Glasgow, an event of no small wonder to estate residents with whom I have spoken. While the SNP rhetoric has shaped political discourse by offering a moralized, multicultural vision of Scotland, Cohen's theory of personal nationalism reminds us that the persuasiveness of such rhetoric depends on its relevance to everyday life and experience.

Sally's experience suggests a close relationship between urban conditions and national political discourse, which in her case has produced self-conscious affirmations of cosmopolitan practices and attitudes. This positive relationship indicates that in the converse, we should consider the impact of alternative conditions, in particular the forced mobilities experienced by refugees or other kinds of lives in exile, on postures toward nation, culture, and identity. That such experiences tend to destabilize processes of individual and group social and political identification (Tihanov 2014) should prompt care when characterizing the affective expressions of cosmopolitanism, lest we inadvertently construct another affect category—the attitudes of idealized cosmopolitans—through which to police refugees and political migrants (Silverstein 2018). The destabilizing effects of forced relocations furthermore suggest that we should not presume that the campaigners' identification with cosmopolitan Scottishness, which has been forged through place-based engagements with a particular city center, will continue to flourish through their forced relocation. In other words, if the Canongate (or other neighborhoods like it) has provided aesthetic arrangements of persons, places, social life, and communal life amenable to a working-class cosmopolitanism, it should not be presumed that such cosmopolitan attitudes will continue to flourish in the absence, particularly a forced absence, of such conditions. We need not ascribe a deterministic relationship to place and politics, but we should reflect on Sally's observations that a socially, culturally, and politically engaged life has been easier to sustain in a place integrated closely with other neighborhoods and proximate to the institutions of urban life. In fact, as patterns of suburban residence and middle-class positions in the United States correlated strongly with votes in 2016 and 2020 for the authoritarian, nationalist populism of Donald Trump, the apparent relationships between geographic residence, class, and political imaginaries suggest a field ripe for exploration.

Sally's national politics bear the distinctive aesthetic traces of the Canongate's moral order, and while she has adapted her self-narration to the SNP discourses of multiculturalism and cosmopolitanism, as I have shown, these political virtues reflect realities rooted in the Canongate, as well as in her current city-center location. In contrast to the elite cosmopolitanism of the Caltongate development, the cosmopolitanism of the SNP does not require her to abandon the Canongate aesthetic but affirms its social and political critiques. Of the three campaigners discussed in this chapter, Sally has most fully embraced the SNP political agenda. She has supported national independence through participation in marches, the distribution of nationalist materials via her social networks, and in regular social media usage that advocated this campaign in its commitment to ideals, she has espoused through her community activism. The connections between ideals championed in the Canongate campaign and the Scottish independence campaigns are direct for Sally. Neither in person nor on social media did she hedge her advocacy for national independence, although she does worry about the SNP's willingness to halt the urban growth machine and exploitative capitalism more generally.

The two campaign leaders discussed in the following sections have also praised some platforms of Scotland's nationalist political rhetoric; in particular, the egalitarian social order and vision of multicultural Scotland. Their willingness to identify as nationalists, however, has been complicated by conditions particular to their own backgrounds and positions. These leaders offer engagements with Scottish nationalism that emphasize the personal nature of nationalist politics and affirm that what is perceived by individuals in any nationalist campaign exceeds the official rhetoric and political platforms.

### Catriona

Of the campaigners, Catriona had the longest history in the Canongate; a great-aunt had lived in the neighborhood, and so Catriona had grown up visiting the place and eventually moved into the flat. Following the start of building works on the Caltongate development site, Catriona traded that Canongate flat and moved to the historically working-class, though gentrifying, area of Leith in a move similar to Sally's. Although her flight from the neighborhood was not forced on her by private or government action, it could not be considered entirely voluntary either; rather, the spatial expression of disappointed hopes and stymied political agency. Catriona's politics stood in the long tradition of Scottish working-class mobilizations; as a third-generation socialist, her views on politics and society were refracted through a deeply felt class identity. It was Catriona, therefore, who was most likely to judge a person on their responsibility to other members of their social class or community and most likely to cite socialist political theory in her judgments.

We reflected on her experiences in political activism when I visited in 2017. I was reminded of the Canongate campaign's invocation of the political activism of the early twentieth century, when Catriona connected her views of communal responsibility to her grandfather's way of thinking, as a Catholic socialist in the same era. She explained to me that he saw working-class individuals as bound to the welfare of their class, concluding that a person should not try to get ahead on her own but should rise up with her people. She reminded me that self-betterment, such as obtaining the undergraduate and graduate degrees she had earned, should benefit the people in a community. This was the neglect that she perceived in the upwardly mobile trajectory prescribed by former council leader Donald Anderson. His exemplary personal narrative of having "made it" from the housing estate to the city council, a narrative that expressed the realization of neoliberal agency (Gershon 2011), was negated in Catriona's eyes by his apparent lack of interest in advocating for the expressed interests of his people, the working classes. When Anderson had commended upward social mobility broadly to the working classes, Catriona had replied exasperatedly, "But not everyone can *be* middle-class!" Her activities in the CCF/SOOT campaign had sought to protect a "place for the working class in the city center," as did her bid as a Scottish Socialist candidate running for council office, in which she sought to fundamentally discredit neoliberal property-based accumulation strategies and the homogenizing narratives of individual aspiration.

So Catriona's engagement with the Caltongate planning process and CCF/SOOT campaign had been, to a heightened degree even when compared to the other campaigners, shaped by a class-based politics, and through that class-based aesthetic, she addressed national politics as well. Working-class politics in Scotland has long claimed national independence as a means to the improvement of working-class welfare (Brown, McCrone, and Paterson 1996; Gilfillan 2011), and although analysis of the 2014 independence referendum votes suggests that independence may appeal as much to middle-class Scots as well (Paterson 1997), the connection between working classes and nationalism in Scotland remains strong. While Catriona's support for independence may seem to typify working-class Scottish nationalism, she takes exception to that label and in doing so demonstrates again the complexities hidden under the veil of electoral outcomes. Catriona emphasized to me that her interest in Scottish nationalism is purely instrumental, a political means to add teeth to her critiques of neoliberalism. An independent Scotland, she explained, could become a society more attuned to the experiences of the poor and working classes, a version of the "Scottish Socialist Republic" that she envisions. She added that, were she English, she would probably vote Labour to strengthen the effectiveness of working-class politics through that party's influence. The reason she was not voting Labour, however, was due to "the history of the Union." She explained, "I'm not anti-English, but I am anti-UK. There have been times that it's worked out for Scotland to be part of Britain [said grudgingly], but for the most part it's not been good for Scotland. People just don't understand that it's not about nationalism."

When I interjected to clarify my understanding, "It's not about Scotland," Catriona retorted, "Och. I don't care about '*Scotland*'!" She was voting, she insisted, "for a change" and for "something better." Like Sally, Catriona's politics had been charged by the affect of hope generated by the rise of the SNP, but Catriona's vision of "something better" has included more radical solutions than the SNP or Sally have pursued. A favorite photo features Catriona standing with her partner before a yellow banner that reads, "Scottish Socialist Party" across the top, with the byline "Defy All Cuts" below and "Unite*Strike*Occupy" across the bottom. Catriona's socialist politics had been recognized as a distinctive of hers throughout the CCF/SOOT campaign, and they were generally respected by other campaigners as representing an idealistic, local, and historic strand of working-class political activism, one compatible with a liberal democratic state.

As the narrative of the CCF/SOOT campaign illustrated, the values of community empowerment and of people's right to a home, which became important to that campaign, bore significant continuities with the objectives of socialist politics in Glasgow and Edinburgh. Catriona could and did bring her socialist principles to campaign meetings and assert them as moral alternatives to the neoliberal urbanism being pursued via Caltongate. As the SNP rose in prominence, however, the space for SSP representation shrunk to insignificance. The SNP's "social justice frame" (Breeze et al. 2015, 427), introduced in 2009–2015, presented a national platform of values quite sympathetic to both Catriona's socialist politics and the community activism of CCF/SOOT. An independent Scottish nation, although represented by the SNP as a form of Scottish liberal democracy, thus proved resonant with Catriona's values, especially in light of her experience fighting unsuccessfully to realize these values during the Caltongate's depoliticized development process. So Catriona came to support the Scottish independence movement, from a position further to the left of the SNP but satisfied for the moment to be advocating a change "for the better." She continued to distinguish her support for independence from national*ism*, however, which she associated, despite the inclusive rhetoric of the SNP, with an exclusionary politics that were anathema to her socialist principles of global solidarity.

### Tom

As both academic and media commentators on Scotland have observed, although the political promises of an independent Scotland have affirmed communitarian empowerment and egalitarian values, the accessibility of these promises to everyone in Scotland remains at best fuzzily defined and at worst strategically avoided (Davidson et al. 2018; McCollum 2020). Research detailing discrimination on the part of international, especially nonwhite, immigrants in Scotland has identified breakdowns in public discourse and private practice. One white resident of the Canongate, Tom, related his experiences of marginalization and anxiety that point to an enduring fracture in the image of an inclusive Scottish nation: the uncertainty of English residents in an independent Scotland. In popular and academic discourse about the character of Scottish nationalism, the positive characteristics of the Scottish nation (liberal/civic nationalism, egalitarianism) are often defined in contradistinction to English nationalism and Englishness (ethnic nationalism, hierarchy). This historic comparison seems to be legitimated by recent votes regarding Brexit (2016) and the 2019 general UK election, in which Scottish voting patterns contrasted dramatically with voting in England in particular. As Hearn has noted, this strategic contrast has been most evident when comparisons between Scotland and South East England are invoked rather than between Scotland and the northern industrial towns of England (2017), but the recent success of the BNP and the UK Independence Party (UKIP) in England in capitalizing on characterizations of the neglected "indigenous" English residents has heightened differences even between those more similar regions.

In Scottish nationalist discourse, England often becomes the "backward country," to use Sally's turn of phrase, from which Scots distance themselves politically and morally. The actions and discourse of the SNP encourage such framings. When SNP party leader and Scottish first minister Nicola Sturgeon directed her public statement to EU citizens in Scotland in April 2019, assuring them, "You are welcome here," the not-so-suppressed subtext amid turmoil between the England-led Conservative and Labour Parties over the terms of Brexit was "You are welcome *here*" (Brooks 2019). In nationalist political rhetoric, this distinctiveness grants Scotland a moral minority status within the UK, and the divergence of Scottish voting patterns, suggesting a distinctive national political perspective, has become the primary argument that Sturgeon and her party have instrumentalized as the rationale for a second independence referendum. At the time of writing (autumn 2020), public opinion in Scotland seemed to be embracing the rationale: a record high of 58 percent support for Scottish independence, following not only performances of electoral distinction via

Brexit but also Scottish responses to the COVID-19 pandemic, which have exercised greater caution more quickly than those in England and have been perceived favorably by most Scots.[3] As Scotland's independent future rests ever more heavily on its distinction from the habits of thought and practice of English people, the impacts of that distinction on the English, and the relations between Scots and English, must be considered.

Tom was one of the leaders of the CCF/SOOT campaign; born and raised in England, he migrated to Scotland in the 1970s, where he raised his family. He occupied the flat he owned in the Canongate at the time of the campaign, in a stair shared with three other families. Like Sally and Catriona, he became increasingly disillusioned with life in the neighborhood following the approval of the Caltongate proposal, and as construction on the New Waverley (formerly Caltongate) development progressed, the other families moved out, and Airbnb renting took over the remaining flats—all but two of the thirteen flats in his building, he estimated in 2017. Although he had become deeply invested in the Old Town community, having joined the Old Town Community Council and participated in this instrument of neighborhood politics for more than three decades, he recalled that at first he and his family's transition to Scotland was difficult. As "incomers," his family found it difficult to get to know people in Edinburgh, and the children at school were distinctly cool toward their new English classmates. But moving on quickly from this uneasy description, Tom highlighted the role of the Canongate neighborhood in easing his introductions, "When I first arrived here, it was just great to be able to go into the shops and have a talk with somebody and just meet people in the street and have a bit of gossip. Just, sort of, social stuff really!" That neighborhood community experience and his background in Old Town politics motivated his activism in the CCF/SOOT campaign.

Tom had worked closely with Sally and Catriona on the Canongate campaign, continuing with the work of the Edinburgh Old Town Development Trust (EOTDT) afterward. He and his family worked through the initial discomforts and exclusions they felt at being English in Scotland, such that Tom became both an integrated community member and political representative. In his community politics and relationships, Tom helped to articulate the distinctive Canongate aesthetic, and his long tenure in a flat there made him one of the neighborhood's most recognizable figures. In short, Tom appeared to be a model of English belonging in Scotland.

When we talked politics, he praised the work of the SNP and laughingly admitted that he, an Englishman, supported the SNP because he was "so disillusioned with the other parties" and because the SNP was managing "actual effective governance for everyday issues."

It was the question of Scottish independence, however, that raised Tom's concerns, and perhaps the specter of his earliest years in Scotland. He recalled an uneasy comment from a friend, also English, who had asked Tom privately, "Does that mean if it [the independence referendum vote] is 'Yes,' we have to move [back to England]?" Tom made it clear that he harbored no such fears, but he suggested that the comment pointed out a lack of inclusion, an English blind spot of sorts, in the nationalist rhetoric. Reflecting on his position, he admitted that he felt uncomfortable with the nationalist public discourse, despite the reality that "I've made most of my life in Scotland, my children have been in Scotland most of their lives, and there would be no reason to go down south. So really what I'm saying is, my home is here, in Scotland."

Tom's more than thirty years of local political engagement in Edinburgh, shaped by his social and political networks in Edinburgh and Glasgow, could be identified as a "lowercase" nationalist, the kind whose politics are distinctively Scottish but who may not identify with SNP-brand nationalism (Nairn 1995). In fact, Tom expressed the hope that the SNP would continue managing "everyday issues," which he judged they did well, and set independence as a long-term goal. When I asked him whether he thought Scotland should eventually pursue independence, he paused before replying, "It has a long way to go at the moment. I think there's potential there. And, that's the way I see it, I think it really has got potential. . . . But yes, I think it's a long way to go yet."

That Tom could express confidence in SNP governance and yet empathize with concerns about the prospects of English people in an independent Scotland, suggests some limits to the egalitarianism and civicness of Scottish nationalism. The distinctiveness of Scotland still relies on favorable comparison with a less liberal, more stratified England, and so for people born and raised in England but living in Scotland, even for decades, the question of full belonging remains fraught. To be sure, my fieldwork and interviews contain multiple affirmations from Scots of working and middle classes to the effect of "everybody's Scottish at the end of the day" (Breeze et al. 2015, 429), including all who live within the borders of Scotland and who by that fact have both right and responsibility to engage the question of independence. Tom's experience, however, suggests that Englishness remains one of the unresolved lacunae of Scottish nationalism, marking the affective limits of inclusion and of the long arm of Scotland's cosmopolitanism.

### From Neighborhood to Nation: Possibilities and Political Agency

The narratives of campaigners' engagement with nationalist politics in Scotland described in this chapter convey a nuanced portrait of nationalisms both personal and communal, formed in the crucible of their aesthetic activism against the property engines of neoliberal development. The Scottish nation was not, in these engagements, regarded as a more experience-distant scale of identification but rather as a potentially more effective instrument for the democratic pursuit of political ideals honed and cultivated through what felt like a failed community campaign. That is, the aesthetics of neighborhood and national politics were interpreted through and made to cohere with one another by the former CCF/SOOT campaign leaders. Sally, who identified personally with the Scottish nation, supported the SNP independence campaign directly, as a scaled-up attempt to realize the social and political ideals of the CCF/SOOT campaign. Catriona's affinity with the working-class politics of socialism motivated her to support the independence movement as a means to realizing the "social justice" aims of socialism without embracing the Scottish nation itself as a matter of identity. While Tom approved of the platforms and policies of the SNP and fashioned his political activities in support of them, his Englishness and his memory of its impacts on his family's initial efforts to gain acceptance in Scotland stopped him short of advocating for independence in the short term or identifying as a nationalist. Throughout these narratives, the former campaigners pursued congruence between neighborhood and national political aesthetic, refracted through their histories and desires.

The long duration of my fieldwork among these former Canongate residents has traced connections between political agency in neighborhood-level activism, which is often treated as expressing attachments between people and place but not necessarily addressing global concerns, and national political engagement. It has highlighted the significance of affect to the management of both municipal and national politics and of political aesthetics for the cultivation of coherence between scales of political action. As Sally, Catriona, and Tom all expressed in their own words, the failure of the CCF/SOOT campaign to protect and enrich the Canongate neighborhood dealt a profound blow to their sense not only of political efficacy but of moral empowerment as well. When walking through the Canongate in 2017, Catriona recalled the experience with dismay, "You think, well we've got the right on our side, and if we just get everyone together, then we can do it—but you can't!" This conversation reminded me of another walk through the Canongate, this time with Sally, who spotted some word art on a T-shirt for sale in a pricey women's shop, which read, "Remember: You can change the world." She had read it out loud dramatically, then turned back to me and proclaimed, "No, you cannot. That's not true. That's a lie." Following the disillusionment that they had experienced through the CCF/SOOT campaign, however, the aesthetic activism of the SNP surprised even these self-described "burnt-out" activists with a sense of hopeful possibility, which they sometimes struggled to reconcile with their emotive proclamations that they had given up on activism. While these former campaigners described to me their lost sense of confidence that good will prevail, all of their social media accounts continue to feature petitions to stop Caltongate-reminiscent reconfigurations across Edinburgh.

If the field of politics in Scotland can be described as a more "disputatious environment" (Hassan 2018), then the means by which the politics of dissensus manifest in particular campaigns and projects seeking transformation—and occasionally achieving it—necessitate examination. The inaccessibility of depoliticized urban development practices as helmed by a Labour-led city council has produced a long affect of exhaustion, among campaign leaders in particular. But while in the byzantine processes of city council governance, the clench of neoliberal logics has continued to shrink the space for public voice, the extension of direct democracy via national referenda on both independence and Brexit has made the neoliberal aesthetic appear most vulnerable at the scale of the nation. As the example of the Edinburgh Against Stock Transfer campaign has shown, working-class organization has found more pliable instruments of influence through such directly democratic events (see Interlude 3). The efficacy of community mobilization also increased in step with the onset of economic recession, when the former campaigners observed that good things can grow through the small spaces, cracks, and crevices of neoliberal capitalism (cf. Tsing 2015). It was in 2008–2009 that they managed to save the facades of the historically listed buildings and gain a voice for the EOTDT in future negotiations with the new developers. Similarly, the delay in organizing and settling the terms of Brexit has fostered intensification of discourse on national independence and helped insert a second independence referendum (IndyRef2) back into the conversation about democracy in Britain, where it gained traction in light of the COVID-19 pandemic.

Scotland's new civic debates have opened up spaces for community members' contestations and contributions, and the rhetoric of Scottish national independence, as promoted by the SNP, has resonated with campaigners' experiences of marginalization in their city. Disaffection with neoliberal policies of the working-class residents of the Canongate compares, in broad strokes, with that of urban working classes in England. But the leftist critiques of neoliberalism's competitive aesthetic order that have been leveraged by the SNP despite the party's ambivalent record navigating neoliberal policies, have given voice to the working-class disaffection of the Canongate residents, even while they appeal to the left-leaning middle classes (Paterson 1997). The collaboration between Canongate residents and heritage professionals, itself an adaptation of older interclass alliances, is affirmed through this political discourse and its performance of interclass solidarity. Scottish urban communities like the Canongate, which had lost their sense of political efficacy under neoliberalization guided by local governance, are finding it again in the political movement for Scottish independence.

If independence does come, only difficult and critical democratic work sorting the multitude of voices and visions that have bound their visions and strategies together in this movement can produce a genuinely cosmopolitan, egalitarian, and socially democratic Scotland. Although the prevalent nationalist social and political ideals reflect the influence of liberal democratic philosophy, the realization of an independent Scotland requires the sober recognition of racist, sexist, and classist streams of Scottish culture and social life, as well as a clear-eyed evaluation of resources and limitations within the geographic, environmental, social, and economic realities of the nation. On the tail of a turbulent history that follows the collapse of the British welfare state, the stripping back of the state, and the implementation of austerity measures led from Westminster, the rhetoric, parties, and policies that have seemed to support a Scottish welfare state have sketched an outline of political possibilities and a vision for a society in which working-class Scots are not pushed to the periphery but contribute meaningfully to political direction and priorities. In the coming years, the possibility of independence will be assessed according to the realization of—or at least progress toward—this vision, by working-class cosmopolitans like the Canongate campaigners.

## Notes

1. The "imperative of public space" for each of these campaigns suggests further the dynamics of spatial restructuring and privatization at play through neoliberal urbanism since the 1980s (Low and Smith 2006).

2. In such projects of collective identification, England is the most proximate and powerful foil. Indeed, the posture adopted in Scottish national narratives is that of England's more virtuous, less powerful neighbor. Owing to the structural position of Scotland in the UK, such comparative approaches tempt social scientists as well.

3. It is worth noting that by the *editing* stage of this book (autumn 2022), Scottish votes for independence have been wobbling up and down for months and are currently appearing to trend upwards of 50% again, reminding us to resist any impulses to call this race.

# CONCLUSION
# Urban Scotland, Working-Class Politics, and National Futures

AS NATIONALIST POLITICAL VISIONS CAPTURE an ever-widening proportion of democratic electorates across Europe, situating these particular nationalisms within their geographic, historical, social, and economic contexts becomes a project of pressing significance. In Scotland as elsewhere, working-class mobilizations have featured prominently within nationalist politics, and yet support for nationalism in Scotland is at least as strong among the middle classes, particularly among those who identify with the working classes (Paterson 2015). The prominence of working class as a popular identity in Scotland, the cultural mythology of Scots as a supposedly egalitarian people, and almost a century of electoral distinctiveness on social and economic issues within the British state have shaped the political and social imaginaries invoked in contemporary formations of the Scottish nation (McCrone 2017). Despite its proximity to some of the foremost centers of anthropological study in Europe, Scotland—and the city of Edinburgh in particular—has received comparatively little anthropological attention. The distinction of Scottish nationalism from other European nationalisms—even construed in the most sweeping binary rhetorical terms: civic rather than ethnic, liberal rather than conservative—indicate the importance of careful consideration of the social, political, and economic conditions that have given expression to a political movement seemingly out of step with its contemporaries, in Britain and beyond.

This book has contributed to an understanding of working-class political mobilization in urban Scotland, arguing that such mobilization should be viewed within a longer history of mixed-class political agency and alliances. From the perspective of a city-center neighborhood in Edinburgh called the Canongate, negotiation over the built environment has been presented as a significant subject of contemporary working-class political concern due to dominant practices of neoliberal development in the city and the narrowing of political possibilities that these practices effect in working-class lives. With a view to the history of Edinburgh's built environment, political activism seeking influence on the city's structures and spaces reflects a historic lever of working-class politics, of particular concern in issues relating to the provision of urban housing. That activism in the twentieth century produced intermittent alliances with middle-class conservationists as well as a key conceptualization of the built and social environment that gave expression to the shared interests of this alliance, Patrick Geddes's paradigm of conservative surgery. The Canongate residents' twenty-first-century campaign, with its place-specific historical impulses, invoked its past through Geddes as well as projects of activism by which earlier generations of residents had achieved political influence, both of which shaped their convictions about the appropriately political nature of the processes of urban development.

When faced instead with depoliticized processes of urban development, an affective politics that precluded their influence, and its characterization of moral economic behavior in terms they rejected, the Canongate residents developed critiques about neoliberal logic and governance grounded in their everyday practices of dwelling and experiences of thwarted political agency, critiques that would resonate with the political rhetoric and affect of the Scottish National Party (SNP). As residents of an urban center rife with international connections, the Canongate campaigners would not identify internationalism or multiculturalism as the culprits for their disempowerment but rather the local government's privileging of commercial business interests over those of city residents like themselves and its lack of commitment to the ideals of equality and political provision. The campaign for Scottish independence came to offer—in different ways, as represented by three of the campaign leaders discussed in this book—an opportunity to translate their concerns and welfare state—or socialist state—political vision to the national stage. These political imaginaries of the Scottish nation were negotiated through the spaces of the city, affirming Lefebvre's characterization of the essentially political nature of space and suggesting that the politics of urban space has direct implications for the politics of the nation.

As this book has shown, residents' political mobilizations in Scottish national politics are continuous with their political engagements in Edinburgh's processes of urban development. In light of the experience of the Canongate residents, several insights may be suggested to the study of Scottish nationalism, in particular highlighting factors that distinguish the working-class political activism in Edinburgh's city center from the participation of the working classes in other European nationalisms. The viability of centrally located council housing has maintained a presence of working classes in the center of this capital Scottish city, and through that location, residents have been able to engage development-related issues; (re)build alliances with middle-class professionals in the city; share criticisms over capital-focused development; and, by invoking the legacy of Geddes, find common ground in a social, political, and economic vision that unites accommodations to economic growth with provision for the working classes and conservation of the built environment.

We should also consider significant political moments and bridging movements that have contributed to a belief in the potential for working-class political efficacy among twenty-first-century activists. One such legacy that influenced the campaign of the Canongate residents is that of socialist activism in urban Scotland; such activism shaped the accommodations of the state to working-class housing provisions in particular (McCrone and Elliot 1989) and was regarded as an example of working-class political empowerment by the campaigners. Among participants in the Canongate campaign, this activism was not singled out as antidemocratic but rather was invoked as a kind of successful working-class political agency within a democratic state. As Catriona's accommodations to the Scottish independence movement indicate, some individuals like herself who identified with socialist political ideals have found in an independent Scottish welfare state an acceptable compromise, reaching agreement on issues relating to equality, fairness, and concern for the working classes and poor. Although both she and the official Scottish Socialist Party (SSP) position agree on the long-term goal as the formation of a Scottish Socialist Republic, joining cause with the SNP on its electorally ascendant path to pursue an independent Scotland appeared to offer the greatest, or most likely, hope for change. Canongate residents, wearied from political embattlement, did not perceive an independent Scotland as a utopian social vision but rather pursued it as an opportunity to chasten the neoliberalization of their urban political economy and reinvigorate a contentious, conflictual, and ultimately responsive politics.

As the case of Scotland indicates, a long-standing mythology of social equality and national exceptionalism can shape behavior and its interpretation, even while those ideals remain not fully or even satisfactorily realized (McCollum 2020). Cosmopolitanism rather than exclusivism continues to be championed in Scottish nationalist political rhetoric (Knight 2017), and for the Canongate campaigners, these ideals corroborated their experiences of living in a multicultural city center. That the negation of campaign claims levied by the Canongate residents paralleled the council's apparent disregard for concerns expressed by the middle-class conservationists with whom they allied themselves provided grounds for solidarity rather than a class-based isolation, and such alliances resonate with the interclass collaboration within the movement for national independence. I have argued not that the national political agency of the Canongate campaigners should be derived solely from their political activities in urban development but rather that the conditions and moral narratives in both these spaces have reinforced, reacted to, and built on one another. In the project of bettering our understandings of national political imaginaries and agency, exploring those political activities with which they are continuous and with which they cohere in meaningful ways directs us to the ongoing politics of city space. To consider this claim in light of one more city space in Edinburgh, this book ends with a scene set in Leith.

### Looking to Leith

In 2018, Sally and I met up at the foot of her stairs for a morning walk. She wanted to take me to the site of a proposed development, again for a hotel and again in a working-class neighborhood. This time the location was Leith, the community whose historic roots lay in the docks where the Firth of Forth joined the North Sea. Like the Canongate, Leith maintained its independence until the burgh was absorbed into Edinburgh in 1920, adding both a deep port and a considerable working-class population to the city. As we walked, Sally filled me in on the events I had been missing since we had last met in Edinburgh a year previous, and when we approached the site for which the hotel was intended, I noted that instead of residences, it consisted of a low-rise row of shops, now empty and fronted by gray hoarding.

Although she insisted she was done with such campaigns, Sally read with interest the messages painted, and in one case yarn-bombed, onto the hoarding, chuckling with appreciation at the caustically witty jibes directed at the city council. After reading each panel along the strip, she wished the community campaigners well, and we turned to proceed farther along the sidewalk. As we did so, Sally gestured across the street to a small glass-paned storefront: "It's happening already—here's your hipster bakery!" When I laughed at her light-hearted jab, she shrugged. "It's not their fault, really. They're just making brioche and coffee and trying to make a living. It's the council who've done this, selling off the shops and letting a developer build another hotel here."

This response was a familiar one. Although Sally might indulge in some mild hipster-mocking, her concern was not fundamentally with middle-class consumer lifestyles but with the political will to prioritize amenities for these lifestyles above the provision of services for working classes and the poor. As we walked on, we passed an open-air pedestrian mall at the entrance to a council housing development, which drew Sally's attention. "There—these are the stores that serve the poor," and she identified loan shops, a Poundsavers, and a frozen food store. "These wouldn't be for hipsters. Hipsters just like to live *near* poor people." This element, the aesthetic appeal of "grit" to the middle classes described by Sharon Zukin (2010) and identified by Sally with hipsters, represented a departure from the sweeping "upmarketing" development logic that had motivated the Caltongate proposal. The sale of grit—suggesting a posture of willfully blind proximity to poverty—Sally found more objectionable than the bakers' desire to make a living. As we continued on walking through the council housing block, she interrupted our conversation with a nod toward a pair of young men who had just strode rather forcefully past us, silently shoulder to shoulder, close-shaved hair, battered jean jackets, and cigarettes locked in their fingers. They had not spared us a glance, and Sally drily observed, "There are a couple of indigenous Leithers. Hipsters wouldn't stand a chance against them." As we walked on, I wondered again at the profuse modes of encroachment produced by neoliberal development practices.

The displacement of working-class residents to make way for new development projects has been documented in cities across Europe and North America, such that this depoliticized displacement may be defining the new typical experience of urban working-class precarity. Neoliberalizing development produces a kind of forced mobility, whether through formal requirement or through defamiliarization, as in the case of the Canongate campaigners. As these practices become ever more normalized and the working classes displaced from central urban locations, their ability to anchor themselves, individually and collectively, to the histories, events, and persons signified by the built environments of the city centers, themselves the cultural and political hubs of the nation, is correspondingly diminished. The Canongate case suggests that, in the inverse, material isolation may objectify social and symbolic exclusion from streams of social memory embedded in the built environment (Connerton 2009). Given the significance that has been attributed to centrally located housing by not only the present-day Canongate campaigners but their precursors in the nineteenth-century Old Town as well, the diverse impacts of working-class displacement to peripheral locations around the city must be carefully considered. Particularly in an era in which working-class discontent is feeding populist nationalisms across Europe (Kalb and Halmai 2011), supports for cosmopolitan attitudes among these populations, and factors that serve their sense of social and political integration, demand attention.

Today, much of the working-class population of the Canongate has been replaced by an encroaching wave of transients, and the tenements previously redeveloped by City Architects Ebenezer MacRae and Robert Hurd transformed into Airbnb rentals, student lodging, and hotels. Its former residents have sought new working-class communities that are integrated into the built and social fabric of the city rather than isolated at its margins. Leith has remained a popular destination for these working-class relocators, even as it increasingly attracts a middle-class population—including those "hipsters" Sally identified, along with some young professionals, university lecturers, and civil servants. In these ways, Leith, once a solidly working-class burgh, may today be characterized by the heterogeneous social mix that once typified the Old Town—and indeed that some, through the Edinburgh Old Town Development Trust (EOTDT), continue to pursue there. The juxtaposition of grime-streaked council houses, tidy and bright council houses, and new-build tenements managed by a housing cooperative, strung out all along a single stretch of road, fits poorly with the segregating property-development logic of neoliberal urbanism. But inasmuch as it facilitates the interclass proximity that Johnson and Rosenburg once identified in the Old Town, this juxtaposition may present a material and social environment conducive, if not sufficient in itself, to the sharing of social and political concerns. This is not to offer a utopian proposal for consensus by tenement stair; plenty of evidence from social science analysis demonstrates that proximity can be as harmful as it is helpful to the correcting of prejudice and building of solidarity. But the cosmopolitan working-class attitudes among the (former) Canongate residents discussed in this book suggest possibilities for solidarity based in a politics of home, a politics operative from neighborhood to nation. As the electoral negotiations of Brexit and grapplings with the devastations of a national pandemic continue to highlight political differences between Scotland and England, the ordinary politics of Scottish nationalism may signify the power and limits of these solidarities in a neoliberal era. The degree to which Scottish national politics delivers a more inclusive, just, and accessible state, or continues to smooth the path in its pursuit, constitutes a question—or, rather, a larger project—of pressing urgency, which demands that we take seriously the hopes and intentions of Scots like the Canongate activists.

# REFERENCES

Abbasi, Ayah, Chaham Alalouch, and Glen Bramley. 2016. "Open Space Quality in Deprived Urban Areas: User Perspective and Use Pattern." *Procedia: Social and Behavioral Sciences* 216:194–205.
Abélès, Marc. 2017. *Thinking beyond the State*. Translated by Phillip Rousseau and Marie-Claude Haince. Ithaca, NY: Cornell University Press.
Adamson, Alex, Lynn Kilpatrick, and Miriam McDonald. 2016. *Pints, Politics and Piety: The Architecture and Industries of Canongate*. Edinburgh: Historic Environment Scotland.
Allan, Vicky. 2008. "The End of Heritage?" *The Herald*, November 15. Accessed November 29, 2022. https://www.heraldscotland.com/default_content/12767123.end-heritage/.
Allen, Chris. 2008. *Housing Market Renewal and Social Class*. London: Routledge.
Anderson, Benedict. 1991. *Imagined Communities: Reflections on the Origins and Spread of Nationalism*. New York: Verso.
Andersson, Ruben. 2014. *Illegality, Inc.: Clandestine Migration and the Business of Bordering Europe*. Oakland: University of California Press.
Andrews, Malcolm. 1989. *The Search for the Picturesque: Landscape Aesthetics and Tourism in Britain 1760–1800*. Stanford: Stanford University Press.
Appadurai, Arjun. 1986. *The Social Life of Things*. Cambridge: Cambridge University Press.
———. 2006a. *Fear of Small Numbers: An Essay on the Geography of Anger*. Durham, NC: Duke University Press.
———. 2006b. "The Thing Itself." *Public Culture* 18 (1): 15–21.
Arendt, Hannah. 1958. *The Human Condition*. Chicago: University of Chicago Press.
Arnstein, Sherry R. 1969. "A Ladder of Citizen Participation." *Journal of the American Institute of Planners* 35 (4): 216–24.
Art, David. 2011. *Inside the Radical Right: The Development of Anti-Immigrant Parties in Western Europe*. Cambridge: Cambridge University Press.
Avila, Eric. 2014. *The Folklore of the Freeway: Race and Revolt in the Modernist City*. Minneapolis: Minnesota University Press.
Bahloul, Joëlle. 1996. *The Architecture of Memory: A Jewish-Muslim Household in Colonial Algeria, 1937–1962*. Cambridge: Cambridge University Press.
Baiocchi, Gianpaolo, Elizabeth Bennett, Alissa Cordner, Peter Taylor Klein, and Stephanie Savell. 2014. *The Civic Imagination: Making a Difference in American Political Life*. Boulder, CO: Paradigm.
Baker, Brian. 2006. "Edinburgh's New Leader Promises to Listen over City's Transport Plans." *City Mayors*, September 28. Accessed November 7, 2020. http://www.citymayors.com/politics/edinburgh_aitken.html.

Bald, John. 1999a. "Arthur's Street." In *Collective Views*, 19–20. Edinburgh: Dumbiedykes Writers Group.
———. 1999b. "The Not So Good Old Days." In *Collective Views*, 22–23. Edinburgh: Dumbiedykes Writers Group.
Balthazar, Ana Carolina. 2021. *Ethics and Nationalist Populism at the British Seaside*. New York: Routledge.
Barclay, Katie, and Rosalind Carr. 2013. "Rewriting the Scottish Canon: The Contribution of Women's and Gender History to a Redefinition of Social Classes." *Études Écossaises* 16:11–28.
Barnett, Clive. 2008. "Political Affects in Public Space: Normative Blind-Spots in Non-Representational Ontologies." *Transactions of the Institute of British Geographers* 33 (2): 186–200.
Bartha, Eszter. 2011. "'It Can't Make Me Happy That Audi Is Prospering:' Working Class Nationalism in Hungary after 1989." In *Headlines of Nation, Subtexts of Class: Working Class Populism and the Return of the Repressed in Neoliberal Europe*, edited by Don Kalb and Gábor Halmai, 92–112. New York: Berghahn.
Baxstrom, Richard. 2008. *Houses in Motion: The Experience of Place and the Problem of Belief in Urban Malaysia*. Stanford: Stanford University Press.
BBC News. 2005. "Residents Reject Housing Transfer." December 15. Accessed November 16, 2022. http://news.bbc.co.uk/2/hi/uk_news/scotland/4530106.stm.
Bechhofer, Frank, and David McCrone. 2015. *Understanding National Identity*. Cambridge: Cambridge University Press.
Beck, Ulrich. 1992. *Risk Society: Towards a New Modernity*. Translated by Mark Ritter. London: Sage.
Bell, Henry. 2018. *John Maclean: Hero of Red Clydeside*. London: Pluto.
Bianchini, Franco, and Michael Parkinson, eds. 1993. *Cultural Policy and Urban Regeneration: The West European Experience*. Manchester: Manchester University Press.
Billig, Michael. 1995. *Banal Nationalism*. London: Sage.
Biressi, Anita, and Heather Nunn. 2013. *Class and Contemporary British Culture*. London: Palgrave Macmillan.
Blackburn, Lucy, and Michael Keating. 2012. "Scottish Policy Innovation Forum. Localism and Local Governance: Scotland in Context." *Scottish Affairs* 81:98–109.
Blackley, Michael. 2007. "City Red Tape 'Driving Firms to Glasgow.'" *Edinburgh Evening News*, August 16.
Bloch, Maurice, and Jonathan Parry. 1989. *Money and the Morality of Exchange*. Cambridge: Cambridge University Press.
Bonino, Stefano. 2019. "Discrimination against Muslims in Scotland." In *The Routledge International Handbook of Islamophobia*, edited by Irene Zempi and Imran Awan, 161–74. London: Taylor and Francis.
Bort, Eberhardt. 2010. "Review: History of Edinburgh." *Scottish Affairs* 72 (1): 119–26.
Bourdieu, Pierre. 1991. *Language and Symbolic Power*. Cambridge, MA: Harvard University Press.

Bowd, Gavin. 2013. *Fascist Scotland: Caledonia and the Far Right*. Edinburgh: Birlinn.
Breeze, Maddie, Hugo Gorringe, Lynn Jamieson, and Michael Rosie. 2015. "'Everybody's Scottish at the End of the Day': Nationalism and Social Justice among Young Yes Voters." *Scottish Affairs* 24 (4): 419–31.
Breitenbach, Esther. 1993. "Out of Sight, Out of Mind? The History of Women in Scottish Politics." *Scottish Affairs* 2 (1): 58–70.
Brenner, Neil, and Nik Theodore. 2002. "Cities and the Geographies of 'Actually Existing Neoliberalism.'" *Antipode* 34 (3): 347–79.
Brooks, Libby. 2019. "Nicola Sturgeon Tells EU Citizens in Scotland: 'You Are Welcome Here.'" *Guardian*, April 5, 2019.
Brown, Alice, David McCrone, and Lindsay Paterson. 1996. *Politics and Society in Scotland*. London: Palgrave.
Buch, Elana D. 2015. "Postponing Passage: Doorways, Distinctions, and the Thresholds of Personhood among Older Chicagoans." *Journal of Psychological Anthropology* 43 (1): 40–58.
Bunzl, Matti. 2005. "Between Anti-Semitism and Islamophobia: Some Thoughts on the New Europe." *American Ethnologist* 32 (4): 499–508.
Caltongate. 2006. *Living*. Accessed February 22, 2011. http://replay.waybackmachine.org/20080725082532/http://www.caltongate.com/Living.aspx.
Calvino, Italo. 1972. *Invisible Cities*. New York: Harcourt.
Campbell, Ian, and Margaret Stewart. 2005. "The Evolution of the Medieval and Renaissance City." In *Edinburgh: The Making of a Capital City*, edited by Brian Edwards and Paul Jenkins, 21–41. Edinburgh: Edinburgh University Press.
Canongate Community Forum. 2007. "Jock the Weathercock Disappears." Accessed July 5, 2012. http://eh8.org.uk/jock_the_weathercock_disappears.
Cant, Alanna. 2019. *The Value of Aesthetics: Oaxacan Woodcarvers in Global Economies of Culture*. Austin: University of Texas Press.
Carlyle, Andrew. 1910. *Autobiography of Dr. Alexander Carlyle of Inveresk, 1722–1805*. Edited by J. H. Burton. London: T. N. Foulis.
Carrier, David G. 2006. *A Handbook of Economic Anthropology*. Northampton, MA: Edward Elgar.
Carrier, David G., and Don Kalb, eds. 2015. *Anthropologies of Class: Power, Practice and Inequality*. Cambridge: Cambridge University Press.
Carsten, Janet, and Stephen Hugh-Jones. 1995. *About the House: Lévi-Strauss and Beyond*. Cambridge: Cambridge University Press.
Challinor, Ray. 1977. *The Origins of British Bolshevism*. London: Croom Helm.
Chesluk, Benjamin J. 2008. *Money Jungle: Imagining the New Times Square*. New Brunswick, NJ: Rutgers University Press.
City of Edinburgh Council. 2005. *The Edinburgh Business Assembly*. May 10. Accessed November 2, 2020. https://silo.tips/download/this-report-outlines-the-principles-underlying-the-new-edinburgh-business-assemb.
City of Edinburgh Council. 2006a. *Caltongate Masterplan*. October 5.
City of Edinburgh Council. 2006b. "Scottish Executive Consultation: Draft PAN on Community Engagement." *Planning Committee Report*.

Clark, Colin. 2018. "Sites, Welfare and 'Barefoot Begging': Roma and Gypsy/Traveller Experiences of Racism in Scotland." In *No Problem Here: Understanding Racism in Scotland*, edited by Neil Davidson, Minna Liinpää, Maureen McBride, and Satnam Virdee, 145–61. Edinburgh: Luath.

Coates, David. 1981. "Labourism and the Transition to Socialism." *New Left Review* 129:3–22.

Cohen, Anthony P. 1996. "Personal Nationalism: A Scottish View of Some Rites, Rights and Wrongs." *American Ethnologist* 23 (4): 802–15.

Cole, Jennifer. 1998. "The Work of Memory in Madagascar." *American Ethnologist* 25 (4): 610–33.

Coleman, Leo. 2018. "Building Scotland, Building Solidarity: A Scottish Architect's Knowledge of Nation." *Comparative Studies in Society and History* 60 (4): 873–906.

Collier, Stephen J. 2012. "Neoliberalism as Big Leviathan or…? A Response to Wacquant and Hilgers." *Social Anthropology* 20 (2): 186–95.

Connerton, Paul. 2009. *How Modernity Forgets*. Cambridge: Cambridge University Press.

Creed, Gerald W. 2006. *The Seductions of Community: Emancipations, Oppressions, Quandaries*. Santa Fe, NM: School of American Research Press.

Crummy, Helen. 1992. *Let the People Sing! A Story of Craigmillar*. Edinburgh: H. Crummy.

Daly, Guy, Gerry Mooney, Lynne Poole, and Howard Davis. 2007. "Housing Stock Transfer in Birmingham and Glasgow: The Contrasting Experience of Two UK Cities." *European Journal of Housing Policy* 5 (3): 327–41.

Darling, Elizabeth. 2015. "A World in Action: Women's Work and Children's Work in the Canongate's St. Saviour's Child Garden, 1906-1914." In *The Evergreen: A New Season in the North*, edited by Sean Bradley, 111–23. Edinburgh: Word Bank.

Davidson, Neil, Minna Liinpää, Maureen McBride, and Satnam Virdee, eds. 2018. *No Problem Here: Understanding Racism in Scotland*. Edinburgh: Luath.

Davidson, Neil, and Satnam Virdee. 2018. "Introduction: Understanding Racism in Scotland." In *No Problem Here: Understanding Racism in Scotland*, edited by Neil Davidson, Minna Liinpää, Maureen McBride, and Satnam Virdee, 9–12. Edinburgh: Luath.

DeFilippis, James, Roger Fisher, and Eric Shragge. 2010. *Contesting Community: The Limits and Potential of Community Organizing*. New York: Taylor and Francis.

Degnen, Cathrine. 2013. "'Knowing,' Absence and Presence: The Spatial and Temporal Depth of Relations." *Environment and Planning D: Society and Space* 31:554–70.

Degnen, Cathrine, and Katharine Tyler. 2017. "Reconfiguring the Anthropology of Britain: Ethnographic, Theoretical and Interdisciplinary Perspectives." *Sociological Review Monographs* 65 (1).

Dekkers, Wim. 2011. "Dwelling, House and Home: Towards a Home-Led Perspective on Dementia Care." *Medicine, Health Care and Philosophy* 14 (3): 291–300.

Deleuze, Gilles, and Felix Guattari. 1987. *A Thousand Plateaus: Capitalism and Schizophrenia*. Translated from the French by Brian Massumi. Minneapolis: University of Minnesota Press.

Dennison, E. Patricia. 2005. *Holyrood and Canongate: A Thousand Years of History*. Edinburgh: Birlinn.
Desmond, Matthew. 2016. *Evicted: Poverty and Profit in the American City*. New York: Penguin.
Devine, T. M. 2003. *Scotland's Empire: The Origins of the Global Diaspora*. Harmondsworth: Penguin.
Dickie, Mure, and John Burn-Murdoch. 2020. "Scotland's Coronavirus Record Flattered by Comparison to South." *Financial Times*, June 1. Accessed November 8, 2020. https://www.ft.com/content/a3fe315f-610a-4086-a6bc-a466a7f33aa1.
Donaldson, Jean. 1999. "Holyrood Square." In *Collective Views*, 21. Edinburgh: Dumbiedykes Writers Group.
Dorling, Daniel, Dan Vickers, Bethan Thomas, John Pritchard, and Dimitris Ballas. 2008. "Changing UK: The Way We Live Now." A Report Commissioned by the BBC. Accessed November 16, 2022. http://sasi.group.shef.ac.uk/research/changingUK.html.
Doukas, Dimitra. 2003. *Worked Over: The Corporate Sabotage of an American Community*. Ithaca, NY: University of Cornell Press.
Durrenberger, E. Paul. 2009. "The Last Wall to Fall: The Anthropology of Collective Action and Unions in a Global System." *Journal of Anthropological Research* 65 (1): 9–26.
*Edinburgh Evening News*. 2006a. Letters, May 9.
*Edinburgh Evening News*. 2006b. Letters, May 11.
*Edinburgh Evening News*. 2006c. Letters, May 12.
*Edinburgh Evening News*. 2006d. Letters, May 31.
*Edinburgh Evening News*. 2006e. Letters, June 21.
*Edinburgh Evening News*. 2006f. Letters, July 20.
*Edinburgh Evening News*. 2007a. Letters, April 5.
*Edinburgh Evening News*. 2007b. Letters, May 27.
*Edinburgh Evening News*. 2007c. Letters, May 29.
Edinburgh Old Town Development Trust. 2009. Accessed 3 March 2017. https://eotdt.org.
Edwards, Jeanette. 2017. "Across Class." *Sociological Review Monographs* 65 (1): 188–95.
Edwards, Jeanette, Gillian Evans, and Katherine Smith. 2012. "Introduction: The Middle-Classification of Britain." *Focaal: Journal of Global and Historical Anthropology* 62:3–16.
Elinoff, Eli. 2016. "A House Is More Than a House: Aesthetic Politics in a Northeastern Thai Railway Settlement." *Journal of the Royal Anthropological Institute* 22 (3): 610–32.
Engels, Friedrich. 2009 (1844). *The Condition of the Working Class in England*. Edited by David McLellan. New York: Oxford University Press.
———. 2010 (1884). *The Origin of the Family, Private Property and the State*. Translated by Tristram Hunt. New York: Penguin.
Etzioni, Amitai. 1993. *The Spirit of Community: Rights, Responsibilities and the Communication Agenda*. New York: Crown.

Evans, Gillian. 2006. *Educational Failure and Working Class White Children in Britain.* New York: Palgrave Macmillan.

———. 2012. "The 'Aboriginal' People of England: The Culture of Class Politics in Contemporary Britain." *Focaal: Journal of Global and Historical Anthropology* 62:17–29.

———. 2017. "Social Class and the Cultural Turn: Anthropology, Sociology, and the Post-Industrial Politics of 21st Century Britain." *Sociological Review Monographs* 65 (1): 88–104.

Fairley, John. 1996. "Scotland's New Local Authorities and Economic Development." *Scottish Affairs* 15 (1): 101–22.

Featherstone, David. 2005. "Towards the Relational Construction of Militant Particularisms: Or Why the Geographies of Past Struggles Matter for Resistance to Neoliberal Globalisation." *Antipode* 37 (2): 250–71.

Fehérváry, Krisztina. 2013. *Politics in Color and Concrete: Socialist Materialities and the Middle Class in Hungary.* Bloomington: Indiana University Press.

Fekete, Liz. 2016. "Hungary: Power, Punishment, and the Christian-National Idea." *Race and Class* 57 (4): 39–53.

Feld, Stephen, and Keith Basso. 1996. *Senses of Place.* Santa Fe, NM: School of American Research Press.

Ferguson, Brian. 2007. "£300m Caltongate Vision Dubbed Grotesque." *Edinburgh Evening News,* May 22. Accessed February 23, 2011. http://edinburghnews.scotsman.com/edinburgh/300m-caltongate-vision-dubbed-grotesque.3288126.jp.

Ferguson, James. 2006. *Global Shadows: Africa in the Neoliberal World Order.* Durham, NC: Duke University Press.

Flyvbjerg, Bent. 1998. *Rationality and Power: Democracy in Practice.* Chicago: University of Chicago Press.

Flyvbjerg, Bent, and Tim Richardson. 2002. "Planning and Foucault: In Search of the Dark Side of Planning Theory." In *Planning Futures: New Directions for Planning Theory,* edited by Philip Allmendinger and Mark Tewdwr-Jones, 44–62. London: Routledge.

Folbre, Nancy. 2009. *Greed, Lust and Gender: A History of Economic Ideas.* Oxford: Oxford University Press.

Fones-Wolf, Elizabeth. 1994. *Selling Free Enterprise: The Business Assault on Labor and Liberalism, 1940–1960.* Urbana: University of Illinois Press.

Foster, Hal. 2013. *The Art-Architecture Complex.* New York: Verso.

Fox, Colin. 2013. *The Case for an Independent Socialist Scotland.* Glasgow: Scottish Socialist Party.

Friedman, Jonathan. 2003. *Globalization, the State, and Violence.* Walnut Creek, CA: Alta Mira.

Gallagher, Cailean, Rory Scothorne, and Amy Westfell. 2016. *Roch Winds: A Treacherous Guide to the State of Scotland.* Edinburgh: Luath.

Gawlewicz, Anna. 2020. "'Scotland's Different': Narratives of Scotland's Distinctiveness in the Post-Brexit-Vote Era." *Scottish Affairs* 29 (3): 321–35.

Geddes, Patrick. 1915. *Cities in Evolution: An Introduction to the Town Planning Movement and to the Study of Civics.* London: Williams and Norgate.

Gershon, Ilana. 2011. "Neoliberal Agency." *Current Anthropology* 52 (4): 537–55.
Ghertner, D. Asher. 2015. *Rule by Aesthetics: World-Class City Making in Delhi*. New York: Oxford University Press.
Gibb, Kenneth. 2004. "At the Margins of Devolution? Fiscal Autonomy, Housing Policy and Housing Benefit." *Scottish Affairs* 48 (1): 130–51.
Giddens, Anthony. 1994. *Beyond Left and Right: The Future of Radical Politics*. Stanford: Stanford University Press.
Gilfillan, Paul. 2011. "Working Class Nationalism in a Scottish Village." In *Headlines of Nation, Subtexts of Class: Working Class Populism and the Return of the Repressed in Neoliberal Europe*, edited by Don Kalb and Gábor Halmai, 173–93. New York: Berghahn.
Gingrich, Andre. 2002. "When Ethnic Majorities Are 'Dethroned': Towards a Methodology of Self-Reflexive, Controlled Macrocomparison." In *Anthropology, by Comparison*, edited by Andre Gingrich and Richard G. Fox, 245–68. London: Routledge.
Gingrich, Andre, and Marcus Banks. 2006. *Neo-Nationalism in Europe and Beyond*. New York: Berghahn.
Glendenning, Miles. 2005. "Housing and Suburbanisation in the Early and Mid Twentieth Century." In *Edinburgh: The Making of a Capital City*, edited by Brian Edwards and Paul Jenkins, 150–67. Edinburgh: Edinburgh University Press.
———. 2013. *The Conservation Movement: A History of Architectural Preservation*. New York: Taylor and Francis.
Goldie, Paul. 2018. "Cultural Racism and Islamophobia in Glasgow." In *No Problem Here: Understanding Racism in Scotland*, edited by Neil Davidson, Minna Liinpää, Maureen McBride, and Satnam Virdee, 128–44. Edinburgh: Luath.
Goldman, Michael. 2005. *Imperial Nature: The World Bank and Struggles for Social Justice in an Age of Globalization*. New Haven, CT: Yale University Press.
Goode, Judith. 2006. "Faith-Based Organizations in Philadelphia: Neoliberal Ideology and the Decline of Political Activism." *Urban Anthropology and Studies of Cultural Systems and World Economic Development* 35 (2/3): 203–36.
Goodwin, Mark. 1993. "The City as Commodity: The Contested Spaces of Urban Development." In *Selling Places: The City as Cultural Capital, Past and Present*, edited by Gerry Kearns and Chris Philo, 145–62. London: Pergamon.
Gordon, Eleanor. 1991. *Women and the Labour Movement in Scotland, 1890–1914*. Oxford: Clarendon.
Gordon, Ian. 1999. "Internationalisation and Urban Competition." *Urban Studies* 36 (5–6): 1001–16.
Goring, Rosemary, ed. 2018. *Scotland Her Story: The Nation's History by the Women Who Lived It*. Edinburgh: Birlinn.
Graeber, David. 2009. *Direct Action: An Ethnography*. Oakland, CA: AK.
———. 2011. "Consumption." *Current Anthropology* 52 (4): 489–511.
Grill, Jan. 2012. "'It's Building Up to Something and It Won't Be Nice When It Erupts': The Making of Roma/Gypsy Migrants in Post-Industrial Scotland." *Focaal: Journal of Global and Historical Anthropology* 62:42–54.

Grillo, Ralph. 1998. *Pluralism and the Politics of Difference: State, Culture and Ethnicity in Comparative Perspective*. Oxford: Clarendon.
———. 2007. "An Excess of Alterity: Debating Difference in a Multicultural Society." *Ethnic and Racial Studies* 30 (6): 979–98.
———. 2008. *The Family in Question: Immigrant and Ethnic Minorities in Multicultural Europe*. Amsterdam: University of Amsterdam Press.
Gullestad, Marianne. 2002. "Invisible Fences: Egalitarianism, Nationalism, Racism." *Journal of the Royal Anthropological Institute* 8 (1): 45–63.
———. 2006. "Imagined Kinship: The Role of Descent in the Rearticulation of Norwegian Neo-Nationalism." In *Neo-Nationalism in Europe and Beyond*, edited by Andre Gingrich and Marcus Banks, 69–91. New York: Berghahn.
Gusterson, Hugh. 2017. "From Brexit to Trump: Anthropology and the Rise of Nationalist Populism." *American Ethnologist* 44 (2): 1–6.
Halbwachs, Maurice. 1992. *On Collective Memory*. Translated by Lewis A. Coser. Chicago: University of Chicago Press.
Hale, Charles R. 2005. "Neoliberal Multiculturalism: The Remaking of Cultural Rights and Racial Dominance in Central America." *Political and Legal Anthropology Review* 28 (1): 10–28.
Hall, Tim, and Peter Hubbard. 1998. *The Entrepreneurial City: Geographies of Politics, Regime, and Representation*. Chichester: Wiley.
Halmai, Gábor. 2011. "(Dis)possessed by the Spectre of Socialism. Nationalist Mobilization in the 'Transition' of Hungary." In *Headlines of Nation, Subtexts of Class: Working-Class Populism and the Return of the Repressed in Neoliberal Europe*, edited by Don Kalb and Gábor Halmai, 113–41. New York: Berghahn.
Hann, Chris M. 1998. *Property Relations: Renewing the Anthropological Tradition*. Cambridge: Cambridge University Press.
Harvey, David. 1985. *The Urbanization of Capital: Studies in the History and Theory of Capitalist Urbanization*. Baltimore: Johns Hopkins University Press.
———. 1989. "From Managerialism to Entrepreneurialism: The Transformation in Urban Governance in Late Capitalism." *Geografiska Annaler. Series B, Human Geography* 71 (1): 3–17.
———. 2004. *The New Imperialism*. New York: Oxford University Press.
———. 2005. *A Brief History of Neoliberalism*. New York: Oxford University Press.
Hassan, Gerry. 2009. *The Modern SNP: From Protest to Power*. Edinburgh: Edinburgh University Press.
———. 2016. *Scotland the Bold: How Our Nation Has Changed and Why There Is No Going Back*. Glasgow: Freight.
———. 2018. "Civil Society, the Rise and Fall of Civic Scotland, and Contextualising Media." *Scottish Affairs* 27 (1): 36–44.
Hassan, Gerry, and Anthony Barnett. 2009. "Breaking Out of Britain's Neo-Liberal State." *Think Pieces*. London: Compass.
Hastings, Annette. 2004. "Stigma and Social Housing Estates: Beyond Pathological Explanations." *Journal of Housing and the Built Environment* 19:233–54.
Hearn, Jonathan. 2000. *Claiming Scotland: National Identity and Liberal Culture*. Edinburgh: Edinburgh University Press.

———. 2003. "Big City: Civic Symbolism and Scottish Nationalism." *Scottish Affairs* 42:57–82.
———. 2014. "Nationalism and Normality: A Comment on the Scottish Independence Referendum." *Dialectical Anthropology* 38:505–12.
———. 2016. "Once More, with Feeling: The Scottish Enlightenment, Sympathy and Social Welfare." *Ethics and Social Welfare* 10 (3): 211–23.
———. 2017. *Salvage Ethnography in the Financial Sector: The Path to Economic Crisis in Scotland*. Manchester: Manchester University Press.
Heidegger, Martin. 1954. "Building, Dwelling, Thinking." In *Poetry, Language, Thought*, translated by Albert Hofstadter, 143–62. New York: Harper & Row.
———. 2008. *Being and Time*. New York: Harper Perennial Modern Classics.
Henderson, Ailsa, Rob Johns, Jac Larner, and Chris Carman. 2020. "Scottish Labour as a Case Study in Party Failure: Evidence from the 2019 UK General Election in Scotland." *Scottish Affairs* 29 (2): 127–40.
Herzfeld, Michael. 2009. *Evicted from Eternity: The Restructuring of Modern Rome*. Chicago: University of Chicago Press.
Hinton, James, and Richard Hyman. 1975. *Trade Unions and Revolution: The Industrial Politics of the Early British Communist Party*. London: Pluto.
Hirsch, Eric. 2010. "Property and Persons: New Forms and Contests in the Era of Neo-liberalism." *Annual Review of Anthropology* 39:349–60.
Hohmann, Jessie. 2013. *The Right to Housing: Law, Concepts, Possibilities*. Oxford: Hart.
Holston, James. 1989. *The Modernist City: An Anthropological Critique of Brasilia*. Chicago: University of Chicago Press.
———. 2009. *Insurgent Citizenship: Disjunctions of Democracy and Modernity in Brazil*. Princeton: Princeton University Press.
Hughes, Annmarie. 2010. *Gender and Political Identities in Scotland, 1919–1939*. Edinburgh: Edinburgh University Press.
Hunter, Alistair, and Nasar Meer. 2018. "Is Scotland Different on Race and Migration?" *Scottish Affairs* 27 (3): 382–87.
Huyssen, Andreas. 2003. *Present Pasts: Urban Palimpsests and the Politics of Memory*. Stanford: Stanford University Press.
Ibrahim, Youssef M. 1996. "Rethinking 'Harm Reduction' for Glasgow Addicts." *New York Times*, August 18. Accessed April 26, 2021. https://www.nytimes.com/1996/08/18/world/rethinking-harm-reduction-for-glasgow-addicts.html.
Innes, Judith, and David Booher. 2004. "Reframing Public Participation: Strategies for the 21st Century." *Planning Theory and Practice* 5 (4): 419–36.
Irving, Andrew, and Nina Glick Schiller. 2015. "Introduction: What's in a Word? What's in a Question?" In *Whose Cosmopolitanism? Critical Perspectives, Relationalities and Discontents*, edited by Nina Glick Schiller and Andrew Irving, 1–22. New York: Berghahn.
Jacobs, Jane. 1961. *The Death and Life of Great American Cities*. New York: Random House.
Jenkins, Paul, and Julian Holder. 2005. "Creation and Conservation of the Built Environment in the Later Twentieth Century." In *Edinburgh: The Making of a Capital City*, edited by Brian Edwards and Paul Jenkins, 185–203. Edinburgh: Edinburgh University Press.

Johns, Robert, James Mitchell, and Christopher J. Carman. 2013. "Constitution or Competence? The SNP's Re-Election in 2011." *Political Studies* 61 (1): 158–78.
Johnson, Jim, and Lou Rosenburg. 2010. *Renewing Old Edinburgh: The Enduring Legacy of Patrick Geddes*. Glendaruel, Scotland: Argyll.
Jones, Owen. 2012. *Chavs: The Demonization of the Working Class*. London: Verso.
Joseph, Miranda. 2002. *Against the Romance of Community*. Minneapolis: University of Minnesota Press.
Kalb, Don. 2011. "Headlines of Nation, Subtexts of Class: Working-Class Populism and the Return of the Repressed in Neoliberal Europe." In *Headlines of Nation, Subtexts of Class: Working-Class Populism and the Return of the Repressed in Neoliberal Europe*, edited by Don Kalb and Gábor Halmai, 1–36. New York: Berghahn.
Kalb, Don, and Gábor Halmai, eds. 2011. *Headlines of Nation, Subtexts of Class: Working-Class Populism and the Return of the Repressed in Neoliberal Europe*. New York: Berghahn.
Kallin, Hamish, and Tom Slater. 2014. "Activating Territorial Stigma: Gentrifying Marginality on Edinburgh's Periphery." *Environment and Planning A: Economy and Space* 46 (6): 1351–68.
Keating, Michael. 2009. "Nationalist Movements in Comparative Perspective." In *The Modern SNP: From Protest to Power*, edited by Gerry Hassan, 204–18. Edinburgh: Edinburgh University Press.
Kelly, Katherine, and Tullio Caputo. 2011. *Community: A Contemporary Analysis of Policies, Programs and Practices*. Toronto: Toronto University Press.
Kerr, Derek. 2005. "Preparing for the 21st Century: The City in a Global Environment." In *Edinburgh: The Making of a Capital City*, edited by Brian Edwards and Paul Jenkins, 204–30. Edinburgh: Edinburgh University Press.
Kipnis, Andrew. 2007. "Neoliberalism Reified: Suzhi Discourse and Tropes of Neoliberalism in the People's Republic of China." *Journal of the Royal Anthropological Institute* 13:383–400.
Klaufus, Christien, and Arij Ouweneel, eds. 2015. *Housing and Belonging in Latin America*. New York: Berghahn.
Knight, Daniel M. 2017. "Anxiety and Cosmopolitan Futures: Brexit and Scotland." *American Ethnologist* 44 (2): 237–42.
Koch, Insa. 2015. "'The State Has Replaced the Man': Women, Family Homes and the Benefit System on a Council Estate in England." *Focaal: Journal of Global and Historical Anthropology* 73:84–96.
———. 2016. "Bread-and-Butter Politics: Democratic Disenchantment and Everyday Politics on an English Council Estate." *American Ethnologist* 43 (2): 282–94.
———. 2017. "What's in a Vote? Brexit Beyond Culture Wars." *American Ethnologist* 44 (2): 225–30.
Koch, John T. 1997. *The Gododdin of Aneurin: Text and Context from Dark-Age North Britain*. Cardiff: University of Wales Press.
Kopytoff, Igor. 1986. "The Cultural Biography of Things: Commoditization as Process." In *The Social Life of Things*, edited by Arjun Appadurai, 64–91. Cambridge: Cambridge University Press.

Krzyzanowski, Michal. 2013. "From Anti-Immigration and Nationalist Revisionism to Islamophobia: Continuities and Shifts in Recent Discourses and Patterns of Political Communication in the Freedom Party of Austria." In *Right-Wing Populism in Europe: Politics and Discourse*, edited by Ruth Wodak, Brigitte Mral, and Majit Khosravinik, 135–48. New York: Bloomsbury.

Lawrence-Zúñiga, Denise. 2015. "Residential Design Guidelines, Aesthetic Governmentality, and Contested Notions of Southern California Suburban Places." *Economic Anthropology* (2): 120–44.

Leary, John Patrick. 2018. *Keywords: The New Language of Capitalism*. Chicago: Haymarket.

Lefebvre, Henri. 1953. *Contribution a L'Aesthetique*. Paris: Editions Sociales.

———. 1974. *The Production of Space*. Translated by Donald Nicholson-Smith. New York: Blackwell.

———. 1991. *Critique of Everyday Life*. Translated by John Moore. New York: Verso.

———. 1996. "The Right to the City." In *Writings on Cities*, edited by Eleanor Kofman and Elizabeth Lebas, 147–59. Cambridge, MA: Wiley-Blackwell.

Leith, Murray Stewart, and Daniel P. J. Soule. 2011. *Political Discourse and National Identity in Scotland*. Edinburgh: Edinburgh University Press.

Lévi-Strauss, Claude. 1955. "The Structural Study of Myth." *Journal of American Folklore* 68 (270): 428–44.

Li, T. M. 1996. "Images of Community: Discourse and Strategy in Property Relations." *Development and Change* 27:23–51.

Liinpää, Minna. 2018. "Nationalism and Scotland's Imperial Past." In *No Problem Here: Understanding Racism in Scotland*, edited by Neil Davidson, Minna Liinpää, Maureen McBride, and Satnam Virdee, 14–31. Edinburgh: Luath.

Loftman, Patrick, and Brendan Nevin. 2003. "Prestige Projects, City Centre Restructuring and Social Exclusion: Taking the Long-Term View." In *Urban Futures*, edited by Malcolm Miles and Tim Hall, 76–91. London: Routledge.

Logan, John, and Harvey Molotch. 1987. *Urban Fortunes: The Political Economy of Place*. Berkeley: University of California Press.

Loopstra, Rachel. 2020. *Vulnerability to Food Insecurity since the Covid-19 Lockdown*. Preliminary Report. London: Kings College London.

Low, Setha, and Neil Smith. 2006. *The Politics of Public Space*. New York: Routledge.

Macdonald, Murdo. 2009. "Patrick Geddes and the Scottish Generalist Tradition." *Scottish Affairs* 69 (1): 40–56.

MacLaren, A. Allan. 1976. *Social Class in Scotland*. Edinburgh: John Donald.

MacLennan, Stuart. 2016. "Safer and Stronger? The Decline of Managerial Competence and Liberal Welfarism in Justice Policy." *Scottish Affairs* 25 (1): 62–82.

Madgin, Rebecca, and Richard Rodger. 2013. "Inspiring Capital? Deconstructing Myths and Reconstructing Urban Environments, Edinburgh, 1860–1910." *Urban History* 40 (3): 507–29.

Malpas, Jeff. 2021. *Rethinking Dwelling: Heidegger, Place, Architecture*. New York: Bloomsbury.

Marx, Karl. 1978 (1846). "Society and Economy in History." In *The Marx-Engels Reader*, edited by Robert C. Tucker, 136–42. New York: Norton.

Matthews, Peter. 2015. "Neighborhood Belonging, Social Class and Social Media—Providing Ladders to the Cloud." *Journal of Housing Studies* 30 (1): 22–39.
———. 2016. "Social Media, Community Development and Social Capital." *Community Development Journal* 51 (3): 419–35.
McCollum, David. 2020. "Scotland and Brexit: Identity, Belonging and Citizenship in Uncertain Times." *Scottish Affairs* 29 (3): 419–30.
McCollum, David, Beata Nowok, and Scott Tindal. 2014. "Public Attitudes towards Migration in Scotland: Exceptionality and Possible Policy Implications." *Scottish Affairs* 23 (1): 79–102.
McCrone, David. 1992. *Understanding Scotland: The Sociology of a Stateless Nation*. New York: Routledge.
———. 2005. "Cultural Capital in an Understated Nation: The Case of Scotland." *British Journal of Sociology* 56 (1): 65–82.
———. 2017. *The New Sociology of Scotland*. Edinburgh: Edinburgh University Press.
McCrone, David, and Brian Elliott. 1989. "The Decline of Landlordism: Property Rights and Relationships in Edinburgh." In *Scottish Housing in the Twentieth Century*, edited by Richard Rodger, 214–35. Leicester: Leicester University Press.
McCrone, Gavin. 1999. "Industrial Clusters: A New Idea or an Old One?" *Scottish Affairs* 29 (1): 73–77.
McDonogh, Gary. 1999. "Discourses of the City: Policy and Response in Post-Transitional Barcelona." In *Theorizing the City: The New Urban Anthropology Reader*, edited by Setha Low, 34–76. London: Rutgers University Press.
McGarvey, Darren. 2017. *Poverty Safari: Understanding the Anger of Britain's Underclass*. Edinburgh: Luath.
McKean, Charles. 2001. *The Scottish Chateau: The Country House of Renaissance Scotland*. Phoenix Mill: Sutton.
McKee, Kirsten Carter. 2018. *Calton Hill and the Plans for Edinburgh's Third New Town*. Edinburgh: Birlinn.
McKenzie, Lisa. 2015. *Getting By: Estates, Class and Culture in Austerity Britain*. London: Policy.
McKibbin, Ross. 1984. "Why Was There No Marxism in Great Britain?" *English Historical Review* 99:305–22.
McLean, Iain. 1983. *The Legend of Red Clydeside*. Edinburgh: John Donald.
Meer, Nasar. 2018. "What Do We Know about BAME Self-Reported Racial Discrimination in Scotland?" In *No Problem Here: Understanding Racism in Scotland*, edited by Neil Davidson, Minna Liinpää, Maureen McBride, and Satnam Virdee, 114–27. Edinburgh: Luath.
Melling, Joseph. 1989. "Clydeside Rent Struggles and the Making of Labour Politics in Scotland, 1900–39." In *Scottish Housing in the Twentieth Century*, edited by Richard Rodger, 54–88. Leicester: Leicester University Press.
Mepschen, Paul. 2017. "A Discourse of Displacement: Super-Diversity, Urban Citizenship, and the Politics of Autochthony in Amsterdam." *Ethnic and Racial Studies* 42 (1): 71–88.
Miller, Daniel. 1987. *Material Culture and Mass Consumption*. Oxford: Blackwell.
———. 1988. "Appropriating the State on the Council Estate." *Man* 23:353–72.

———. 2010. *Stuff*. Malden, MA: Polity.
Miller-Idriss, Cynthia. 2009. *Blood and Culture: Youth, Right-Wing Extremism, and National Belonging in Contemporary Germany*. Chicago: University of Chicago Press.
Mollona, Massimiliano. 2009. *Made in Sheffield: An Ethnography of Industrial Work and Politics*. Oxford: Berghahn.
Mookherjee, Nayanika. 2011. "The Aesthetics of Nations: Anthropological and Historical Approaches." *Journal of the Royal Anthropological Institute* 17 (S1): S1–S20.
Morris, Robert J. 2013. "White Horse Close: Philanthropy, Scottish Historical Imagination and the Re-Building of Edinburgh in the Later Nineteenth Century." *Journal of Scottish Historical Studies* 33 (1): 101–28.
Morton, Graeme. 1999. *Unionist Nationalism: Governing Urban Scotland, 1830–1860*. East Linton: Tuckwell.
Mostafa, Iqbal. 2018. *Migration of Farm Workers to Rural Scotland: Equality, Cultural Capital and the Process of Social and Cultural Transitions*. Bloomington, IN: AuthorHouse.
Muehlebach, Andrea. 2012. *The Moral Neoliberal: Welfare and Citizenship in Italy*. Chicago: University of Chicago Press.
Nadin, Vincent, and Dominic Stead. 2014. "Spatial Planning in the United Kingdom, 1990–2013." In *Spatial Planning Systems and Practices in Europe: A Comparative Perspective on Continuity and Changes*, edited by Mario Reimer, Panagiotis Getimis, and Hans Heinrich Blotevogel, 189–214. New York: Routledge.
Nairn, Tom. 1977. *The Break-Up of Britain: Crisis and Neo-Nationalism*. London: New Left.
———. 1995. "Upper and Lower Cases." *London Review of Books* 17 (August 24): 14–18.
Ong, Aiwa. 2007. "Neoliberalism as a Mobile Technology." *Transactions of the Institute of British Geographers* 32 (1): 3–8.
Partridge, Damani J. 2012. *Hypersexuality and Headscarves: Race, Sex, and Citizenship in the New Germany*. Bloomington: Indiana University Press.
Paterson, Lindsay. 1997. "Scottish Autonomy and the Future of the Welfare State." *Scottish Affairs* 19:55–73.
———. 2015. "Utopian Pragmatism: Scotland's Choice." *Scottish Affairs* 24 (1): 22–46.
Paterson, Lindsay, Ian Bechhoffer, and David McCrone. 2004. *Living in Scotland: Social and Economic Change since 1980*. Edinburgh: Edinburgh University Press.
Pawson, Hal. 2004. "Reviewing Stock Transfer and the Transformation of British Social Housing." Paper delivered to the International Sociological Association conference, Adequate and Affordable Housing for All: Research, Policy, Practice, Toronto, Canada.
Pawson, Hal, and Cathie Fancy. 2003. *Maturing Assets: The Evolution of Stock Transfer Housing Associations*. Bristol: Policy.
Peck, Jamie, and Nik Theodore. 2012. "Reanimating Neoliberalism: Process Geographies of Neoliberalisation." *Social Anthropology* 20:177–85.
Peck, Jamie, and Adam Tickell. 2002. "Neoliberalizing Space." *Antipode* 34 (3): 380–404.
Pinson, Gilles, and Christelle Morel Journel. 2017. *Debating the Neoliberal City*. New York: Routledge.
Plotnicov, Leonard. 1990. "Work and Play: An Urban Lifestyle Ideally Portrayed." *City and Society* 4 (1): 3–19.

Purcell, Mark. 2002. "Excavating Lefebvre: The Right to the City and Its Urban Politics of the Inhabitant." *GeoJournal* 58:99–108.
Rabinow, Paul. 1989. *French Modern: Norms and Forms of the Built Environment*. Chicago: University of Chicago Press.
Radin, Margaret Jane. 1982. "Property and Personhood." *Stanford Law Review* 34 (5): 957–1015.
Ramadan, Tariq. 2014. "Cosmopolitan Theory and the Pluralism of Daily Life." In *Whose Cosmopolitanism? Critical Perspectives, Relationalities and Discontents*, edited by Nina Glick Schiller and Andrew Irving, 57–64. New York: Berghahn.
Rancière, Jacques. 2004. *The Politics of Aesthetics: The Distribution of the Sensible*. New York: Continuum.
Rancière, Jacques, and Mark Foster Gage. 2019. "Politics Equals Aesthetics: A Conversation between Jacques Rancière and Mark Foster Gage." In *Aesthetics Equals Politics: New Discourses across Art, Architecture, and Philosophy*, edited by Mark Foster Gage, 9–26. Cambridge: Massachusetts Institute of Technology.
Rankin, Ian. 2004. *Fleshmarket Close*. London: Orion.
Rapport, Nigel, and Andrew Dawson. 1998. *Migrants of Identity: Perceptions of Home in a World of Movement*. New York: Berg.
Rasza, Maple. 2015. *Bastards of Utopia: Living Radical Politics after Socialism*. Bloomington: Indiana University Press.
Robinson, Peter. 2005. "The Development of Tenement Housing." In *Edinburgh: The Making of a Capital City*, edited by Brian Edwards and Paul Jenkins, 103–25. Edinburgh: Edinburgh University Press.
Rodger, Derek. 2017. "Come into the Light." In *The Evergreen: A New Season in the North*, edited by Sean Bradley, 109–17. Edinburgh: Word Bank.
Rodger, Richard, ed. 1989. "Crisis and Confrontation in Scottish Housing 1880–1914." In *Scottish Housing in the Twentieth Century*, 25–53. Leicester: Leicester University Press.
———. 2004. *The Transformation of Edinburgh: Land, Property and Trust in the Nineteenth Century*. Cambridge: Cambridge University Press.
———. 2014. "(N)evergreen? Auld Reekie Absolved." In *The Evergreen: A New Season in the North*, edited by Sean Bradley, 33–38. Edinburgh: Word Bank.
Rodger, Richard, and Hunain Al-Qaddo. 1989. "The Scottish Special Housing Association and the Implementation of Housing Policy, 1937–87." In *Scottish Housing in the Twentieth Century*, edited by Richard Rodger, 184–213. Leicester: Leicester University Press.
Rogan, Pat. 1997. "Re-Housing the Capital: The Crusade against Edinburgh's Slums." In *Re-Building Scotland: The Post-War Vision 1945–1975*, edited by Miles Glendenning, 66–74. East Linton: Tuckwell.
Rose, Nikolas. 1999. *Powers of Freedom: Reframing Political Thought*. Cambridge: Cambridge University Press.
Rosenburg, Lou. 2016. *Scotland's Homes Fit for Heroes: Garden City Influencers on the Development of Scottish Working Class Housing 1900–1939*. Edinburgh: The Word Bank.
Rosie, Michael, and Ross Bond. 2008. "National Identities and Politics after Devolution." *Radical Statistics* 97:47–65.

Rutheiser, Charles. 1999. "Making Place in the Nonplace Urban Realm: Notes on the Revitalization of Downtown Atlanta." In *The New Urban Anthropology Reader*, edited by Setha Low, 317–41. Piscataway, NJ: Rutgers University Press.

Saalman, Howard. 1971. *Haussmann: Paris Transformed*. New York: George Braziller.

Sabljak, Ema. 2020. "Glasgow Magnet Fishing: Gun Pulled Out of Forth and Clyde Canal." *The Herald*, August 23. Accessed December 2, 2022. https://www.heraldscotland.com/news/18670191.glasgow-magnet-fishing-gun-pulled-forth-clyde-canal/.

———. 2021. "Magnet Fishing Given Go-Ahead from Today on Scottish Canals." *Glasgow Times*, April 24. Accessed December 2, 2022. https://www.glasgowtimes.co.uk/news/19256541.magnet-fishing-given-go-ahead-today-scottish-canals/.

Sa'di, Ahmad H., and Lila Abu-Lughod. 2007, *Nakba: Palestine, 1948, and the Claims of Memory*. New York: Columbia University Press.

Sansi, Roger. 2015. *Art, Anthropology and the Gift*. New York: Bloomsbury.

———. 2020. "Utopia and Idiocy: Public Art Experiments in the Metropolitan Region of Barcelona." *City and Society* 32 (2): 250–71.

Sawalha, Aseel. 2010. *Reconstructing Beirut: Memory and Space in a Postwar Arab City*. Austin: University of Texas Press.

Schellekens, Elisabeth. 2007. *Aesthetics and Morality*. New York: Continuum.

Schiller, Nina Glick. 2005. "Racialized Nations, Evangelizing Christianity, Police States, and Imperial Power: Missing in Action in Bunzl's New Europe." *American Ethnologist* 32 (4): 523–32.

Schiller, Nina Glick, and Andrew Irving. 2015. *Whose Cosmopolitanism? Critical Perspectives, Relationalities and Discontents*. New York: Berghahn.

Scothorne, Rory. 2018. "1968 and the Rise of Campus Radicalism in Scotland." *Sceptical Scot*, March 4. Accessed November 5, 2020. https://sceptical.scot/2018/03/1968-rise-campus-radicalism-scotland.

———. 2020. "Scotland's Dreaming: Why the SNP Appears Unstoppable." *The New Statesman*, August 18. Accessed November 5, 2020. https://www.newstatesman.com/politics/scotland/2020/08/scotland-s-dreaming-why-snp-appears-unstoppable.

Sigona, Nando, and Marie Godin. 2019. "EU Families in Scotland after the Brexit Referendum: Fears, Hopes and Belonging." Eurochildren Research Brief Series, no. 8. Accessed October 29, 2020. https://eurochildrenblog.files.wordpress.com/2019/09/eurochildren-brief-8-sigona-godin-scotland.pdf.

Silverstein, Paul. 2018. *Postcolonial France: The Question of Race and the Future of the Republic*. London: Pluto.

Simpson, Ludi, and Andrew Smith. 2014. "Who Feels Scottish? National Identities and Ethnicity in Scotland." Centre on the Dynamics of Ethnicity. University of Manchester. Accessed January 12, 2020. http://hummedia.manchester.ac.uk/institutes/code/briefings/dynamicsofdiversity/code-census-briefing-national-identity-scotland.pdf.

Smith, Harry, and Emilio José Luque-Azcona. 2012. "The Historical Development of Built Heritage Awareness and Conservation Policies: A Comparison of Two World Heritage Sites: Edinburgh and Salvador do Bahia. *GeoJournal* 77 (3): 399–415.

Smith, Katherine. 2017. "'You Don't Own the Money, You're Just the One Who's Holding It:' Borrowing, Lending and the Fair Person in North Manchester." *Sociological Review Monographs* 65 (1): 121–36.

Smith, Laurajane, Paul A. Shackel, and Gary Campbell. 2011. "Introduction: Class Still Matters." In *Heritage, Labour and the Working Classes*, 1–16. New York: Routledge.

Smith, Neil. 2002. "New Globalism, New Urbanism: Gentrification as Global Urban Strategy. *Antipode* 34 (3): 427–50.

Smith, P. J. 1989. "The Rehousing-Relocation Issue in an Early Slum Clearance Scheme: Edinburgh 1865–1885." *Urban Studies* 26 (1): 100–14.

Smyth, James J. 2019. "The Power of Pathos: James Burn Russell's *Life in One Room* and the Creation of Council Housing." *Scottish Historical Review* 98 (1): 103–27.

SNP. 2019. "New Scots." Accessed December 17, 2019. https://www.snp.org/groups/new-scots/.

Spark, Muriel. 1961. *The Prime of Miss Jean Brodie*. New York: Harper Perennial.

Spencer, Jonathan. 1997. "Post-Colonialism and the Political Imagination." *Journal of the Royal Anthropological Institute* 3 (1): 1–19.

———. 2000. *A Sinhala Village in a Time of Trouble: Politics and Change in Rural Sri Lanka*. New York: Oxford University Press.

Spirou, Costas. 2011. *Urban Tourism and Urban Change: Cities in a Global Economy*. New York: Taylor and Francis.

Starecheski, Amy. 2019. "Squatters Make History in New York: Property, History and Collective Claims on the City." *American Ethnologist* 46 (1): 61–74.

Stewart, John. 2004. *Taking Stock: Scottish Social Welfare under Devolution*. Bristol: Policy.

Stolz, Klaus. 2020. "Scotland, Brexit, and the Broken Promise of Democracy." In *Contested Britain: Brexit, Austerity, and Agency*, 189–202. Chicago: Bristol University Press.

Strathern, Marilyn. 1996. "Potential Property: Intellectual Rights and Property in Persons." *Social Anthropology* 4 (1): 17–32.

Swanson, Ian. 2016. "Donald Anderson Discusses Highs and Lows of Leading City Council." *Edinburgh Evening News*, September 14. Accessed July 19, 2019. https://www.edinburghnews.scotsman.com/news/politics/donald-anderson-discusses-highs-and-lows-of-leading-city-council-1-4229851.

Taylor, Erin B. 2013. *Materializing Poverty: How the Poor Transform Their Lives*. Lanham, MD: Rowman & Littlefield.

Tihanov, Galin. 2014. "Whose Cosmopolitanism? Genealogies of Cosmopolitanism." In *Whose Cosmopolitanism? Critical Perspectives, Relationalities and Discontents*, edited by Nina Glick Schiller and Andrew Irving, 29–30. New York: Berghahn.

Todd, Selina. 2015. *The People: The Rise and Fall of the Working Class, 1910–2010*. London: John Murray.

Tooley, Christa Ballard, and Julia Yezbick. 2020. "Appearances That Matter: Aesthetic Practices in the City." *City and Society* 32 (2): 244–49.

Torrance, David. 2009. *"We" in Scotland: Thatcherism in a Cold Climate*. Edinburgh: Birlinn.

Trevor-Roper, Hugh. 1983. "The Invention of Tradition: The Highland Tradition of Scotland." In *The Invention of Tradition*, edited by Eric Hobsbawm and Terence Ranger, 15–42. Cambridge: Cambridge University Press.

Tsing, Anna Lowenhaupt. 2015. *The Mushroom at the End of the World: On the Possibility of Life in Capitalist Ruins*. Princeton: Princeton University Press.
Tuan, Yi-Fu. 1996. *Cosmos and Hearth: A Cosmopolite's Viewpoint*. Minneapolis: University of Minnesota Press.
Tyler, Imogen. 2013. *Revolting Subjects: Social Abjection and Resistance in Neoliberal Britain*. London: Zed.
Tyler, Katharine. 2004. "Reflexivity, Tradition and Racism in a Former Mining Town." *Ethnic and Racial Studies* 27:290–309.
———. 2012. *Whiteness, Class and the Legacies of Empire*. London: Palgrave Macmillan.
Vertovec, Steven, and Susanne Wessendorf. 2010. *The Multiculturalism Backlash: European Discourses, Practices and Policies*. New York: Routledge.
Wade, Mike. 2008. "Holyrood Named as Britain's Loneliest Place." *The Times*, December 1. Accessed November 11, 2022. https://www.thetimes.co.uk/article/holyrood-named-as-britains-loneliest-place-hh3hbmjj298.
Walley, Christine J. 2017. "Trump's Election and the 'White Working Class': What We Missed." *American Ethnologist* 44 (2): 231–36.
Warner, Deborah. 2014. "Woman Painting." In *The Evergreen: A New Season in the North*, edited by Sean Bradley, 49. Edinburgh: Word Bank.
Waterson, Roxana. 2014. *The Living House: An Anthropology of Architecture in South-East Asia*. Rutland, VT: Tuttle.
Weszkalnys, Gisa. 2010. *Berlin, Alexanderplatz: Transforming Place in a Unified Germany*. New York: Berghahn.
Williams, Raymond. 1976. *Keywords: A Vocabulary of Culture and Society*. New York: Oxford University Press.
Wodak, Ruth. 2013. "'Anything Goes!' The Haiderization of Europe." In *Right-Wing Populism in Europe: Politics and Discourse*, edited by Ruth Wodak, Brigitte Mral, and Majit Khosravinik, 23–38. New York: Bloomsbury.
Yale, Lawrence. 1992. *Architecture, Power and National Identity*. New Haven, CT: Yale University Press.
Yezbick, Julia. 2020. "Domesticating Detroit: Art Houses, Blight, and the Image of Care." *City and Society* 32 (2): 316–44.
Youngson, A. J. 2002. *The Making of Classical Edinburgh*. Edinburgh: Edinburgh University Press.
Zhang, Li. 2010. *In Search of Paradise: Middle-Class Living in a Chinese Metropolis*. Ithaca, NY: Cornell University Press.
Zigon, Jarrett. 2014. "An Ethics of Dwelling and a Politics of World-Building: A Critical Response to Ordinary Ethics." *JRAI* 20 (4): 746–64.
Zukin, Sharon. 2010. *Naked City: The Death and Life of Authentic Urban Places*. New York: Oxford University Press.

# INDEX

Acts of Union (1707), 41, 71, 203: effects on Edinburgh, 41; and Scottish sovereignty, 71, 203; *see also* Scottish Parliament, devolution

Aesthetic: Canongate, 10, 17, 23, 109-110, 154-157, 172, 177, 196-197, 208; defamiliarization, 129-131; denigration, 125-129; discourse, 60, 82-84, 126-129, 158; nations, 16, 25, 122-123, 199, 203, 207-208, 219-221; neoliberal, 111-112, 123, 198, 203, 229; relationship to affect, 200; working-class, 58, 190-193

Affect: political, 16-20, 122, 198-201, 206-208, 216-219; 223; 227-228; 232; relationship to aesthetic, 17, 200, 122-123. *See also* Neoliberalism: affect of urgency

Airbnb, 61-63, 140, 160, 225, 236

Architecture, 7, 33, 40-44, 47, 53, 64, 80, 129, 141; Caltongate masterplan, 60, 123-129; Canongate campaign, 178-179

Architectural Heritage Society of Scotland, 60, 161

Arendt, Hannah, 4, 17, 167-168, 177, 180

Artisan Real Estate, 65-66

Bank of Scotland (Halifax, HBOS), 74; and development, 83, 134.

Brexit, 12, 228, 237; English nationalism and, 224; Remain vote in Scotland, 12; Scottish nationalism and, 19, 204, 224-225, 229

Calton Hill, 85, 87, 110

Caltongate development: aesthetics, 127-129; developer, *see* Mountgrange PLC; immediate reception of proposal, 93-96; instrument of council's economic development hopes, 75-86; masterplan, 87-93; naming of, 87-88;

Caltongate Liaison Group, 120

Canongate: clearances, 46; Edinburgh Old Town Development Trust community center, 130-131, 138; housing provision within, 41, 46, 48-50; industrial economy participation, 44-45; medieval history of, 38-41; Scottish Enlightenment, 41-42; redevelopment schemes (pre-Caltongate), 46, 48-50; walking in, 159-162, 169-170; women's work in, 49-50

Canongate Community Forum: influence in Edinburgh, 113, 194-196; meetings of, 24-26, 112-113, 117, 155, 178-179, 206-207, 223; origins, 112-116; relationship to Save Our Old Town, 112

Canongate-Corstorphine Scheme (1927), 48-49

Canongate Project: 131-134, 176-177, 187, 212

Canongate Venture building, 32, 34, 139: proposed demolition of, 33, 89; proposed redevelopment of, 65, 135

City of Edinburgh Council: Caltongate decision, 95-96; community planning consultation 26, 69, 82-84, 116-122, 138; Development Management Subcommittee meeting, 94-95, 130; headquarters, 8, 85-86, 111-112, 123, 125, 140, 181

Cockburn Association: 59-60, 64, 161, 179

Common Good property claims, 173-174

Community: competition between organizations, 66-67; conflict with affect of urgency in city planning, 74-75, 77, 119; moralized idea, 23, 60, 108-109, 118-119, 121-122; planning theory, 115, 118-120; in Caltongate planning consultation, 95, 111-112, 120-122; questions of representation, 117-118, 132

Connerton, Paul, 4, 17, 129, 157

257

Conservation: alliances between conservation*ists* and community residents, 19-20, 24-25, 28, 30, 36, 43, 50-55, 57, 60, 62-68, 114, 117-118, 122, 129, 131-132, 136, 138, 141, 157, 161-163, 178-181, 196, 213-214, 232-234; community-proposed projects, 134-137; locations of concern in Edinburgh, 194-195; professionalization of, 53-54

Conservative surgery: original conceptualization by Geddes, 47-48; influence in Edinburgh's development schemes, 36, 50-52, 54, 56-58; invoking in response to Caltongate, 28, 114, 232

Consultation. *See* Community: in planning consultation

Cosmopolitanism: among Canongate campaigners, 20, 30, 217-220, 227, 234; banal, 123, 128; elite, 197, 219; multiculturalism and, 12, 209, 215; neoliberalism and, 19, 25, 31; origins, 19; place and, 19, 202, 219; Scottish National Party rhetoric, 64, 215, 220, 227, 234; working-class, 18-20, 25, 31, 150, 196-197, 202, 220

Council housing, 7, 22, 71, 79: Canongate, 8, 22, 108, 112, 162-163, 196, 217-218; construction of, 53, 162, 165, 186; in Dumbiedykes, 117, 143, 145, 147-149, 186; Edinburgh's peripheral housing estates, 8, 78, 114, 162, 165, 186, 187, 217-219; Glasgow, 187; Leith, 235; Right to Buy, 159-160, 162

Covid-19, 13, 193: SNP electoral record, 204, 225, 229

Craigmillar Festival Society, 54, 66, 114, 187, 219

Development: depoliticization of, 23, 29, 35, 68-69, 73, 77, 109, 115. Neoliberal logic of, *see* Neoliberalism, logic of development.

Devolution, 28, 69-72: impacts on Scottish Labour, 72, 92, 205; referenda, 71, 85. *see also* Scottish Parliament

Disaffection, 1, 229

Dispossession, 1, 11: instruments of, 5, 29-30, 109, 115, 126; neoliberal urbanism, 23, 126

Doocots, 27: Scottish Canals, 192-193; spatial claims, 184-185, 192-193; working-class pastime, 185

Dwelling, 4, 18, 96, 116, 157-158, 160, 164, 167, 218, 232

Edinburgh Against Stock Transfer campaign, 147-149

Edinburgh Business Assembly, 82-83

Edinburgh community and neighborhood organizations, beyond the Canongate:
Dumbiedykes Writers Group, 146
Edinburgh At Risk, 155, 195-196
Edinburgh Old Town Renewal Trust, 55
Friends of Corstorphine Hill, 113, 194
Grassmarket Area Housing Association, 54
Mushroom Trust, 54
Patrick Geddes Gardening Club, 137
Porty Greenkeepers, 113, 194
Save Glenogle Baths, 113, 194
Save Meadowbank, 194

Edinburgh Old Town Development Trust (EOTDT): origins, 65-66; proposals, 135-136; community center in Canongate, 66, 137-139; relationship to SOOT/CCF activists, 141-142, 225, 228-229, 236

Elsie Inglis Maternity Hospital, 108-109

Entrepreneurial city governance, 21, 59, 76, 80, 82, 84-85, 118-119, 124, 140-142, 161

European Union, 19, 134, 204

Forgetting. *See* Memory.

Geddes, Patrick, 28, 36, 44, 46-51, 114, 118, 135-137, 232-233

Glasgow: clearances, 48; comparison with, 44-46, 48, 80, 83, 148, 184, 212. *See also* Possilpark, Glasgow

Green Party, Scotland, 94-95, 174, 179, 207

Halifax. *See* Bank of Scotland

Halifax Bank of Scotland. *See* Bank of Scotland

Heritage. *See* Conservation. *See also* UNESCO: World Heritage site

Heroin in working-class community life, 150-151, 188
Home, collective solidarity, 30, 161-162, 164, 169, 179-180, 237; inalienability of, 30, 154-155, 174-175, 177, 180; indivisibility of, 154-155, 172; singularity of, 170-171, 173, 175, 177, 180; in art, 154, 156; politics of Scotland, 164, 237; relationship to knowing, 157-158, 167; site of resistance, 7, 148-149, 154-155, 157-158, 161-163, 172-173,175-177; windows, 159-160, 182
Housing activism, 28, 158, 162-163; relationship to labor activism, 164-165, 168; women's role in, 45, 54, 113, 165;
Hurd, Robert, 50, 236
Identity, 2; class, 10, 15, 66-67, 221; British, 14, 70; English, 13-14, 214; national, 10, 15, 19, 198, 208; place, 122, 129, 131, 157-158, 174, 179, 197; Scottish, 13-15, 203-204, 209, 212-214; working-class, 11-12, 15, 91, 231

Independence. *See* Scottish independence
Indwelling. *See* Dwelling
IndyRef2. *See* Scottish independence
Interurban competition, 82, 95, 119

Jeffrey Street arches, 139, 169
Jock the Weathercock, 32-34

Labour Party: British, 14, 36, 71, 148, 214-215, 224; City of Edinburgh Council, 28, 58, 69, 73, 75-80, 84, 92, 95, 127, 148-149, 161, 198, 200-201, 206-207, 228; relationship to rise of SNP, 12, 72, 93, 202, 205-206, 222; Scottish, 21, 64, 71, 74, 78, 162, 211;
Liberal democracy in Scotland, 2, 5, 10, 25, 110, 137, 197, 210, 212, 223, 229
Liberal Democrat Party, Scotland: 79, 95, 206 207

MacRae, Ebenezer, 50; Canongate tenement, 56, 89, 129, 139, 181-182, 236; Canongate-Corstorphine development, 49;
Materiality: endurance of, 157, 177; neoliberal urbanism, 69, 73, 76, 219; quality of world-building, 4, 167-168; relationship to memory. *See* Memory: relationship to built environment.
Memory: relationship to built environment, 4, 9, 17, 30, 125; 129, 131, 157-158, 178, 236
Middle classes: alliances with community activists, 24, 28, 31, 36, 38, 49-50, 53-54, 57-58, 63-64, 66-67, 161-162, 196, 232-234; aspirations for class mobility, 20, 91, 222; Edinburgh neighborhoods, 42, 47, 49-50, 78, 236; image of Edinburgh, 7, 42, 44, 52, 235; national politics in Scotland, 10, 15, 19-20, 197, 222, 231;
Moralization: Canongate aesthetics and practices, 3, 23, 97, 109, 172, 196-197; community, 118-119, 121; neoliberal affects and practices, 21, 28, 74, 76-77, 90-92; visions for Scotland, 2, 200, 208, 212, 215 219
Mountgrange Capital, PLC, 86, 96, 118, 133-134
Multiculturalism: Europe, 1; politics of Canongate campaigners, 2, 5, 10, 13, 16, 20, 23, 197, 215, 220-221, 232, 234; Scotland, 150, 199, 213-214; SNP rhetoric, 2, 9, 13-14, 197, 215, 218-220;
Myths of Scottish distinctiveness, 209-211, 213, 216, 231, 234

Nationalism: civic, 209-210, 214, 224, 226; European, 11, 13, 30, 116, 198, 231, 233, 236; ethnic or racial, 10; 31, 201, 214, 224; liberal, 2, 18, 25, 210, 214, 224; personal, 30, 202, 219, 221; populist, 1-2, 11-12, 15, 220; resurgence of, 10, 24; social democratic, 19, 23 unionist, 14, 205;
Nationalism, English, 110, 202, 209, 214, 217, 224
Nationalism, Scottish: affecting black and brown Scots, 13-14, 214; cosmopolitan characteristics of, 12, 18-20, 24, 30, 64, 208-209, 213-220, 227, 229, 234; distinct from electoral support for SNP, 222-223, 226-227; electoral support for, 194, 200, 204-205, 207; liberal democratic values of, 2, 14, 210; rhetorical contrast to English ethnic nationalism, 12-15, 202, 209, 224; Scottish distinctiveness. *See* Myths of Scottish distinctiveness

Neoliberalism: affect of urgency, 75-76, 79-80, 83-84, 86, 94-96, 119, 198, 200, 207; boosterism, 20, 101; policies of Prime Minister Margaret Thatcher, 28, 36, 56, 69-72, 75, 91, 106, 119, 123-124, 148, 166; regeneration proposal for, 126; regeneration proposal for, 126; virtues of competition in, 74-75, 90
Neonationalism. *See* nationalism
New Town, Edinburgh: construction of, 38, 42; relationship to Old Town, 42-43
New Waverley, 22, 60, 137-138, 140, 170, 225; Edinburgh Old Town Development Trust engagement, 65-66; developer: *see* Artisan Real Estate

Old Town, Edinburgh: civil society in, 47; conservative surgery in, 47-50, 54-55; geography of, 6, 37-39; housing in, 38-39, 41-42, 45-50, 56, 61, 64, 114, 159-161, 166-167, 169, 175-176, 236; overcrowding, 25, 40-41; regeneration proposal for, 126; relationship to Scottish Enlightenment, 41-42; sanitary improvement schemes, 46-49; *see also* Waverley Valley Redevelopment Strategy

People's Story Museum, 107-109
Political aesthetic, 36-37, 69, 73, 180, 196, 213
Populism; leftist, 2; nationalist, 2, 11, 220; working-class, 12, 14
Possilpark, Glasgow: Claypits Nature Reserve, 189-193; *see also* Doocots

Racial minorities: in England, 214-215; in Scotland, 13-14, 199, 213-214. *See also* Nationalism, Scottish: as affecting black and brown Scots
Rancière, Jacques, 3-5, 17-18, 69, 200, 204-205, 213
Red Clydeside, 45, 165, 211
Right to Buy program, 56, 106-107, 148-149, 162, 176
Royal Mile, 62, 88-89, 91, 94, 111, 127, 132

Save Our Old Town (SOOT): campaign meetings, 24-27, 112-113, 117, 155, 178, 206-207, 223; campaign poster, 133; origins, 110-113; relationship to Canongate Community Forum, 112; relationship to Dumbiedykes, 117, 143, 145-146;
Scottish Executive: *see* Scottish Parliament
Scottish independence: IndyRef 2 (second independence referendum) possibility, 204, 224, 229; popular referendum, 194, 203, 219, 222, 226; referendum votes as distinct from support of Scottish nation, 204
Scottish National Party (SNP): affect of hope, 20, 31, 110, 116, 194, 198-201, 206-208, 228; electoral support, 12, 14, 72, 79, 202, 204-206; engagement with the Caltongate development, 94-96, 206-207; immigration, 13, 214, 224; imperialism, 13; multiculturalism, 9, 13, 197, 213, 215, 219-220; neoliberalism, 64, 74-75, 110, 137, 219, 229, 232
Scottish Parliament: building, 8, 85, 87, 98; members' engagement with Caltongate, 173-174, 207; members' engagement with Dumbiedykes, 151; Planning bill, 121-122; *see also* Acts of Union, 1707; Devolution
Socialism: Scottish Socialist Party, 206, 212, 223, 233; support for Scottish independence, 206, 212, 233; and working-class politics, 45, 148, 164-165, 211-213, 221, 227
Slum clearance, 41, 45-46, 48, 51, 56, 145-146. *See also* Canongate: clearances
St. James Centre, 53, 87, 111-112

Tartan tat, 98, 111, 170
Tenements: Canongate, 38-40, 45, 49, 100, 128, 130, 140, 149, 156, 169-170, 177; Dumbiedykes, 143-145, 147, 151; Glasgow, 45, 188; Edinburgh's Old Town, 42-43, 47; impact of Caltongate development on, 89, 128, 181, 236; place in Canongate campaigners' politics, 7, 107, 178, 196

Thatcher, Margaret: proponent of neoliberalism, 28, 56, 69-72, 75, 119, 148, 166; reception in Scotland, 71-72, 91, 123-124

UNESCO, 7: inspectors, 134; World Heritage site, 8, 25-26, 158, 178

Waverley Valley, 6, 169: cultural history, 137; regeneration of, 80, 87, 110, 138; *see* New Waverley
Waverley Valley Redevelopment Strategy, 80
Welfare state: British, 1, 36, 69-70, 72, 117, 119, 142, 152, 229; Scottish, 18, 20, 28, 70-72, 93, 97, 209, 212, 229; and SNP rhetoric, 63, 232-233; working-class politics, 107, 142, 147, 152, 164, 196-197, 202, 211

West End, Edinburgh, 101-102
Women in Scottish political movements, 9, 24, 45, 49-50, 54, 113-114, 162, 165-166, 187
Working classes: displacement from Edinburgh's city center, 21, 54, 114, 155-156; heritage, 131-132; right to the city, 35, 115-116, 126; role in housing activism, 28, 54, 147-149, 152, 154, 157, 164-165, role in nationalist movements, 11-12; 14-15, 34-35, 219, 221-223, 233; self-identification in Scotland, 15, 186, 221, 231; visibility in Edinburgh, 7-8, 24, 50
World Heritage site. *See* UNESCO: World Heritage site

CHRISTA BALLARD TOOLEY is Professor in the Department of Sociology and Academic Director of the Belmont Innovation Labs for Social Impact at Belmont University.

www.ingramcontent.com/pod-product-compliance
Lightning Source LLC
Chambersburg PA
CBHW031804220426
43662CB00007B/520